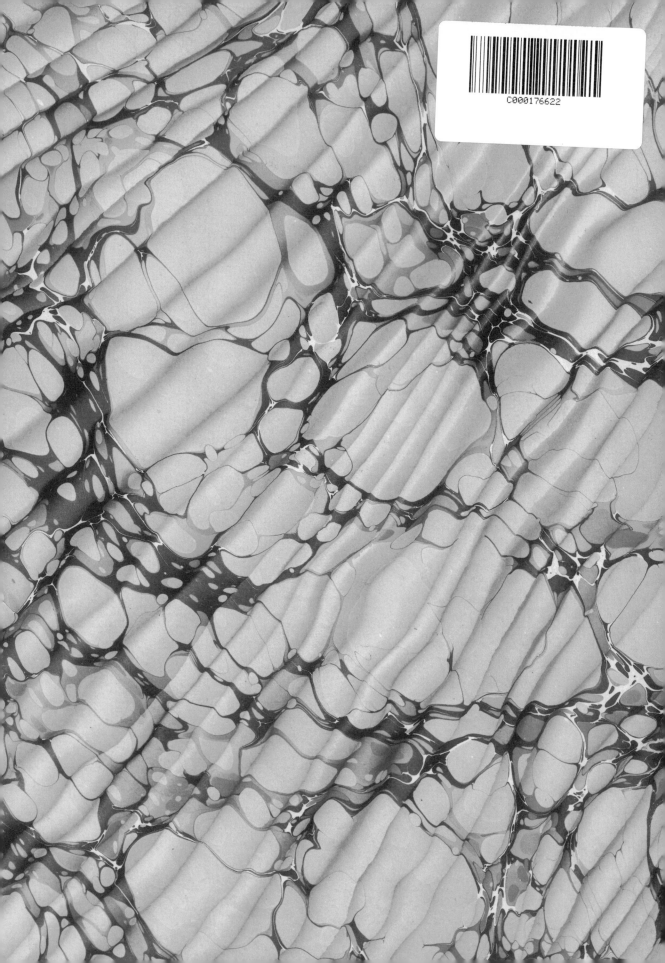

Pretty
GENTLEMEN

PETER McNEIL

Pretty
GENTLEMEN

MACARONI MEN AND THE
EIGHTEENTH-CENTURY FASHION WORLD

Yale University Press, New Haven and London

Contents

ACKNOWLEDGEMENTS

Many people have encouraged my research over the years with intellectual, moral and practical support and I remain indebted to them. My first thanks go to my mentors and supervisors, John Clarke and Michael Carter from the University of Sydney. John Clarke's erudite lectures on Shanghainese neck-ties were a revelation of content and method for me in 1990. Michael Carter remains today the expansive thinker and generous soul that he was nearly thirty years ago. Jennifer Milam helped me prepare for the perils and joys of the 'old' Bibliothèque Nationale and its challenging catalogue in the early 1990s. And Virginia Spate, Julian Pefanis and Terry Smith sponsored my research trips to Paris and London well before online catalogues, with their encouragement and financial support. My parents, now in their ninth decades, and Ian Henderson gave me a solid foundation from which to pursue both my dreams and my academic ideals.

The recent research has been supported by a Lewis Walpole Library / Yale University Fellowship, following on from an earlier visit to Farmington, Connecticut. This space of inspiration is dear to my heart and I remember fondly the late Joan Sussler and the other staff working there. Thanks to the taxi driver and Yale University gardener who drove me to and from the bus stop near West Hertford. A Gervers Fellowship at the Royal Ontario Museum in 1998 enabled me to understand the materiality of eighteenth-century dress much better, and I thank Alexandra Palmer, Anu Livandi, Shannon Elliott, Esther Methé, Howard Collinson, Virginia Wright, Lynne Milgram and Edward Maeder for their kindness while I was in Toronto.

A myriad of experts in academies, museums and collections have assisted with this research over many years, to all of whom I am grateful. The staff of the following libraries and archives: the Power Institute of Fine Arts Research Library, University of Sydney; the British Library, especially John Stokes; the State Library of New South Wales; the Bibliothèque Nationale de France, Paris; the Bibliothèque Forney, Paris; the Fashion Research Centre, Bath; the Royal Ontario Museum Library, Toronto. The staff of the following museums, galleries, collections and other institutions: the Art Gallery of Ontario – Katharine Lochnan and Brenda Rix; the Bata Shoe Museum, Toronto – Jonathan Walford and Elizabeth Semmelhack; Calke Abbey, Derbyshire – John Parkinson; the Colonial Williamsburg Foundation – Linda Baumgarten; the Gallery of English Fashion, Platt Hall, Manchester City Art Galleries – Miles Lambert; the George R. Gardiner Museum of Ceramic Art, Toronto – Patricia Ferguson; the Los Angeles County Museum of Art – Clarissa M. Esguerra, Sandra Rosenbaum, Kaye Spilker, Gail Stein

and Sharon Sadako Takeda; the McCord Museum of Canadian History, Montreal – Jacqueline Beaudoin-Ross; the Metropolitan Museum of Art, Costume Institute – Alexandra Kowolsky and the late Richard Martin; the Metropolitan Museum of Art, Department of European Paintings – Eleanor S. Hyun; Musée Ariana / Musée Suisse de la Céramique et du Verre, Geneva – Isabelle Naef Galuba; the Museum at the Fashion Institute of Technology, New York; National Historic Sites, Canadian Heritage – Gail Cariou; Spencer House, London – Jane Rick; Peter Finer, Fine Antique Arms, Armour and Related Objects, London – Peter Finer and Nickki Eden. And the following scholars, curators and others: Chloe Chard; Michelle Compton, formerly of the Australian Embassy, Paris; Kristi Cooper; Erika Esau; John Gascoigne, School of History, University of New South Wales; Heather Johnson, Sydney; Peter Kohane, University of New South Wales; Louise Marshall, University of Sydney; Margaret Maynard; Peter Raissis, Art Gallery of New South Wales; the late Sue Rowley; Anthony O'Brien; Elizabeth McCrum, Keeper of Applied Art at the Ulster Museum, Belfast; Moira Bonnington; Gillian Russell; Kimberly Chrisman-Campbell; Daniel Claro; Dominic Janes; Kelly Olson; Patrik Steorn, Louise Wallenberg, Andrea Kollnitz and Ingela Herne at the Centre for Fashion Studies, Stockholm University; Margareta Gynning and Martin Olin at the Nationalmuseum, Stockholm; Elizabeth Fischer, Head of the Jewellery Design Division, Haute École d'Art et de Design, Geneva; Desley Luscombe, Charles Rice, Bronwyn Clark-Coolee, Masafumi Monden and Kevin Alexander Su at the University of Technology Sydney; Anne Kjellberg at Kunstindustrimuseet, Norway; Naomi Tarrant, formerly of the National Museum of Scotland.

Titi Halle, Michele Majer, William de Gregorio, Valerie Steele and Patricia Mears have been supportive for many years in New York. Nicolas and Antoine of Diktats Bookstore have been generous with their time and knowledge. Beverly Lemire has been another inspiration and academic friend. Catriona Fisk, Giorgio Riello and Virginia Wright kindly commented on many aspects of the work. Ann Hobson and Hazel Baker helped to 'manage' the manuscript and were supportive in many other ways. I would like to thank Gillian Malpass for commissioning the book, and the professional staff at the Yale University Press London office, particularly Sophie Oliver, for their kind assistance.

My most recent research and thinking have been supported intellectually and financially by the Humanities in the European Research Area / 'Fashioning the Early Modern Project', under the magisterial direction of Evelyn Welch. I have benefited greatly from discussions there with Christopher Breward, Giorgio Riello, Lesley Miller, John Styles, Paola Höhti and Patrik Steorn. In Australia I am grateful to the curators and art historians Matthew Martin and Richard Read, who have commented on aspects of this work. At the National Gallery of Victoria, Roger Leong, Paola

Di Trocchio and Katie Somerville were very helpful. Anonymous readers helped to sharpen my argument. Simon Lee is a daily tonic and inspiration.

The funding bodies and programmes that have supported this research include the Australian Research Council – 'Discovery Projects' scheme; University of New South Wales College of Fine Arts Faculty Grant; University of New South Wales Research Support Program; Yale University, Lewis Walpole Library; Veronika Gervers Fellowship in the History of Textiles and Dress, Royal Ontario Museum, Toronto; the Centre for Contemporary Design Practices at the University of Technology Sydney; and the Humanities in the European Research Area. I also wish to thank the organisers of the 'Politeness and Prurience' conference at the University of Edinburgh in 2013, particularly Christopher Breward, Viccy Coltman, Freya Gowrley and Jordan Mearns. I thank the Academy of Finland for funding my Distinguished Professorship from 2014 to 2018 in the field of 'Costume Methodologies', as well as Dr Sofia Pantouvaki, the PhD and postdoctoral candidates at Aalto University, Donatella Barbieri and other participants at the 'Critical Costume Conference' held there in 2015.

The draft of this work was completed in the historic setting of a little 'queer cottage' that once belonged to the inter-war artist Donald Friend in a remote community called Hill End in New South Wales, thanks to the Bathurst Regional Art Gallery Artists in Residence Program, 2014 and 2016. I was surrounded by my favourite things: flowers, friends (on weekends), food, wine and birds, and I could imagine the pleasures of the British traveller journeying abroad on his or her own Grand Tour. Particular thanks go to the many local artists there, as well as Richard Perram OAM, Bathurst Regional Art Gallery Director, and Christine LeFevre at Bishopscourt in the central tablelands of New South Wales.

The work is dedicated to Martin Kamer, an extraordinary collector, true friend and fashionable inspiration. His passion for fashion and the eighteenth century, his wit and erudition are a daily inspiration for me, even though I generally reside in a different hemisphere and continent. The macaroni bow to him daily across the Zugersee, as do I.

Peter McNeil

The Field of Men's Fashion

The study of history is the progression of shifting priorities and changing interests, amid a great deal of serendipity, especially in relation to the memory of once-important historical figures.

In May 2014 I went looking for the elaborate marble commemorative tablet erected to that great macaroni of his day, the miniature-painter Richard Cosway (1742–1821). His monument is housed in Marylebone Parish Church. After attending the wrong Marylebone Church, which had been turned into a data-business office, I headed off in a taxi, finally arriving at the correct church on the busy pavements near the location of Madame Tussaud's. Once the church would have been more genteel, as it elegantly faces Regent's Park. Today the area teems with tourists and a few homeless people and is rather down-at-heel. A young man runs a coffee cart on the steps. Inside, just to the right of the vestibule, a group of enthusiastic youth broke their meeting for tea and biscuits. 'Where's the manager please?' I asked, assuming that the vicar was long gone. 'I'd like to see Cosway's tomb, but I can't seem to find it.' I was greeted with polite incredulity. I became anxious as well as curious; a journey of 10,500 miles from Australia, and I was not leaving without seeing Cosway's memorial. Peering around the corner, as art historians tend to, I looked into the tea room. 'Where's Cosway, please?' I asked a young person. 'Oh, he's there, over the stove,' she replied. And there he was, crammed in above a cupboard, up tight against another monument and hanging over an array of plastic cups and wine glasses. Much abraded, and barely legible, was the inscription 'Cosway . . . erected by Maria'.

Cosway was once a celebrated painter, a lavish collector and a fine 'macaroni' dresser. Outside the field of eighteenth-century British art he is not a household name today. Reputations go in and out of fashion, just as clothes change. Appearances, too – even the shape and form of the human body – are subject to flux. As the historian Keith Thomas notes: 'The human body, in short, is as much a historical document as a charter or a diary or a parish register (though unfortunately one which is a good deal harder to preserve) and it deserves to be studied accordingly.' He goes on to note that two things can be concluded from the study of history: 'Those who study the past usually find themselves arriving at two contradictory conclusions. The first is that the past was very different from the present. The second is that it was very much the same.'[1]

Richard Westmacott, Richard Cosway's memorial tablet, erected by Maria Cosway, Marylebone Parish Church, London

This is the first book-length study devoted to that famous male fashion figure of the 1760s and 1770s, the 'macaroni'. A series of interlinked questions will be posed. How can we understand this ultra-fashionable male of the last third of the eighteenth century? Was he a self-absorbed young man fascinated by the fashion world around him, much like followers of fashion today? What did clothing mean for men – in the drawing rooms of England, on the stage and in the street? Are young men of all times and places likely to engage with fashionable luxuries, particularly those that improve their appearance? After all, this is an idea that extends back at least to the Greeks, and many eighteenth-century subjects continued to frame such thinking through classical and later Christian concepts.[2] Fashion changed very rapidly for men in the years 1760–90. The 'macaroni period' allows us to study more closely the swiftness of these changes in the wardrobes of men, as they shifted from wearing tightly cut and short French-style suits to long, informal 'frock' coats with Anglophile accessories and soft hats. Their whole bodily appearance changed, from the rather pear-shaped man of the middle third of the century, with his courtly accessories of slipper-like shoes, snuff-box and cane, to the tall, lanky elegant of the end of the century, wearing long boots to the knee, droopy riding hat and carrying a riding crop.

Fashion culture, biography and historical events are brought together in this book with the broader visual and material culture of the day. 'History and fashion' come together, to supplant what still tends to be marginalised as the 'history of fashion', which is a linear narrative account of fashion change over time. I aim to contribute to a 'new art-historical fashion studies' (as opposed to the 'art history of fashion' – my terms) that is being pursued by figures including Marcia Pointon and Susan Siegfried.[3] It seems that the empirical and theoretical divide that continues to shape parts of fashion studies today might be overcome by connecting history with strategies drawn from theories of fantasy, spectacle and reading 'across the grain'.

Although theory has been very important in developing this framework – particularly feminist, spectatorship and queer theory – the 'record' is far too untidy, complex and multifaceted to be managed by any one of these theoretical approaches. If anything, this study questions dominant theoretical attempts to explain late eighteenth-century fashion change, from the Freudian psychology advanced by J.C. Flügel in the 1920s and 1930s, to the post-structural Lacanian readings of men's dress undertaken by researchers such as Kaja Silverman. As such, the work encompasses a wide range of sources and approaches, to argue that fashion carries within it a significant aesthetic dimension that drives aspects of social change.

CHAPTER 1

Introduction: *'The Vulgar Tongue'*

*M*accaroni, *An Italian paste made of flour and eggs; also, a fop; which name arose from a club, called the Maccaroni Club, instituted by some of the most dressy travelled gentlemen about town, who led the fashions; whence a man foppishly dressed was supposed a member of that club, and, by contradiction, stiled a Maccaroni.*

Grose's Classical Dictionary of the Vulgar Tongue, 1785[1]

In 1823, when this term was included in Pierce Egan's new edition of *Grose's Classical Dictionary of the Vulgar Tongue*, 'macaroni' had been circulating in the English language for 60 years, denoting a species of foppish man.[2] It was a term mainly used between 1760 and 1780, but was still in everyday use in 1795, when a verse described men shopping in the spa town of Bath thus: 'booted and spur'd, the gay macaronies, / Bestride Mandell's counter, instead of their ponies'.[3] The word continues to echo on a daily basis within the refrain of the famous patriotic tune 'Yankee Doodle' (published in 1767), referring to the appearance of troops during the French and Indian War (or the 'Seven Years War' of 1754–63):

> Yankee Doodle Came to Town
> Riding on a Pony,
> Stuck a feather in his cap
> And called it Macaroni![4]

The macaroni were remembered in the nineteenth century as colourful fashion eccentrics from a romantic past long surpassed by Victorian materialism, until the cataloguers of the British Museum's eighteenth-century satirical prints gave the topic greater potential for study with their comprehensive published catalogue cross-referenced to historical events. The catalogue had been undertaken in the 1860s, building on the earlier notes of Edward Hawkins, by Frederic George Stephens, a member of the Pre-Raphaelite Brotherhood and supporter of late nineteenth-century aestheticism (hence the co-authorship of 'Stephens and Hawkins' for the first part of the British Museum catalogue). It was continued in the first decades of the twentieth century by the indefatigable M. Dorothy George, one of several notable women to set themselves the task of cataloguing British caricature prints with detailed explanatory keys.

Not well known to the general public apart from those who have a particular interest in late Georgian England, the macaroni evokes bemused puzzlement when his name is mentioned today. Slippery like the pasta that his name connotes, the term 'macaroni' was once widely recognised in daily life, just as the word 'punk' or 'hipster' is in our own. Eclipsed by the fame of the masculine Regency bucks and swells, and not embedded in tumultuous political events as was the *incroyable* of post-revolutionary Paris, the macaroni

Opposite

1.1 Coat and breeches, Italian, probably Venice, *c.*1770. Green silk, coat centre-back length 90.8 cm, breeches length 62.2 cm. Los Angeles County Museum of Art, Costume Council Fund, M.83.200.1a–c

Waistcoat, French, *c.*1770. Pink silk, centre-back length 66 cm. Los Angeles County Museum of Art. Purchased with funds provided by Suzanne A. Saperstein and Michael and Ellen Michelson, with additional funding from the Costume Council, the Edgerton Foundation, Gail and Gerald Oppenheimer, Maureen H. Shapiro, Grace Tsao, and Lenore and Richard Wayne, M.2007.211.688a

existed 30 years before the justly famous figure of the dandy. Although many people today say, 'Aha! A dandy' when they hear the term 'macaroni', his ethos and appearance were completely different from that figure.

This book aims to bring the macaroni 'back to life' by considering what his sense of fashion enabled. As well as being a study of men and their sartorial fashions, it is a social, sexual and general cultural history, because for a period of 30 years 'macaroni' was a highly topical term, yielding a complex set of meanings and associations. 'Macaroni' indicated either fine or ultra-fashionable dressing, but it was not a static fashion movement with simply one form. Macaroni men dressed in a manner that asserted a cosmopolitan, fashion-centric outlook (fig. 1.1). Desirous of the rich and colourful textiles that countries such as France and Italy were renowned for, their attitude towards fashion was exclusive and undemocratic. Many macaroni men wore the tightly cut suit or *habit à la française* that derived from French court society, which also became the transnational and up-to-date fashion for many European men at this time (Swedish courtiers rushed to get out of their imposed national dress and into the modern French suit as soon as they could whilst travelling). Such clothing, and the accessories expected to accompany it, were expensive and unsuitable for many forms of work. It differed from the woollen suits of varying quality that tended to be worn by everyday men. Yet it was possible to copy certain aspects of the macaroni appearance, particularly the hairstyle, and it seems many did so, including young men from the countryside. Judging by engravings, as well as the clear depiction in several oil paintings, some men embraced the tighter and shorter broadcloth woollen suits and soft hats, including 'jockey caps', that characterised the pan-European desire for a new English taste in the last third of the eighteenth century (fig. 1.2). This might be the dress that is depicted on a Bohemian milk-glass painted tankard in the collection of the National Gallery of Victoria, possibly taken from a German print with an Anglophile focus (fig. 1.3).

Macaroni dress was not restricted to members of the aristocracy and gentry, but included men of the artisan, artist and upper servant classes, who wore versions of this visually lavish clothing with a distinctive cut and shorter jackets. Wealthier shopkeepers and entrepreneurs also sometimes wore such lavish clothing, particularly those associated with the luxury trades, such as mercers and upholsterers – the cabinet-maker John Cobb, for example. A famous painter (Richard Cosway), a garden designer (Humphry Repton), a freed slave (Julius Soubise), a criminal parson (the Reverend William Dodd) and a great botanist-explorer (Sir Joseph Banks) were amongst those considered macaroni in their day.

Contemporary interest in male sartorial display was amplified by the great expansion of printed satirical caricatures that occurred concurrently,

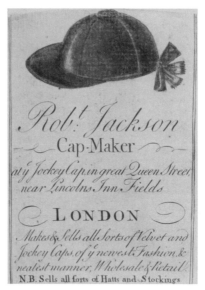

of which the macaroni phenomenon formed a major topic. The repetition of
certain motifs within these caricatures – the very high hairstyle, a tiny hat,
the cane and sword, spying glasses, high-heeled shoes and use of a snuff-box
– indicates that these objects had a powerful charge for male participants in
this type of dressing.

This is certainly the view taken by the late historian Paul Langford,
who notes that 'young men with too much money and too few inhibitions
prospered in the permissive climate of the years between two great wars' in
the eighteenth century.[5] Here he is referring to the cessation of the Seven
Years War (which involved all the great powers of Europe, as well as colonial
struggles overseas between Britain and France), at which point many young
well-to-do men rushed to the continent to see what was going on with the
French and Italian fashion they had so missed during wartime. The Seven
Years War was a disaster for France and marked an according ascendancy
for Britain, hence the even stronger significance of clothing styles adopted
at a time of national confidence. The American Revolutionary and
Napoleonic wars that reshaped borders and colonies mark the conclusion
of the period under consideration.

Other issues may be raised at this point in understanding the
significance of men's fashion. Some of these acquisitions were status-
conscious purchases to signal cosmopolitanism and success; others
were crafted by close female relatives and therefore inscribe chains of
attachment, and possibly also eroticism. Eighteenth-century women
frequently worked waistcoats and made sword-knots for their husbands,
particularly on marriage, a custom that was explicit for the aristocracy in
France.[6] A charming painted fan in the collection of the Museum of Fine

Arts, Boston, depicts a lady of leisure on the right, clearly embroidering a men's waistcoat panel on her tambour frame (fig. 1.4).[7] There was therefore a personal charge to aspects of gift exchange and the making of sartorial fashions. Such associations could carry social and cultural associations negatively framed as feminised and licentious. Some of these attitudes were transferred in what we would now call a 'homophobic' manner to a group of 'queer embroiderers' described in a scurrilous pamphlet mocking such men and entitled *The Pretty Gentleman* (1747), from which this work takes its title.

Fundamental to the general notion of macaroni fashion was the hairstyle. Fashionable men in the late 1760s and 1770s replaced the small 'scratch-wig' of the older generation, a prosthetic that supplemented the natural hair and was often worn for riding, with elaborate hairstyles that matched the towering heights of contemporary female coiffure. For men, a very tall toupee rising in front and a thick club of hair behind required extensive dressing with pomade and white powder. Other wigs had very long and thin tails, looking rather like horses. Wigs became a widespread fashion item, able to be copied by men 'up from the country'; and barbers and hairdressers were common, even in rural areas of England and France. The new fashionable macaroni queue of hair was held in a large black satin wig-bag, often trimmed with a rosette, to protect the back of the jacket. The wig-bag was requisite for attendance at court and therefore became striking when worn in the street and in everyday life; it also carried an added

expense. The effect of the hair could be copied with real and partial wigging – many men wore a mixture of their own plus false hair. The macaroni 'big hair' silhouette dominates the fashion ideal of many of the men of this era, and it is a signature of the notable portraiture associated with the most important artists of the day, including Joshua Reynolds, Thomas Gainsborough, Pompeo Batoni and Richard Cosway.

What did men's fashion have to do with the wider picture of social change so familiar to readers acquainted with the pre-revolutionary period? Many conclusions have been drawn regarding the changing appearance of men's dress in eighteenth-century western Europe. The distinguished French social historian Daniel Roche notes of the 'great cultural transformation' that was the Enlightenment: 'the hierarchy of the signs of social differentiation weakened'; 'there was a shift in the significations of appearances to emphasise social personalities in other ways, and operate differently on social space'.[8] Writing earlier and in a more general way, the dress historian François Boucher argued that whereas men in pre-eighteenth-century Europe were as splendid as, or more splendidly dressed than, women, in the eighteenth century women surpassed men for the first time in their pursuit and wearing of rich and elaborate clothing.[9] American art historian and theorist Kaja Silverman draws a theoretical conclusion concerning this issue: the richness of male dress surpassed female dress at times, 'so that in so far as clothing was marked by gender, it defined visibility as a male rather than a female attribute'.[10] She writes that the history of western fashion poses a serious challenge to the 'naturalised' equation of spectacular display with female subjectivity, and the assumption that exhibitionism is synonymous with woman's subjugation to a controlling male gaze.[11] Silverman notes that ornate dress was a 'class' (the term would more precisely be 'hierarchical status') rather than a gender prerogative from the fifteenth to the seventeenth century, a privilege protected in many European countries and principalities by sumptuary laws. Sartorial extravagance was thus a mark of power, a mechanism for tyrannising rather than surrendering to the gaze of the (class) 'other', and other social groupings.

A close study of the macaroni episode tests these historical and theoretical claims. Being fashionable and looking at fashionable people are part of a complex power relationship that still puzzles and perturbs us today. As Joseph Monteyne argues in his recent work regarding eighteenth-century prints, peep shows and optical tricks, a new sense of 'self-hood', which drew on philosophy and science as well as new spaces of leisure and new forms of visual culture, was being conjured up in the second half of the eighteenth century.[12]

Macaroni origins and migrations

The first use of the term 'macaroni' appeared in actor and theatre-manager David Garrick's play *The Male-Coquette* (1757), which included the foppish character 'il Marchese di Macaroni'. The term was occasionally used to refer to women noted for their conspicuous gambling, which was described, like fashion, as a form of endless and ephemeral expenditure – but it generally referred to the styling of men. The famous observer of manners Sir Horace Walpole made numerous references to these new fashionables. In the first relevant letter, dated February 1764, Walpole discussed gambling losses amongst the sons of foreign aristocrats at the 'Maccaroni club, which is composed of all the travelled young men who wear long curls and spying-glasses'.[13] Although he was never explicit, it would seem that the club involved was Almack's (see Chapter 2). Invoking Almack's generated a series of associations connected with patrician status, profligacy, folly and waste, as well as fun.

Macaroni men enjoyed wearing and carrying accessories characteristic of societies with a court at their pinnacle. These included the hanger or dress small-sword, traditionally the preserve of the nobility, but worn also by this date as a fashion statement; red-heeled and thin-soled, slipper-like black leather shoes with leather rosettes or decorative buckles of diamond, paste or polished steel; a tiny tricorn hat, known as the *nivernais*, or jokingly as the *nivernois* for the French Ambassador in London, Louis Jules Mancini Mazarini, duc de Nivers (translator of Walpole's essay on gardening into French), called the duc de Nivernois in England; large floral corsages, or 'nosegays'; chatelaines or hanging watches and seals suspended around the waistline; and elaborate or finely turned canes. Decorative neoclassical metal snuff-boxes and spying or eye-glasses also feature in the many varied descriptions and images of the macaroni wardrobe.

The macaroni departed from the trembling erotics of rococo taste in that symmetry and new textile preferences were often enforced in his dressing. The newly fashionable textiles were often spotted or thinly striped, moving away from the large-patterned meandering brocades characteristic of the period of George II and Louis XV. The macaroni often balanced a pocket watch hanging from the waistcoat with a bunch of seals, or perhaps a *fausse-montre*, a dummy watch. His clothing therefore matched developments in architecture and interior design: 'Here, then, we have a sartorial fondness of symmetry which is so clearly manifested in architectural and interior design, through false fireplaces, false doors and so on', notes Karin Tetteris in her study of French-influenced court taste in Sweden during this period.[14]

New materials also set new fashion trends. Fine examples of this development include the 'jockey'-style printed cotton waistcoats associated

1.5 **Vest, English**, 1790–1800.
Cotton plain weave with
supplementary-weft patterning,
centre-back length 61 cm. Los
Angeles County Museum of Art.
Gift of Jack Cole, 63.24.6

with late macaroni taste; such garments created novel fashions for men,
which must even have felt different, being soft, pliable and easily washed
(fig. 1.5). These clothing innovations replicated the effects of the much more
expensive trimmings that were used on more costly urban dress, but they
also had a new jauntiness that must have been enjoyed by the young. By
the 1770s the fashion was for steel rather than silver accessories, including
buttons; and sometimes a combination of materials was used in the one
piece of jewellery or shoe-buckle. A maker such as Henry Price 'at the Two
Chains & Buckles', near Red Lion Square, London, advertised that he made
and sold 'all Sorts of Mens, and Womens Steel Chains, and Buckles' as well
as spurs, snuffers, watch keys and the very useful corkscrew (fig. 1.6). His
elegant but rather old-fashioned rococo trade-card illustrates the longer,
thinner men's chatelaine to the left, and probably a woman's cage-like

structure to the right, as well as buckles in two sizes: large for a man and small for a woman. Their design is almost exactly the same, although the smaller buckle might also be for fastening men's knee breeches.

Bobbing just below the waist was the sword-knot, which garnished the small-sword. Although sword-knots were generally made from textiles, and few seem to survive, some were made of steel itself, such as the beautiful example attributed to the great entrepreneur of metals Matthew Boulton, or his workshop (fig. 1.7). As its cataloguer notes, 'The hilt is formed entirely of highly burnished steel, fluted in part and applied with elaborate designs of steel beads cut in imitation of brilliants, both inlaid and carried threaded as openwork designs ... The original tassel is formed of lengths of steel beadwork wound about the knuckle-guard and developing to a series of clustered loops.' The original owner of this sword was Colonel Lord Evelyn

1.7 English small-sword with chased cut-steel hilt, attributed to Matthew Boulton, *c*.1790. Length 104 cm, blade length 83 cm. Courtesy of Peter Finer, London

James Stuart, politician and soldier, second son of John Stuart, 1st Marquis of Bute.[15] As he was a young man in the 1790s, this is an indication of the longevity of certain courtly fashion tastes.

The carrying of such fashion accessories contributed to an emphasising of what was seen as either polite or courtly manners in posture, gesture and speech, further underlined by the use of cosmetics such as face-whiteners and rouge, breath-fresheners and even preferred drinks such as asses' or donkeys' milk. According to contemporary reports, there was a mannered macaroni accent and idiom, captured in popular ditties and joke-books of the period.

The interest in the macaroni was not confined to one visual or literary genre, or even to England. Macaroni dress was amplified in its influence because it appeared concurrently with the marked expansion of English caricature prints, which were perused far beyond the borders of that

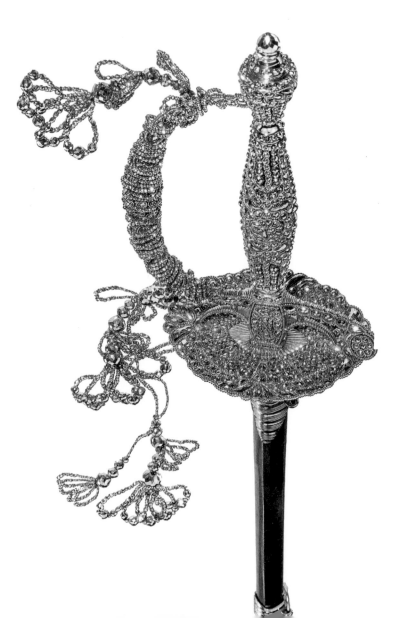

country. Almost immediately, plays, joke-books and songs were written about the macaroni, and glass and ceramics were painted with his likeness. He developed a wide European appeal, particularly through the caricature print published by Matthew Darly, *Ridiculous Taste or the Ladies Absurdity*, first issued in July 1771 (fig. 1.8), republished in reverse by Sayer and Bennett in 1776 (fig. 1.9). A man who might represent a husband, but whose figure also refers to the South Seas explorer Sir Joseph Banks, uses a sextant (for celestial navigation) to observe the top of the head of a female fashionable, who is tended by an ugly *frizeur*, or hairdresser, up a ladder, in macaroni dress. Hanging on the wall in the background is a severe portrait of an unfashionable man, perhaps Oliver Cromwell. The image was clearly very popular, as another version was published in the *Oxford Magazine* as 'The Female Pyramid', a nice joke about exploring exotic and unbelievable places (fig. 1.10). It finds an echo in Thomas Patch's painted caricature of *c.*1760 of an Italian gallery with the Medici Venus (see fig. 2.1), in which the painter himself, dressed in seaman's trousers, scales the classical statue and uses dividers to measure its proportion. As art historian David Cast notes of such Grand Tour images, they are not simply about laughing at others, but often concern the self-assurance of the arrogant and well-to-do.[16]

The Darly print of the macaroni hairdresser reappeared in many surprising formats, both direct and indirect copies, indicating the usefulness and malleability of print culture within wider design and decoration. It was copied in the unusual medium of an oil painting that is extant in Sweden (see fig. 6.5) and on a Swedish Marieberg-made ceramic tray (fig. 1.11) painted with a macaroni hairdresser tending a lady client, dated 1772, hence just a few months after the first appearance of the image (if the date can be believed). The painter of the ceramic tray simplified the details of the rich interior so that it did not disrupt the expanse of glossy white glaze and the striking impact of the leaf-form handles that are modelled in relief.

The translation across borders and media was not a simple act of copying; an extant Swedish painted copy of the English caricature – an extremely rare survival – is set in a recognisably Swedish type of interior, with fictive *boiserie* and a *trompe-l'œil* painted perspectival floor typical of that region. The oil was painted on the back of a panel decorated with flowers, possibly by a sign-painter. The composition was also reworked in wools and silks into a picture, possibly eighteenth-century or later, that was purchased at auction in Stockholm in 1895, probably made by a lady (fig. 1.12). The strong interest in this image in Sweden is not surprising, as the research of Patrik Steorn has discovered that the first illustrated cover of a Swedish newspaper (*Stockholms Posten*) carried a crude woodcut interpretation of the print in July 1779, noting that it was after an English original, but not naming Darly (fig. 1.13).[17] The image was connected to an article by the

RIDICULOUS TASTE OR THE LADIES ABSURDITY.

Left
1.8 **M. Darly,** *Ridiculous Taste or the Ladies Absurdity*, 15 July 1771. Etching with engraving, plate 35 × 24.7 cm, sheet 37 × 26 cm. Courtesy of The Lewis Walpole Library, Yale University

Below left
1.9 **R. Sayer and J. Bennett,** *Ridiculous Taste*, 10 June 1776 (reduced copy after M. Darly). Mezzotint, 15.1 × 12.2 cm. British Museum, London

Below right
1.10 'The Female Pyramid', *Oxford Magazine*, 1771. Facing p.129. British Museum, London

Ridiculous Taste.
London Printed for R. Sayer and Bennett N° 53 Fleet Street, as the Act directs 10 June 1776

The Female Pyramid.

Below
1.11 Erik Borg, *Ridiculous Taste
or the Ladies Absurdity*, tray
produced by Marieberg, 1772.
Faience, sepia paint, 46 × 30.5 cm.
National Museum of Fine Arts,
Stockholm, NMK 78/1943

Below left
1.12 *Ridiculous Taste or the
Ladies Absurdity*, embroidery,
*c.*1800. Wool and silk yarn on fabric,
41 × 35.5 cm. Nordiska Museet,
Stockholm. Purchased 1895 from
Bukowski auction house, Stockholm,
NM.0080638

Below right
1.13 'Ridiculous Taste or the
Ladies Absurdity', front cover of
Stockholms Posten, 17 July 1779.
Woodcut. Kungliga Biblioteket,
National Library of Sweden,
Stockholm

newspaper's editor, Johan Holmberg, who, Steorn writes, 'defended the rights of authors of texts and images to remain anonymous by discussing the necessity of satire, for example of women's fashion exuberance'. Steorn suggests that the use of such satires of fashion in Sweden related to the restriction of the press by Gustav III in 1774, and that such exaggerated fashion images were useful in underscoring the corrective power of satire.[18] Visual satires of macaroni fashion played multifaceted roles in their incarnations inside and outside England.

The German ceramic works of Ludwigsburg, which specialised in fine-quality porcelain figural groups, created another version of a hairdresser group in which the lady sits at her *toilette* table (fig. 1.14). Numerous men with very high hair tend her, with the support of stepladder and spying glass, suggesting that men's business has been reduced to frippery. The design was possibly by Gottlieb Friedrich Riedel, director of painting and design at Ludwigsburg from 1759 to 1779 and an independent engraver as well. Whether such models had any corrective potential, or were simply made to decorate mantels or dressing tables, remains unclear, although Walpole and others complained about the invasion of china figurines and knick-knacks into women's private cabinets and lives at this time. Another hard-paste figure group of the time depicts a courtier sporting an enormous black wig-bow attempting to walk through the arch of a classical ruin (fig. 1.15). He is watched by another fop and a poorly dressed man, but there is empathy, sweetness and charm in the expressions and the selected palette. The allusion here would include a ludicrous participation in the Grand Tour. A painting of this period by the Swedish painter Carl Pehr Hilleström, *Petter Pehr Hilleström Studying a Sculpture*, indicates the complex relationship between artistic practice, fashionable clothing, bodily posture and an observation of the classical tradition, in this case a cast of the Apollo Belvedere (fig. 1.16). These Swedish and German survivals indicate the topicality and mobility of images of the Grand Tourist abroad and the enjoyment of print culture as a part of everyday life for those with leisure, access to imported images and education.[19] The Swedish artist who copied Darly's print created the sense of a proscenium stage, and this is significant, as many such prints might have had their basis in performances at the theatre or been associated with that giddying world. Satirical prints inspired the theatre and other 'real life' situations. A contemporary report of the London Pantheon masquerade ball in 1773, for example, noted that a woman wore 'a tall Head-dress and a little ladder to it, after Darley's print'.[20]

It is undoubtedly the case that the influence of the macaroni was amplified by their coincidence with the great expansion of satirical print production in England, and this reference point has shaped much of their subsequent interpretation.[21] The cataloguers of the British Museum

1.15 Figure group, German, attributed to Ludwigsburg, Württemberg, c.1770. Porcelain, h. 11.2 cm. British Museum, London, 1923, 0314.102.CR

caricature collection, Frederic George Stephens, in 1883, and Dorothy George, in 1935, published within their very different times and mindsets a treasure of primary material relating to the macaroni that has formed the basis of all further studies. Aileen Ribeiro wrote the first article devoted to this body of prints in 1978 for *History Today*, and has included them in her subsequent magisterial studies of eighteenth-century dress, where they are discussed as visually splendid and as a good example of the sartorial folly of young men.[22] Other approaches have emphasised social and political influences; the definition of English character vis-à-vis the French; the macaroni's role in 'an age of extravagance' but also as 'polite and commercial people'; and their function as a leitmotif of urban sociability, and of private character, leadership and innovation in Enlightenment culture.[23] Gillian

1.16 Carl Pehr Hilleström, *Petter Pehr Hilleström Studying a Sculpture, c.*1770. Oil on copper, 50 × 39 cm. Konstakademien / The Royal Academy of Fine Arts, Stockholm

Russell has argued that macaronism is part of the shifting authority of court factions, popular entertainments and 'voices' in eighteenth-century London life, and she has emphasised the role of female 'macaronesses'.[24] Russell points to the very high hair of the period as a type of 'voice' for women participating in urban fashionable pursuits and public life. The high hair of men and women seems to have been used at times to suggest the complementary nature of the sexes in the new polite society of mid-eighteenth-century England, as in the caricature *Macaroni Courtship or the two Insignificants* (fig. 1.17), which at the same time connotes that men have become as shallow as women, despite their fine clothes and hair.

None of the recent scholarship on the macaroni focuses much on what was actually worn by these men. What was 'actually worn' in the past is a

MACARONI · COURTSHIP.

or the two Insignificants.

Publish'd acord.to Act Feb^y1.1772.by M.Darly 39 Strand.

1.17 M. Darly, *Macaroni Courtship or the two Insignificants*, 1 February 1772. Etching with engraving, plate 18 × 24.9 cm, sheet 19 × 27 cm. Courtesy of The Lewis Walpole Library, Yale University

topic that has been emphasised by Aileen Ribeiro, who has argued that theoretical understandings of dress and fashion sometimes get in the way of understanding exactly what we are talking about in the pursuit of fashion studies.[25] Writers to date have not much enquired what the macaroni resembled. What did he look like and how are we to recognise him? Did he look at all different from someone attending court? If we rely mainly on caricatures, then what impression do we acquire? Do we arrive at a caricature of a caricature? That was certainly the impression re-presented in period films such as James Ivory's *Jefferson in Paris* (1995), which included a greatly exaggerated vignette of the painter Richard Cosway.[26]

At a time when English dress generally consisted of more sober cuts and the use of monochrome broadcloth, macaronism emphasised the effects associated with French, Spanish and Italian textiles and trimmings, such as brocaded and embroidered silks and velvets; pastel colours; fashionable patterns of spots (fig. 1.18), stripes and small-field motifs; and refined textile surfaces such as those created with the use of chenille threads that were integral to the brocade and further embellished with metallic sequins, paste or simulated gemstones and raised metal threads (fig. 1.19). So 'over-the-top' were some Italian silks and velvets that the painter Venceslao Verlin depicted

Above left
1.18 M. Darly, *Sam Spot Esq.,*
1 July 1778. Etching with drypoint,
plate 35.2 × 24.9 cm, sheet 37 × 26
cm. Courtesy of The Lewis Walpole
Library, Yale University

Above right
1.19 Detail of embroidered
waistcoat and buttons, English
or French, *c.*1770. Silk droguet with
silver *filé* ground, embroidered in
coiled metal wire (gold bullion), gold
and silver sequins, silver foil and
glass paste. Royal Ontario Museum,
Toronto, 909.33.4.B

a man wearing leopard-skin-pattern breeches in a Grand Tour scene of 1768
(private collection, sold Carlo Orsi, Milan, 1997). Contemporary viewers were
probably able to identify domestic and imported silks, as they had a highly
refined sense of materiality, colours and cloth. It was sometimes suggested
that French silks resembled colours as seen under artificial light, whereas
the English (or so it was claimed) used a palette drawn more from nature.[27]
French silks were banned from 1766 and were excluded from the Free Trade
Treaty of 1786, 'a prohibition which lasted until July 1826'.[28] Macaroni men
therefore embodied a tension in English society between native interests,
manufactures and prerogatives, and a cosmopolitan outlook that privileged
travel, urbanity and access to outside ideas.

Being a macaroni was about more than wearing fashion. There
were strong links between modes of appearance in dress and in interior
decoration. The architect Robert Adam's designs for fine London
townhouses such as Chandos House (1770–71) and 20 St James's Square
(1772–4) were being erected at this time. The preferred colour combinations
and effects of macaroni men were not without meaning; they related to
broader fashion schemes for goods and spaces as diverse as snuff-boxes and
boudoirs. The colours that were particularly associated with macaronism

1.20 Snuff-box, English, possibly Birmingham, 1765–75. Enamelled copper with chased gilt-metal mounts, 3.5 × 8.3 × 6.4 cm. V&A, London. Bequeathed by Myles Burton Kennedy, Esq., C.470–1914

include those used in the designs of this neoclassical architect: pea-green, pink, red and deep orange, garnished with a great deal of gilt. Adam's use of 'patches of bright colour in a non-constructional way' was a departure from the more tonal approach of his rival William Chambers, and surprised viewers and critics alike.[29] The striking colours and light effects created for patrons by Adam in the 1770s, such as the red foil set behind glass and simulating porphyry for the drawing room of Northumberland House, London (1774), find their corollary in the foiled buttons and jewels of this period worn by men and women of fashion. Boxes or bonbonnières of a pink-gold ground inlaid with spots of black enamel simulating leopard skin were fashionable luxuries in the 1770s.[30] A cornucopia of vegetables might adorn an English green enamelled and spotted snuff-box with its hinged lid, enabling the taking of snuff in a conspicuous manner (fig. 1.20). The clashing components of macaroni dress were not always 'harmonious', but suggested a mode of dressing that carried ludic overtones and hints of carnivalesque *mentalités* that reached far back in time.

Fashion and food: macaroni men

Food has profound cultural meaning in all parts of the world. The
slipperiness – and instability – of the food preferred by the macaroni finds
its corollary in the fact that a flaccid penis is still compared with a 'noodle' by
some Mandarin speakers. To what extent did people associate this fashion
figure with jokes concerning food? Quite a lot, it would seem. A French
dictionary of 1768 specified that 'macaroni etits morceaux de pâtes coupés
par tranche' ('macaroni were pieces of pastry cut in slices', and hence akin
to what we call gnocchi).[31] A macaroni caricature played directly with the
analogy between food and fop: *The Salutation Tavern* (H.W. Bunbury,
publisher J. Bretherton, 20 March 1773) is subtitled 'Macaroni & other
Soups hot every day'. The macaroni was firmly embedded within popular
conceptions of food culture, carnival and the *commedia dell'arte* and can
accordingly be connected to earlier *mentalités*. 'Maccus' or 'Maco' was the
name of a glutton of noodles in the *commedia*. Pulcinella (later 'Punch') was
famous as a 'lazy, cunning and licentious' stage glutton and, as Gardiner
Museum founding curator Meredith Chilton writes, his preferred foods
were 'spaghetti, macaroni, and gnocchi, which he consumed in vast
quantities whenever possible'.[32] In 1888 W.A. Clouston published *The Book
of Noodles: Stories of Simpletons or Fools and their Follies*. The joke here is
partly that cooked pasta swells up to several times its original size, just as
macaroni were associated with a swollen pride.

The commonly held explanation for the title 'macaroni' – that it was
derived from a fondness for that dish – may be supplemented in that
'macaronic' also refers to a type of Latin poetry that revolved around wit
and foolery, a hallmark of the macaroni stereotype. 'Macaroni' therefore
suggested the world of the medieval carnival, burlesque and carousing,
which was closely connected to the glutton. The carnival reference was
also related to the topos of the macaroni as 'numbskull' or 'noodle-head';
cauldrons of the food macaroni had been paraded in early-modern
European carnivals, accompanying a fat man (in German carnival, the
food is more generally sausage).[33] Images of pasta-eaters consuming huge
amounts and lengths of the food were particularly associated with Naples.
Porcelain figures of 'spaghetti eaters' were made at factories in Italy
(Capodimonte) and Spain (Buen Retiro) from mid-century until the 1780s.[34]
Reproduced here for perhaps the first time, *A French Macarony Eating of
Macaroons* makes explicit the connection between a foreigner and his food
choice (fig. 1.21). A fop in a fine striped suit, hanger sword and buckled shoes,
with an elaborate and high hairstyle, holds an incongruous spoon, lifting
his head up to eat some slippery pasta from the dish below. A small dog fouls
the pot on the ground from which he is eating. The psychoanalyst Jacques
Lacan once remarked that 'everyone makes jokes about macaroni, because

it is a hole with something around it'; that is, as Juliet Fleming notes, an object organised around emptiness.[35]

The satirical image of the empty-headed man sometimes emerging fully born from an egg (which is also subsequently empty) might also relate to folklore and carnival uses of eggs, in which witches were said to fly. There is another joke at work here: Eros 'is an ancient mythic figure at the centre of creation mythology who is said to have emerged from an enormous egg to create the earth'.[36] Such references provide an explanation for the distinctive image of a well-dressed macaroni hatching from an egg, published as the frontispiece to *The Macaroni Jester, and Pantheon of Wit* (see fig. 5.10). 'An Account of a Macaroni', published in *The London Magazine* in April 1772, described the macaroni as 'the offspring of a *body*, but not of an individual. This same body was a many headed monster in Pall-Mall, produced by the Daemoniack committee of depraved taste and exaggerated fancy, conceived in the courts of France and Italy, and adapted in England. Hence that variety of fantastical beings in all places of publick resort.' There followed a discussion of its digestion: 'The eye is the paunch of a *virtuoso Maccaroni*, as the stomach of the glutton. The *devouring Maccaroni* does not derive the appellation from an immoderate indulgence in animal food; the idea would be too coarse and sensual.'[37]

The macaroni was closely related to the much older notion of the fop, who existed in various guises over the course of both the seventeenth and eighteenth centuries. Foppery was a complex cultural pose. It was not unified, but could range from the sweetness of a sixteenth-century French *mignon*, and the insistent negligence and untidiness of the seventeenth-century English rake, to the strict control of the Regency dandy (not strictly speaking a fop at any rate, as his clothing and bodily 'technology' avoided the most obvious affectation and rested instead in subtle refinement and detail). Fops were considered effeminate, but that did not necessarily correlate with a lack of interest in women. Since the Italian Renaissance the effeminate and finely dressed man was sometimes – but not always – associated with attributes of love and cast as an object of desire.[38]

The macaroni episode redefined such 'effeminate' men. A substantial number of prints, plays and satires cast the macaroni as an indeterminate figure not fitting normative stereotypes of gender and sexuality. Although the aesthetics were different, the attributes of the Regency dandy (*c.*1810) – deviant masculine consumption, non-reproductive irresponsibility, a rejection of 'middling-sort' gendering, a creation of the male body and home into a 'work of Art' – were already present in the macaroni.[39] This book therefore maps a reading of clothing culture onto the history of sexuality. In so doing, it problematises some of the standard theories of male sartorial renunciation, many of which have overlooked the macaroni and turned

directly to the dandy, before commencing with an analysis of modern dressing.

The language and imagery associated with macaronism survived the eighteenth century, being included in the novels of Jane Austen and Charles Dickens and reappearing in the Victorian period 'Cole's Funny Picture Book' as an ailing and ridiculous 'coxcomb'. The term was used in various British novels and short stories in 1930s Australian women's magazines. The macaroni ended up rather old, foolish and feeble, rather than young and sparkling like the men we are about to meet.

CHAPTER 2

Observing the Macaroni

A donis. What every pretty fellow wishes to be, what every macaroni aims at, and what most of them think themselves. Adonise. Every effort used by a complete macaroni to become an Adonis.

Bon Ton, March 1791, p.14

The macaroni are best known today through their representation in printed visual caricature. As F.G. Stephens noted in his part-catalogue of the British Museum satirical print collection (1883), 'The Macaronies are copiously illustrated by a very large body of satires.'[1] M. Dorothy George's revised catalogue of the collection (1935) listed about 150 prints that included the word 'macaroni' in their title; there are many more that allude to the macaroni in their iconography or in the accompanying verbal texts. The macaroni thus form the most substantial subgrouping of the caricatures of manners produced in England in the 1770s. Indeed, classed as a genre, the macaroni are outnumbered only by the enormous body of political caricatures published in the late eighteenth century. Of this category they also form a significant subset, as a political identity such as the Whig politician Charles James Fox was widely caricatured as a macaroni man in his youth, and macaroni status was used to comment on all manner of things, from credit to sodomy.

In recent years, scholarly and popular awareness of the macaroni man has gained momentum among those interested in the fashion culture of the eighteenth century. This might reflect the growing body of interlinked research into consumer practices, print culture and sartorial fashions, as well as the rise of interest in men's dressing. Researchers have begun to resist reading the macaroni simply as illustrative of something occurring in eighteenth-century life – for example, a particular worldview, such as aristocratic excess or anxiety concerning war and the role of the militia. Several reasons can be advanced for this shift. The first is the changing attitude towards the interpretation of caricature prints as complex visual artefacts; the second is the reassessment of dress fashion as an area of serious research within cultural history, rather than as something mainly illustrative of wider cultural forces, policies and trends.

Caricature was generally marginalised within art history until the 1960s. Associated with the ephemeral, the crude and the minor arts, it was, as E.H. Gombrich noted, rarely studied by the art historian unless produced by artists of genius such as Goya or Daumier.[2] Sir Francis Watson was one of the few scholars interested in rescuing the reputation of the artist of painted caricatures, Thomas Patch, first writing about him in 1939. Around 1961 the Grand Tour expert Sir Brinsley Ford discovered a major Patch painting, *A Gathering of Dilettanti in a Sculpture Hall*, which had been turned into a screen and was spotted in the window of a London interior decorator, a work he subsequently purchased and published (fig. 2.1).[3] In his comments on attempts to date the painting, Ford noted that he wished there had been a woman in it, as the dating would therefore have been easier. This is telling as to how little was known about the history of men's fashion, because men's attire of the 1760s to 1770s is distinctive. Ford wrote of the colours:

> Cleaning has revealed an exuberant range of colour in the men's coats . . . [they] are now disclosed as lilacs and pinks, buffs and various shades of grey . . . Cleaning has also brought out the lively touch with which Patch can suggest the sparkle on a sword-hilt, the quality of lace, and the brightness of silver buttons and gold braid.[4]

Ford was correct to notice the spectacular range of colours used by Patch in depicting the clothing worn by his Grand Tourist Englishmen. Hand-coloured macaroni prints of the 1770s most commonly use green, as well as many colours of the rainbow. In one set of prints from 1772 there may be seen pinks, orange, pink trimmed with yellow, violet, yellow, red, white dappled with blue and pink shadows, pink-and-white-striped breeches and waistcoat, violet and green embroidery, blue-and-white-striped stockings,

red-spotted white waistcoats and contrasting tan coats.[5] Such colourings, even if added later, find their corollary in paintings and in written descriptions.

In 1905 'George Paston' – actually Miss Emily Morse Symonds, an unmarried feminist (better known for her writing on the eighteenth-century flower artist Mrs Delaney) – included a lengthy and perceptive discussion on the topic of the macaroni in her *Social Caricature in the Eighteenth Century*.[6] This, along with Dorothy George's detailed catalogue of the holdings of the British Museum, as well as George's richly illustrated social-history studies of Georgian life, provided the main references to the macaroni, until historians of dress and costume began to take some interest in them in the 1970s and 1980s.[7]

Research into eighteenth-century culture has been transformed in recent years with a new focus on many aspects of culture, including the so-called 'material turn', as well as the impetus of interdisciplinary and theoretical work. For example, the research of Shearer West has pointed out that eighteenth-century audiences seemed as interested in the lives of famous actors and actresses as in going to the theatre, and that new categories of visual culture were invented in order to make profits from this reorientation.[8] The macaroni are better understood when reunited with the growth of print and leisure culture of the time, the cult of celebrity and the changing conception of manhood.

Published texts concerning the macaroni are most in evidence in the first half of the 1770s. They appear in periodicals such as *Town and Country Magazine*, *The London Magazine*, *The Universal Magazine* and *The Lady's Magazine*. In 1772 *The London Magazine* noted:

> The only thing to be said in defence of it is, that the character is harmless; it is rather foolish than vicious. As it is now at its height, our print-shops are filled with Macaronies of a variety of kinds, representing with much drollery the absurdity of this species of character in various professions.[9]

Throughout 1772 *Town and Country Magazine* printed a series of satirical letters to the editor and articles that brought the existence of the macaroni to a wide readership. From the beginning, the macaroni was posed as a hothouse exquisite, corrupted by urban mores and in turn inflicting them on his country cousins. The March 1772 entry was a satirical letter to the printer describing a certain F--l--o who had visited London, and also a brothel. 'Having been at the very fountain-head of elegance, he seems to have quaffed pretty copiously of the perfumed springs of Macaroni taste . . .' On returning to his home of Bristol, the macaroni was reported to note: 'Not a moment's felicity can I enjoy with such shocking wretches – hem – where's my shiff box?', a reference both to that essential accessory, the snuff-box (we also find it called a 'snush box' in the sources concerning macaroni men), and to the affected tone that became a hallmark of the macaroni.[10]

'Effeminacy' did not always suggest homosexuality per se, but frequently suggested a softening of manners and morals in a society in which commercial transactions and the consumption of new luxuries overtook older models of the sword. Effeminacy, Philip Carter argues, was not to an eighteenth-century mind primarily about 'sexual behaviour', but rather about 'men's social conduct'.[11] 'Thou call'st me effeminate, for I love women's joys; / I call not thee manly, though thou follow boys,' wrote John Donne in the late sixteenth to early seventeenth century.[12] Writers such as David Hume were concerned that 'modern politeness . . . runs often into affectation and foppery'.[13] Although an attraction to the opposite sex was suggested in the first *Town and Country* description, it disappeared from later accounts. In May 1772 the appearance of effeminate macaroni mocked by outraged women at a masquerade was reported, in a more overt suggestion of homosexuality than is sometimes otherwise encountered.

Two word-plays concerning the macaroni – *Hieroglyphic Epistles*, engraved letters in rebuses and in rhyme – were also published in 1772.[14] A periodical, *Macaroni, Scavoir Vivre, and Theatrical Magazine*, capitalised on their topicality and was published for one year between 1773 and 1774. Interest extended beyond the middling-sort light entertainment represented by these journals to a songbook that included a tune on the subject of the macaroni around this time. This text was printed on cheap paper and may have circulated amongst less affluent areas of the community, its rhyme perhaps drawn from a popular song or ditty.[15] A joke-book with the engaging title *The Macaroni Jester, and Pantheon of Wit; containing All that has lately transpired in the Regions of Politeness, Whim, and Novelty; Including A singular Variety of Jests, Witticisms, Bon-Mots, Conundrums, Toasts, Acrosticks, &c. – with Epigrams and Epitaphs, of the laughable Kind, and Strokes of Humour hitherto unequalled; which have never appeared in a Book of the Kind* was published in around 1773.[16]

The social politics of the macaroni were complex. Many of the first notable macaroni were extremely wealthy, but the most famous of all, Charles James Fox, did not side with the court and came from a Francophile and Jacobite background, later becoming a radical Whig. Others, such as the painter Richard Cosway and the court preacher Reverend Dodd, were court followers who were sycophantic but also creative in their dress and their social motives. The court was peripatetic, moving between St James's, Kensington, Hampton Court and Windsor. The macaroni retained a version of court dress in the streets, whether or not the royal family was in residence. This is one of the reasons for their being mocked; they had the presumption to assume the manners of an elite at a time when the general populace did not dress in such a manner. In this, London differed from Paris, where formal modes were worn by anyone with pretensions, or a claim to *politesse*, and where the court dress was so elaborate and expensive that it could be hired by tourists upon arrival in the city.

The macaroni sources often employ the notion of 'John Bull' being affronted and unseated by the new male urbane fashionability. This reflects less that an interest in fashion on the part of men was new, and more the notion that more men were engaging with fashion. The overall impression of the caricatures is that both sexes were becoming more infected with the 'vice of fashion', a fact that has been confirmed for France in the extensive researches of economic and social historians such as Daniel Roche.[17] If some members of the lower orders emulated macaroni dress, as many sources suggest, then the question of motive becomes even more complicated. Commenting upon precisely this, *The Universal Magazine* noted of the macaroni: 'was it not for an awkwardness in the gait, a clownishness of manners, and a solecism in speech, the Gentlemen of birth and fortune would not be known from him'.[18]

Such people of fortune were willing to pay a substantial part of their income to own foreign-made textiles: *The London Chronicle* noted in 1757 that a gentleman on £2,000 a year in land paid £25 'on foreign manufactured silks, linens, cottons etc.' and that a gentleman on £300 a year paid £3 15s. 'on the same'.[19] £2,000 was a very wealthy income, but this expenditure on imported clothing is not huge if one considers that about 25 per cent of all industrial production at that time was textiles.[20] Such textiles might have included Venetian and Genoan figured velvets, Spanish and Lyons silks and embroideries, as well as the printed and painted cottons from the area around Marseilles, and Indian imports. Even if such textiles were banned at times, efforts were made to smuggle them in.

As G.J. Barker-Benfield has noted, fashion demands display as well as purchase.[21] Expenditure on fine clothes was partly encouraged by the necessity for the aristocracy and gentry to integrate socially and marry for financial reasons, the raison d'être of the establishment of the resort town of Bath, at which macaroni behaviour flourished in the 1760s and 1770s. Mrs Montagu complained of Bath 'Misses who strut about in morning in Riding dresses and uniforms and the Maccaronis who trip in pumps and with Parasols over their heads . . .'[22] Bath was a stage for the display of clothing and manners, more or less fine, as the daughters of merchants tried to tempt those less wealthy than themselves. As the old and new money arrived for the season, so too did the purveyors of luxury and the appearance trades, whose own appearances were walking advertisements for excessive fashions. Successful shopkeepers were expected to be smart and effusive;

a silk mercer 'must have a great deal of the Frenchman in his Manners, as well as a large Parcel of French Goods in his Shop,' noted a mid-century writer.[23] Bath had its own print-shops in which the latest engravings were displayed. And the town itself was fertile ground for the satirist. The caricaturist Matthew Darly played up these associations, producing several images of Bath macaroni, including a figure of obsequious elegance with an enormous wig-bag (fig. 2.2). Christopher Anstey penned two hilarious satires upon the Bath macaroni, as well as the relatively late work *Liberality; or, The Decayed Macaroni. A Sentimental Piece* of *c.*1788 (see fig. 7.8) and Henry Bunbury produced the drawings for certain caricatures of Bath macaroni and fashionables.[24] Macaroni can be seen parading in a painting of 'Orange Grove', Bath, of *c.*1780, where their clothing contrasts with the long, dark frock coats, dark stockings and large hats of the stout older men.[25]

Fine clothes, food and tea-drinking were much complained about after 1750. A group of pessimists led by Dr Price argued that the population was declining owing to the growth of luxury. Given the rise in the death rate, he accounted for the increased consumption of food and goods in terms of luxury rather than population growth. This theory irritated Samuel Johnson: 'Luxury, so far as it reaches the poor, will do good to the race of people; it will strengthen and multiply them.'[26] The population was not, however, declining; between 1700 and 1820 the population of London nearly doubled from 674,000 to 1,274,000. The *British Magazine* noted in 1763, the year in which travel to Paris reopened: 'the present range of imitating high life hath spread itself so far among the gentlefolks of low life, that in a few years we shall probably have no common people at all'.[27]

In *The Man of Manners: or, Plebeian Polished*, the narrator complained, 'We all look above ourselves, and as fast as we can, strive to imitate those, that some way or other, are superior to us':

> Every little Wretch, who plays upon a Pen in an Office, or on an Instrument at a Theatre, must have his large lac'd Hat, and open-sleeve Coat to expose the Gold or Silver Orrice on that of his Waistcoat. Servant Wenches turn up their Noses at Yardwide Stuffs and substantial Camblets; every Trollop of five Pounds a Year appears in her Silk Night-gown, and short Scarlet Cloak: With these last, the Town seems to be quite over-run, every Christening or Crowd that passes the Streets, on any extraordinary Sight or Holiday, looking, at a distance, like a Procession of Popish Cardinals.[28]

This withering comment is in part a comment about religion and the necessity to reform English Protestantism in terms of manners and lifestyle. A dramatic poem by Charles Jenner also mocked the pretension of those

2.2 **M. Darly,** *The Bath Macaroni*, **1 June 1772**. Hand-coloured etching, plate 17.6 × 12.5 cm. Courtesy of The Lewis Walpole Library, Yale University

THE BATH MACARONI.

who followed the dress and manners of their betters by indulging in the pursuit of fashion and leisure, using the Latin title 'avaricious':

> AVARO.
> Time was, when satin waistcoats and scratch wigs,
> Enough distinguish'd all the city prigs,
> Whilst ev'ry sunshine Sunday saw them run
> To club their sixpences at *Islington*;
> When graver citizens, in suits of brown,
> Lin'd ev'ry dusty avenue to town,

Or led the children and the loving spouse,
To spend two shillings at *White Conduit House*:
But now, the 'prentices, in suits of green,
At *Richmond* or at *Windsor* may be seen;
Where in mad parties they run down to dine
To play at gentlefolks, and drink bad wine ...

PRUDENTIO.
'Tis true my friend; and thus throughout the nation
Prevails the general love of dissipation:
It matters little where their sports begin,
Whether at *Arthur's*, or the *Bowl and Pin*;
Whether they tread the gay *Pantheon's* round,
Or play at skittles at *St Giles'* pound,
The self-same idle spirit drags them on,
and peer and porter are alike undone:
Whilst thoughtless imitation leads the way
And laughs at all the grave and wise can say.[29]

The reference here to 'children and the loving spouse' alludes to the companionate marriage and new focus on the loving family; *Prudentio* to Prudence, the enemy of excess; and the expensive dye and the colour green, as we will see, were particularly associated with macaroni fashion of the 1760s and 1770s. The colour green was expensive to dye, and may have had links to the 'Romans of the Decadence', *galbonatus* being a shade of green preferred by homosexuals in the Roman Empire.[30] A nineteenth-century periodical recorded a similar theme in a song entitled 'The Macaroni', set to the air 'Nancy Dawson', which probably reflects a lost eighteenth-century tune. Such popular sources are part of the archaeology of everyday life and attitudes, which are otherwise difficult to retrieve in the case of the macaroni:

... The cits that used, like Jerry Sneak,
To dress and walk out once a week,
And durst not to their betters speak,
Are all grown jolly crony;
Each sneak is now a buckish blade,
When in the Park, but talk of trade,
He thinks you mean him to degrade –
Each cit's a macaroni.[31]

The press was full of complaints of men of 'mean station' getting their hands on superior fashions and making macaroni of themselves – the exhibition of 'abominable vanity in the little'.[32] *Macaroni, Scavoir Vivre, and Theatrical Magazine* reported on a masquerade at the fashionable and notorious Carlisle House run by Mrs Cornelys, at which 'a maccaroni tallow chandler, and another of the same trade with his basket, as greasy as the best of them' were present.[33] The grease of the tallow trade alludes here variously to a slickness of manners, the social stain such types might leave behind, and the smell of the grease of the cheap second-hand or rancid wig. That tallow candles were inferior to wax and much cheaper underscores the mockery.[34]

It was the macaroni attention to wigs that caused most consternation. The small and sensible round 'scratch-wig' of the older generation was replaced by a new form of wig. It matched the towering heights of the female coiffure, with a tall toupee cresting at the centre front. The wig generally had a long tail at the neck ('queue'), which when folded double was called the 'cadogan', all of which required regular dressing with pomade and powder, sometimes in the colours of pink, green or red.[35] The tail of the macaroni wig was often dressed with a black satin wig-bag tied with a large bow ('solitaire'), and when it was placed in this silk bag, which protected clothing from the pomade, it was *à la bourse* (fig. 2.3). The high hair of macaroni men brought them to public attention in new and particular ways.

This excessive new macaroni wig became the subject of fascination and alarm. In visual imagery, macaroni were tailed by hairdressers with devil-like horns and hideous physiognomies; they were mercilessly lampooned as partners in crime, often effete, wizened, satanic (fig. 2.4). Wigs had cost an enormous sum of money in the late seventeenth century – up to £50 in England.[36] The wig was therefore amongst the more expensive items in a gentleman's wardrobe, although the price dropped considerably over the course of the century.[37] The wig's rise across western Europe was almost universal. Even small rural towns in France had several barbers and wig-setters, and in Denmark wigs were taxed from 1710, due to their rising popularity.[38] The Swede Pehr Kalm noted of England in 1748 that 'Farm-servants, clodhoppers, day-labourers, Farmers, in a word, all labouring-folk go through their usual every-day duties with all Peruques on the head. Few, yes, very few, were those who only wore their own hair.' Many journeymen apprentices in England received 'one good and sufficient wig yearly'.[39] Now, it seemed, like many other fashionable items of clothing, a wider range of choices and more wearable styles were produced not just for the eighteenth-century gentleman, but also for the artisan and labourer.

Powdering the hair was satirised as a vigorous and untidy process, in contrast to the fine completed result (fig. 2.5). The powder could be applied with a hollow wooden device that was twisted, called a 'carrot', or with bellows, of which an example survives in a Swedish collection (fig. 2.6). One of the most regular outgoings in a man's weekly expenditure was for the

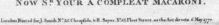

Opposite
2.3 Wig-bag, late 18th century.
Black silk, attached to a coral-pink
silk suit, bag added later as fancy
or theatrical dress. Royal Ontario
Museum, Toronto, 971.164.A

Above left
**2.4 'Brandoin pinxt.', James
Caldwell (printmaker)**, *Now Sr,
You'r a compleat Macaroni*, **6 May
1772**. Etching and stipple engraving,
plate 20.2 × 13.9 cm, sheet 27 × 17 cm.
Courtesy of The Lewis Walpole
Library, Yale University

Top right
**2.5 Ceramic glazed tile depicting
a hairdresser, Liverpool
(manufacturer), after the etching
and engraving by James Caldwell
(printmaker)**, *The Englishman
in Paris*, **published 10 May 1770
by J. Smith and Robert Sayer,
c.1775**. Earthenware, 8 × 12.5 × 12.5
cm. National Gallery of Victoria,
Melbourne. Presented by Mr and
Mrs F. Hodgkin, 1939 (4656.72-D3)

Above
**2.6 Powder bellows, probably
Swedish, probably 18th century**.
Leather and wood. Nordiska Museet,
Stockholm. NM.0059551

services of the hairdresser, and several times each year he bought a new silk wig-bag, as they must have become soiled very quickly.[40] Exaggerated clubs of hair were sometimes described as *à l'Angloise* (*à l'anglaise*, or 'in the English manner') in French fashion periodicals (see fig. 4.10). The macaroni wig was thus a sign of conspicuous consumption, transnational fashionability and a luxury and necessity. If not the clothing, then the general effect of a macaroni hairstyle would have been possible to replicate; real hair could be dressed in the new manner and augmented with false, and there was a large trade in second-hand and stolen wigs. The ragged-looking confections thrust on the heads of caricatured individuals in Darly's engravings might thus have suggested the ridiculous effort to follow an inherently expensive fashion. The wig's symbolism as potentially deceitful was indicated in the following incident from the diary of the young German tourist Sophie Von La Roche, travelling to London in 1786. An English customs official whom she described, even at this early date, as 'Hogarthian', inspected the wig-box of a fellow traveller:

> The customs man raised his voice, flashed his eyes with greater fire, and insisted on opening the box; then, looking important meanwhile, lifted out the wig, lying there in blissful content, and dropped it again scornfully. The foreigner said, 'It is only my wig after all, isn't it?' 'Yes', he replied, 'but a wig often covers a multitude of sins.'[41]

The new macaroni fashions were taken up by youth from the English countryside. Samuel Johnson (b.1754), the young provincial nephew of the celebrated painter Sir Joshua Reynolds, wrote a series of letters to his mother in the countryside whilst he was residing in London. He was convinced by his friends to visit an assembly at Islington (1775), was lent lace ruffles and 'They persuaded me to wear a bag and a sword, but I found myself not singular in a twisted tail.'[42] He must have become accustomed to the style, for in a letter that year to his dismayed mother, who was horrified at the thought of her son's Devonshire curls being plaited and dressed, he wrote:

> This is in defence of my tail, which I must wear in London where none but clergymen and boys wear their hair untied; the place only makes the difference; a tail here is the same as curls in the country, and silk stockings the same as worsted; but if it is only for my hair and not for my head that you are concern'd I can assure you that it is in better order than it has been for months [. . .].[43]

As this young man had to leave London some weekends for lack of a decent suit, clearly elements such as the hairstyle were sufficient to mark one out as a stylish 'macaroni'.[44] William Hickey, upon becoming a young clerk in London in 1765, went straight to the most fashionable Paris hairdresser there, a Mr Nerot, to 'have my hair tied, turned over my forehead, powdered, pomatumed, and three curls on each side, with a thick false tail'.[45] This excitement regarding hairdressing assists in an understanding of Matthew and Mary Darly's macaroni caricatures, which illustrate a wide range of dress, sometimes shabby, but with similar hairstyles.

Although the writer Horace Walpole referred generally to the high-born in his discussion of the macaroni, in an intriguing letter of 1775 he provided a rare insight into the persona of another non-noble or non-gentry macaroni. He discussed the death of 'One of our Maccaronis', identified as 'Captain Mawhood, the tea-man's son'.[46] Captain James Mawhood (d.1775) was a brigadier and lieutenant, and the son of a tea-merchant in the New Exchange.[47] Mawhood is a tantalising reminder that not all men of fashion were high-born; Walpole noted that Mawhood was mocked as Captain 'Hyson' (a green tea) by his fellow officers – green being, once again, a favourite macaroni colour.

Macaroni meanings

This section indicates the derivation of the term 'macaroni', which was probably understood differently by various social groups in the 1760s and 1770s. Dictionaries note that the first recorded use of the term 'macaroni' occurred in the voluminous correspondence of Horace Walpole, although this is not strictly true. Similar words had been used as names of characters in David Garrick's plays as early as 1757. Walpole's trenchant eye did, however, provide the first detailed surviving impression of this phenomenon when it appeared amongst the aristocracy in London. As Stephens noted, it was explained as a novelty. Profligate gaming, associated with continental (and specifically French) manners, was strongly associated with the macaroni type. Gaming was highly fashionable and losses had reached epidemic proportions; Charles James Fox's stakes of £3,000 and total gambling debts of £140,000 were public knowledge, mentioned in macaroni ditties and satires.[48] Walpole, listing the things in the world that were best worth finding, included longitude, the philosopher's stone, the certificate of the Duchess of Kingston's first marriage, the missing books of Livy, 'and all that Charles Fox had lost'.[49] Fox's brother Stephen, also the subject of many macaroni caricatures, lost £13,000 in one sitting.[50] The losses equate to several or many millions in today's money. As in France, the behaviour was widely reported and associated in the public mind with the decadence of a spent aristocracy. Darly included *A Macaroni Gambler* in his third suite of macaroni caricatures (1772), a topical image that referred to Alexander Fordyce, a Scottish banker with the misfortune to have a name so worthy of punning. Fordyce was notorious for the failure of his bank, which caused a great deal of anxiety regarding new models of credit and the manipulation of stocks and bonds that were developing in this period.[51]

2.7 **M. Darly, *The Macaroni Cauldron, to be had with many other Macaronies pubd. by M Darly (39) Strand*, 9 March 1772.** Etching with engraving, plate 24.8 × 35.1 cm, sheet 27 × 36 cm. Courtesy of The Lewis Walpole Library, Yale University

A particular type of dress was associated with the inveterate gambler. The English made a ritual of their dress at the private clubs. Walpole noted:

> They began by pulling off their embroidered clothes, and put on frieze great coats, or turned their coats inside outwards for luck. They put on pieces of leather, such as are worn by footmen when they clean the knives, to save their laced ruffles; and, to guard their eyes from the light, and to prevent tumbling their hair, wore high-crowned hats with broad brims, and adorned with flowers and ribbons.[52]

Men spent such long hours at the table that an engraving depicted a special cap with a wide rim, worn to protect weary eyes from bright candlelight, possibly to deter cheating. Darly's engraving *The Macaroni Cauldron* shows such caps mirroring and protecting the shapes of the high toupee wigs (fig. 2.7). The way in which the men are placed around the table is reminiscent of seventeenth-century English prints of the gathering around the preacher Martin Luther, as in *The Candle is Lighted, We Cannot Blow Out* of *c.*1640 (BM).[53] This was not ultimately the guise that came to be associated in the public mind with the macaroni; instead, the fine clothing they were

2.8 Daniel Gardner (painter), V. Green (printmaker), *George Simon Harcourt, Viscount Nuneham* [later 2nd Earl of Harcourt Stanton], 1772. Mezzotint, 32 × 22.7 cm. Courtesy of The Lewis Walpole Library, Yale University (Horace Walpole's own copy)

protecting beneath was what defined macaroni dress. A play review described 'the Nabob sitting at his table in his gambling dress, the silk night gown, straw bonnet, &c. which the virtuous gentlemen of Almack's use when at play'.[54] References to gaming are significant as they underscore the instability and arbitrary nature of these fashionable appearances.

Walpole's comment on 'all the travelled young men', cited in Chapter 1 (see page 19), clearly refers to those aristocrats who had taken the Grand Tour; he was discussing a group of youth comprising either French or Swiss and Modenese aristocrats, a thoroughly cosmopolitan gaming table. They were the duc de Chaulne's son; 'Virette', possibly a Genevan; the Marchese Giuseppe Paolucci, the Modenese envoy to England; and the duc de Pecquigny. Walpole recorded their names as a feud subsequently developed over their gaming debts. His reference to 'long curls' is, of course, also significant.[55] Such a hairstyle is seen in the engraving dated 1772 after the elegant portrait by Daniel Gardner of George Simon Harcourt, Viscount Nuneham, a friend of Walpole's (fig. 2.8). Although Nuneham was considered an 'exquisite' of his day, the portrait is respectful and does not include the exaggerations seen in contemporary caricature; it thus gives a reasonable idea of the appearance of the macaroni hairstyle. They certainly had a conspicuous appearance. Whether the viscount powdered his hair in unusual shades of red or blue, as Charles James Fox was to do during his macaroni phase, or the nabobs in India did, is not known. The spying glass mentioned by Walpole was either a type of monocle on a decorative string or a retractable device, used for close inspections of others. The expensive glass sets the holder off from the crowd and casts him as observer and, by extension, an outsider.

The issue of the 'macaroni club' established an aristocratic profile for the macaroni when he first appeared. Prominent early twentieth-century historian E. Beresford Chancellor noted that London clubs were associated with food, from their appearance in the reign of Queen Anne: 'their primary object was, more or less, food'.[56] By the 1730s clubs were political, such as the Rumpsteak or Liberty Club (1734), which was in opposition to Walpole's government, or the October Club, which was also Tory. The most exclusive clubs were White's (originally White's Chocolate House); Tom's in Covent Garden; the Cocoa Tree in Pall Mall; and Boodle's and Almack's in St James's Street.[57] Other clubs included the Mohawks, the Society for the Propagation of Sicilian Amorology, the Wet Paper Brigade (which read the papers damp from the presses), the Lying Club, the

Ugly Club, the well-known Hellfire Club and the Dilettanti Society. The existence of the Mohawks club points to the topicality of many of these seemingly frivolous groups. 'The Mohawks' was an intriguing choice of name, as these members of the Iroquois Nations were notable for their longstanding fur-trading association with the Dutch and the French, and for their subsequent decision to support the British in the Seven Years War and the American Revolutionary War. Londoners would have seen portraits of prominent Mohawks, depicted as noble warriors with feathered headdresses. The connection with the feathered headdresses of fashionable English ladies would not have been lost on contemporaries (some Mohawks also visited London in 1762), and such items of dress provide another link with the imperial project of trade and cultural contact that is so significant in Georgian life.

Although the existence of the 'macaroni club' has been stated by several historians of dress, and by the editor of the encyclopaedic Walpole correspondence, none has provided any proof of its existence. Walpole did not name its location. As the press printed articles of a similar nature in 1772, subsequent historians have tended to accept this explanation of the term. The club he referred to was either one of the fashionable clubs in St James's Street: the Robert Adam-designed Boodle's, where vast fortunes were spent gambling by men such as Charles James Fox, or Almack's Assembly Rooms, established by William Almack at 49 Pall Mall, first as a public house in 1759 and then as a private club at number 50 in 1762.[58] The location and ambience of the London clubs were complicated, as their owners were frequently moving and expanding them into adjoining properties. Almack's Assembly Rooms were formed from four houses in adjoining King Street, connected by an alley to Pall Mall in 1764.[59] As Gillian Russell points out, the club was 'formed in opposition to the Tory club of White's' (also 'Arthur's').[60] Almack's moved to St James's Street and was then called Brooks's in 1778. Boodle's stayed at 50 Pall Mall and was distinctive for permitting unlimited gaming. Almack's was Whiggish and was attended by Sheridan, Fox and the Prince of Wales. This would seem to suggest, then, that the aristocratic macaroni met at Almack's. A macaroni print entitled *The Holy Order of St Almac* (BM) depicts a monk with a macaroni toupee, playing cards for a rosary and a bunch of flowers; the song 'The Macaroni's Downfall' accompanied this plate. Walpole's personal scrapbook collection of 280 etchings, prints and drawings gathered by him between 1776 and 1782 includes a pen-and-ink drawing on tracing paper, probably by Bunbury, in which a macaroni is followed by a beggar; the inscription states, 'THIS CLUB was instituted and kept at ALMACKS and called the MACARONNI society' (fig. 2.9).[61] Walpole linked Almack's with the macaroni several other times in his correspondence; there were 'Macaronis lolling out of windows

2.9 'THIS CLUB was instituted and kept at ALMACKS & called the MACARONNI society', in 'Etchings by Henry William Bunbury, Esq. and After His Designs'. Pen-and-ink drawing on tracing paper, dimensions unknown. Album collected by Horace Walpole, 2 vols, fol. 49/3563./v.1.2, at p.2. Courtesy of The Lewis Walpole Library, Yale University

at Almack's like carpets to be dusted'.[62] Furthermore, *The Macaroni, … and Theatrical Magazine* also referred to Almack's, describing 'a compound dish of vermicelli and other pastes, which, unknown in England until then, was imported by our Connoscenti in eating, as an improvement to their subscription table at Almack's'.[63] Walpole's description of the macaroni club was designed to amuse his correspondents who were familiar with the ambience of these Whig establishments, notorious for gaming, feasting and carousing. The Edwardian biographer of the macaroni Walter Stanhope noted that the dish macaroni was 'always placed on the table at their

dinners'.[64] Almack's was later known as the 'Scavoir Vivre', an expression
that occurs in comic journals of the period that included macaroni men.[65]

Other macaroni references are found in Walpole's letters in 1764. In
May of that year he referred to a 'young rich Mr Crewe' as 'a Maccarone';
in June he described a party without heating at which 'All the beauties
were disappointed, and all the macaronies afraid of getting the toothache.'[66]
In November he indicated that macaroni dress was a style of the very young,
when he observed at the Opera: 'You see I am not likely, like my brother
Cholmondeley . . . to totter into a solitaire at threescore.'[67] Distinctive
macaroni colour schemes for various seasons, probably copied from the
vibrant combinations used in French and Italian silks and velvets, were
indicated: 'If I went to Almack's and decked out my wrinkles in pink and
green like Lord Harrington, I might still be in vogue.'[68] The Royal Ontario
Museum holds a fine apple-green silk suit that sums up this taste, with
embroidered floral swags and tassels in the neoclassical manner on the
pockets and back vents, placing a focus on the wearer's rear (figs 2.10, 2.11).

Walpole continued his discussion of the macaroni in his
correspondence in 1775: 'The macaronies will laugh out, for you say I am still
in the fashionable world. – What! They will cry, as they read while their hair
is curling, – that old soul; – for old and old-fashioned are synonymous in the
vocabulary of mode, alas!'[69] In 1775 *Matrimonial Magazine* noted that 'A few

2.12 **Thomas Gainsborough,**
Captain William Wade, 1771.
Oil on canvas, 234.3 × 153 cm.
Victoria Art Gallery, Bath and
North East Somerset Council

months ago most of the Macaronies had got into a sort of jaundiced habit;
a kind of orange-tawney ... and of late there has been a most unseasonable
rage for GREEN CAPES.'[70] 'Capes' was a contemporary term for collars.
This suggestion is borne out in two letters written by Joshua Reynolds's
nephew, the afore-mentioned Samuel Johnson, expressing an enthusiasm
for this colour scheme in that year:

This day I had a new great Coat which am exceedingly pleas'd with;
it is a light colour with a light green collar, made in the new fashion;
the colour of the Coat depends on one's own fancy but the green Capes
[collars] are almost universal ... [26 January 1775]

Went to Mr Lane to talk about another Suit of Cloaths for a best Suit
(I have since chosen a Barri colour, a colour deeper than an orange)
from him [31 January 1775].[71]

Such letters are evidence of the detailed pleasures involved in the pursuit
of fashion at this time by young men.

David Piper states in *The English Face* that there were no painted
portraits of anything resembling macaroni dress. This is not the case.
Thomas Gainsborough's *Captain William Wade* (1771) is a splendid example
(fig. 2.12). This work has not been much discussed in articles concerned
with macaroni dress. Painted at the height of macaroni fashion, its elements
correspond with all the details that became the subject of exaggeration
in visual and verbal caricature of the macaroni man. Wade was Master of
Ceremonies in Bath from 1769 until his divorce case in 1777 and, like Beau
Nash before him (d.1761), was responsible for enforcing rules of dress and
polite behaviour in the resort and encouraging the social but decorous
mixing that made Bath a special place. The painting was commissioned to
hang high in the Card Room at the new Assembly Rooms. Gainsborough,
a resident of the town at that time, painted Wade in a red velvet suit with
lavish gold-embroidered waistcoat.[72] The prominent wig-bag, nosegay,
toupee wig and fine lace of the macaroni type are in evidence. Wade's
painted badge of office hangs from a silk ribbon on his bosom. He adopts
the aristocratic posture of a balletic turned foot and arms akimbo; his face
registers considerable hauteur. Lord Chesterfield wrote about the effect
of such clothing in an earlier generation thus: 'he wore his gold laced
clothes on the occasion, and looked so fine, that, standing by chance in
the middle of the dancers, he was taken by many at a distance for a gilt
garland'.[73] Waistcoats of gold lampas similar to the one depicted by
Gainsborough survive in the Royal Ontario Museum and the Museum
of Costume, Bath (figs 2.13, 2.14). The painters working in Bath for the
summer season were very much a part of the luxury business there,
Gainsborough's sister Mary Gibbon being a milliner in the town and
sharing his painting premises.[74] Gainsborough's charming portrait of
the playwright *Richard Paul Jodrell* (c.1774) shows a young man of
fashion aged about 30, with a macaroni hairstyle and wearing a suit of
pink and green, the colour preference described by Walpole and others
(fig. 2.15).

Right
2.13 Waistcoat, French, *c.*1760–70.
Gold silk lampas, brocaded,
embroidered, tabby ground; winding
band brocaded in pink silk and silver
frisé with floral sprays brocaded in
coloured silks and chenilles and
embroidered with silver *filé*, sequins
and coils of silver wire, buttons
embroidered with silver *lamé* and *filé*.
Royal Ontario Museum, Toronto,
920.28.10

Below
**2.14 Waistcoat, French, *c.*1760–70;
detail of centre front showing
buttons**. Royal Ontario Museum,
Toronto, 920.28.10

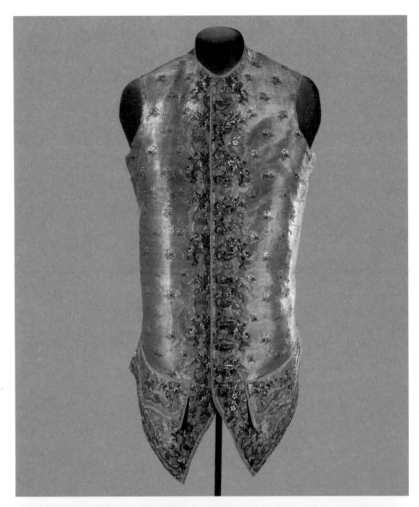

2.15 Thomas Gainsborough,
*Richard Paul Jodrell, c.*1774.
Oil on canvas, 76.8 × 63.8 cm.
The Frick Collection, New York,
1946 1946.1.154

The 1774 portrait *Thomas William Coke*, of 'Young Coke of Norfolk', by the celebrated Italian Grand Tour painter Pompeo Batoni, depicts a young English aristocrat in fancy dress at precisely the height of the macaroni dress (fig. 2.16). Although dressed in a costume, parts of his appearance, such as his hair, show him to be in fashion. Coke was in Rome in 1773, precisely the time when English macaroni manners were at their height. It is striking to see this painting today, with its urbane and cosmopolitan associations, in a rich Palladian setting near a quiet beach in the Norfolk countryside.[75] 'Young Coke of Norfolk' inherited Holkham Hall in 1775; a pioneer of the Agricultural Revolution, he even did some farming himself, to the astonishment of visitors. He was MP for the county and enjoyed his status as 'the first Commoner of England', refusing to be knighted for some time. Coke had taken an enthusiastic Grand Tour and attended the wedding of Bonnie Prince Charlie; it has also been suggested that he was partly

2.16 **Pompeo Girolamo Batoni,**
Thomas William Coke (1752–1842),
Later 1st Earl of Leicester
(of the Second Creation), 1774.
Oil on canvas, 241.9 × 167 cm.
Collection of the Earl of Leicester,
Holkham Hall, Norfolk

educated by émigrés. Batoni's work was commissioned by Princess Louise
of Stolberg, who also happened to be the wife of the Bonnie Prince, and her
features were included in the statue of the Vatican Ariadne in the painting.[76]
'Young Coke of Norfolk' made Holkham Hall, with its magnificent alabaster
entrance hall, a monument to Whig themes, commissioning busts and
reliefs by Sir Francis Chantrey on topics such as *The Passing of the Reform
Bill*; a portrait bust of Charles James Fox still greets the visitor on arrival.

On the Grand Tour he was dashingly painted by Batoni in a version
of fancy or masquerade dress. The work is a harmonious composition in

which the sitter sparkles in dress of grey, silver and coral shades, with a faithful sporting dog suggesting that he should return home to the classical pile he was left to complete. His fallen-lace collar, slashed sleeves and lavish feathered hat refer to the popular Van Dyck dress of the seventeenth century, but the hairstyle, the trim of the pale satin suit and the red-heeled slipper-like shoes refer to macaroni modes. The shoes' grey colour, coral-pink rosettes and matching braid mark them out as fancy, not everyday dress. The clothing is of great luxury, with silver galloon trimming on a plain satin ground, and the cape is lined with ermine. Whereas masquerade dress – Van Dyck dress, the 'dress of Rubens's wife' and other stock costumes – were popular for female portraits (obviating the need to appear in contemporary fashion, which dated very quickly), most men avoided the frivolous associations of the masquerade in their portraits. Few men commissioned their likeness in fancy dress of any type, and of these, Van Dyck dress was the preferred option, with its links to an esteemed aristocratic and artistic past.[77] Thus male masqueraders sporting a version of macaroni dress, about which we read so much in the sources of the day, are commemorated only in the 'minor' arts of engraving and mezzotint, or in genre paintings of crowd scenes and the like. Thomas Coke's portrait is a gift to our imagining such rich assemblies.

Men on the Grand Tour made particular choices about how they chose to be painted. In great contrast to Coke, but painted just three years later, is Batoni's portrait of *Sir Harry Fetherstonhaugh* of 1776, which is now at the beautiful seat of Uppark, West Sussex (fig. 2.17). Sir Harry is coolly modern, wearing one of the very long cloth coats with a standing collar associated with English rather than French taste, but adopted with great enthusiasm by the French nonetheless. The coat appears to be without external pockets and is probably the type of dress described in the 1770s as 'undress' – that is, informal clothing. He is wearing the fashionable combination of pale pink and green, and his needle-lace stock and cuffs are very fine. The elongation of his coat is exquisitely resolved with his long oval face, aquiline nose and thoughtful eyes; it is clear why Batoni was so popular as a portrait painter. The hairstyle is resolutely fashionable and macaroni. Sir Harry's attire might reflect either the mood he wished to convey or the simpler travelling clothes that young men wore on the Grand Tour; in fact a survey of Grand Tour portraits from mid-century onwards suggests that most men appear to be wearing woollen broadcloth laced with galloon, with the exception of the painted caricatures of group scenes by Thomas Patch. There is also every reason to believe that men might have worn a combination of garments of slightly different date, as men and women have always tended to do.

The great Swiss painter Jean-Étienne Liotard depicted another fine example of a young man who accords with macaroni taste. His *Portrait of*

John, Lord Mountstuart, Later 4th Earl and 1st Marquess of Bute (1763) used
pastel to skilfully suggest the texture and detail of clothing (fig. 2.18). The
clothes of the 19-year-old sitter, who was visiting Geneva, cleverly blend with
the colour of the robes worn by a Chinese man depicted in an adjacent exotic
screen, and the mirror provides a second portrait, in profile. Mountstuart's
blue moiré silk winter 'frock' is lined with squirrel, has a fallen collar and
decorative tassels. The hair of the sitter is not terribly high, suggesting that
the fashion for such things was likely subject to individual taste. He wears
a pair of shoe buckles set with paste or diamonds.[78] The Royal Ontario
Museum has an example of such a flamboyant winter garment, a white-
fur-lined ribbed coral-silk coat (fig. 2.19), to which a wig-bag was sewn at a

2.19 Coat, English or French,
*c.***1780**. Coral-pink ribbed silk,
part ermine-lined, ermine cuffs.
Royal Ontario Museum, Toronto

later date, probably for fancy dress (see fig. 2.3). The vents of the coat with
protruding fur would have created a sense of animated movement (fig. 2.20),
nicely captured in William Hickey's description, in his famous memoir, of
the summer dress of a London rake, Charles Horneck, in *c.*1770–71:

> Bob by this time has become quite a London rake. He displayed

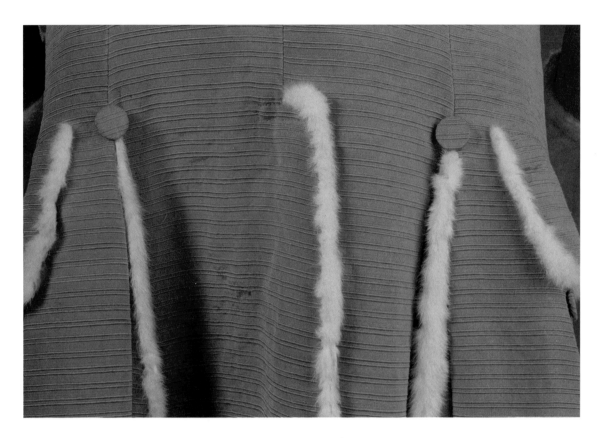

2.20 **Coat, English or French,**
*c.*1780; **detail of rear vents**.
Royal Ontario Museum, Toronto

peculiar taste in dress, though carried to excess in point of fashion, soon becoming the envy of all the young men of his day . . . his dress then being a white coat, cut in the extremity of ton [the fashion], lined with a Garter blue satin, edged with ermine, and ornamented with rich silver frogs; waistcoat and breeches of the same blue satin, trimmed with silver twist a la Hussar, and ermine edges.[79]

The suits and waistcoats of the macaroni years were conspicuous as they marked a very different fashion departure from the previous generation. The large-patterned brocades fashionable for suit jackets and waistcoats of the elites in the 1740s and 1750s were replaced by textiles that relied on smaller repeats and a greater focus on the field of the fabric. Embroidery became smaller in scale and lost its rather overblown or pompous air in the macaroni period, with less use of very large gold and silver thread and raised outlines. In many cases, naturalistic decoration of plants and flowers crept up the edges of the coat, which might also be sprigged all over with buds, insects and leaves, and the buttons embroidered en suite. Light shades were favoured. The National Gallery of Victoria collection includes an exquisite pale-pink French suit embroidered with stylised and newly fashionable

2.21 Three-piece suit (*habit à la française*), French, *c.*1775. Silk satin, silk floss, chenille thread, wood (buttons), shell, metal; frock coat: centre back 115.2 cm, sleeve length 72 cm; waistcoat: centre back 69 cm, waist, flat 44 cm; breeches: outer leg 74.5 cm; waist, flat 35 cm. National Gallery of Victoria, Melbourne. Presented by the National Gallery Women's Association, 1978, D73.a-c-1978

flowers of the time, possibly jasmine and baby's breath (*Gypsophila elegans*), which meander along the embroidered edges of the coat and waistcoat (fig. 2.21). Anthropologists have argued that ornament often adorns the 'entry' points or borders of male dress, such as the edges of the sleeve and the coat. This might have origins in some ancient practices, such as reflective materials rejecting the evil eye; waistcoats from Brittany are extant with protective symbols sewn along the opening of the coat.[80]

Johan Zoffany's oeuvre also provides an excellent indication of the possible appearance of young, pretty macaroni and their older imitators.

2.22 **Johann Zoffany,** *The Tribuna of the Uffizi*, 1772–7/8.
Oil on canvas, 123.5 × 155 cm.
The Royal Collection

His painting *The Tribuna of the Uffizi* includes wonderfully detailed renderings of a young man's gold-coloured silk waistcoat and breeches and typical macaroni club of hair; an older man sports a dove-grey quilted satin waistcoat under a fawn frock coat; another wears rose-pink with a contrasting mouse-grey coat with gold tassels (fig. 2.22). When George III went mad, he became angered at the sight of this painting and attempted to damage it, probably due to the excitement caused by the naked Venus. It has also been asserted that the Queen would not countenance any Thomas Patch works in her presence, as it was felt they depicted dubious characters.[81]

A delicate miniature-painting by Peter Hall, who was born in provincial Sweden and died in Belgium, shows that the fashionable look of the time was recognisable and quite transnational within western Europe, crossing borders and regions that might seem far apart (fig. 2.23). It is a fine representation of the delicate silks and silk velvets associated with fashionable men of the 1760s and 1770s. Thus, despite what has been written

at times concerning a lack of macaroni fashion types being presented in respectful contemporary portraiture, the big hair and fine clothes of the macaroni type were very present, particularly in images of the young.

Acquiring clothes

Where did clothes come from? Coats, breeches and waistcoats were purchased by the wealthy tourist abroad, made up by a tailor from imported cloth or ordered through an intermediary; for example, the actor and celebrity David Garrick was a 'proxy shopper' for his aristocrat friend the Duke of Devonshire, when he was in the countryside.[82]

To achieve the new narrow line that became fashionable in the last decades of the eighteenth century, the outside flapped coat pocket was replaced with an inside pocket from 1777.[83] The coats of the 1760s also tended to be shorter than those of the 1750s, rising to above the knee or mid-thigh in the 1770s. This may have given rise to some of the macaroni wisecracks regarding rumps and rears (fig. 2.24).

A great many jewelled accessories accompanied the macaroni look. They included hanger swords, very long canes, clubs, spying glasses and snuff-boxes. These objects were not new introductions, but marked continuity with earlier details of rich dress. The rewards offered for missing or stolen accessories generally directed the reader to a jeweller, indicating their role as intermediaries, and not just makers and sellers of objects. Canes possessed an extra decorative function when the textile or leather cane-handle was worn around the wrist, rather like a 'twist' bracelet today (see fig. 4.16).

Dress-swords remained a particular feature of court dress. The wearing of swords was 'a formality rather than a necessity: the wearing of swords had been discouraged socially and at public gatherings from the 1760s in England, when Beau Nash banned them at the Assembly Rooms in Bath after a series of fights'.[84] They became the macaroni status symbol, the expensive examples having sterling-silver hilts, often pierced and chiselled, others being parcel-gilt or in two-coloured gold. A very fine French example incorporates enamel and diamonds and represents the most exquisite form of male jewellery of the period (fig. 2.25). The effect of the sword poking through the coat-tails may be seen in Darly's *The St James's Macaroni* (fig. 2.26).

The Cold Rump or Taste Alamode
Pub.d Dec.r 10. 1776.

2.25 Dress small-sword, French, sword cutlers (*fourbisseur*) Bougues and Étienne Giverne, Paris, *c*.1784. Mounted in gold, diamonds and royal-blue translucent enamel, blade etched and fire-gilt, overall length 98.4 cm, blade length 81.7 cm. Formerly collection of the Princes Hohenzollern. Courtesy of Peter Finer, London

Swords were further decorated with large textile tassels or rosettes.[85] In France, noble ladies gifted sword-knots to men on their wedding day; men gave fans to the ladies.[86] Like the sword-knot, the dress-sword probably held an erotic charge in France, at the very least; in Pierre-Antoine Baudouin's *Le Carquois épuisé* (1765, engraving by Nicolas de Launay, *c*.1771), which depicts a young man reclining on a richly decorated bed, gazing up at a young woman, a dress-sword with attached ribbons lies on the floor, the sign of sexual relations to come.[87] That new and modish material, steel, could also be fashioned into a metallic sword-knot wholly integrated with the form of the sword (see fig. 1.7).

Other macaroni accessories include the snuff-boxes of precious and semi-precious materials that survive in large numbers in decorative-arts collections across the world. There were seasonal fashions in snuff-boxes for the rich; they were lighter in weight for summer. Some of the finer and larger examples were not for general use, but were arrayed on tabletops. Horology supplied other men's luxury accessories, although macaroni men were more commonly associated with long, thin chatelaines – chains from which watches and seals depended.

Corsages also commonly recur in macaroni caricatures; they were part of general male attire in the eighteenth century, but the subtle messages were contained in the scale. The key to the macaroni was excess. Walpole characterised the macaroni as sporting massive nosegays or corsages: 'Lord Nuneham's garden is the quintessence of nosegays: I wonder some macaroni does not offer ten thousand pounds for it – but indeed the flowers come in their natural season, and take care to bring their perfumes along with them.'[88] To the Countess of Upper Ossory he wrote that Nuneham had a 'flower-garden

that would keep all Maccaronia in nosegays'.[89] These probably resembled the style of the substantial corsages worn at the French court. It was complained that Viscount Villiers, later Earl Grandison – a notable macaroni – was such a coxcomb that he forced his chairmen to wear 'bouquets in their bosoms'.[90]

Expending the realm

Walpole's correspondence thus established the characteristics of the macaroni stereotype when he first appeared, and indicated a correlation between the verbal and visual caricatures of macaroni that began to appear in popular culture from the early 1770s. Walpole's letters also linked the macaroni with the themes that provided part of the impetus for the scurrilous caricatures that were generated in their hundreds soon afterwards. These commented on fashion and luxury at a time when the terms were the subject of theoretical and economic debate, referred to by some as 'providing employment and spectacle for the poor' and denounced by others as sinful and foolish.[91] References to macaroni in terms of luxury, fashion or folly were connected in Walpole's mind with the extravagant Whig circle around Charles James Fox. The macaroni became a metaphor for problems with the currency and a general draining of the economy:

> Ireland is drained and has not a shilling. The explosion of the Scotch banks has reduced them almost as low, and sunk their flourishing manufactures to low water ebb. The Maccaronis are at their ne plus ultra: Charles Fox is already so like Julius Caesar, that he owes an hundred thousand pounds … What is England now? – A sink of Indian wealth, filled by nabobs and emptied by Maccaronis! A senate sold and despised! A country over-run by horse-races! A gaming, robbing, wrangling, railing nation, without principles, genius, character or allies; the over-grown shadow of what it was![92]

Walpole, as usual, exaggerated; he continued, 'Lord bless me, I run on like a political barber – I must go back to my shop …'[93] An example of the oriental luxury that Walpole refers to may be seen in the engraving *Robert Clive[,] Lord Clive Baron de Plassey … Gouverneur général de tous les établissements de la Compagnie angloise aux judes orientales* (fig. 2.27). His court dress matches the elaborate rococo frame, suggesting general richness, with a palm tree and campaign tents indicating the foreign location. It differs from many other representations of Clive of India, which are more sober in emphasis.

Walpole enjoyed speckling his correspondence with the new term; even the summer arrives 'à la Maccaroni three months too late'.[94] He referred

to some women as 'maccaronesses', but this related to their propensity to gamble in public, although fashionable women generally also had very high hair at this time. A decade later, in 1777, in his copy of *Mason's Heroic Epistle*, Walpole mocked the word 'macaroni', which resonated with the concept of fashion itself:

> Maccaroni is synonimous to Beau, Fop, Cox-comb, Petit Maître, &c. for Fashion having no foundation in Sense, or in the flower of sense, Taste, deals in forms & names, by altering which it thinks it invents. Maccaroni was a name adopted by or given to the young Men of fashion who returned from their Travels in the present reign, and is supposed to have been derived from the Italian paste of that denomination … The Chiefs of the Maccaronis became known beyond the limits of their fantastic Dominion by their excessive gaming.[95]

Petit-maître was perhaps the most common counterpart for 'macaroni'. The *Dictionnaire Critique* described him thus in 1768:

Petit-Maitre. C'est un surtout de caprices & de futilités, qui prend toutes sortes de figures, & qui paroît je ne sais combien de couleurs … Il est au jeu, au spectacles, à la Cour, à la ville, aux boulevards, au Palais-Royal; de sorte qu'on l'a vu par-tout presqu'au même instant, & c'est sa fureur de se multiplier.[96]

High and low

The macaroni figure may have achieved currency as he played a role, along with a myriad other images, plays, sounds and songs, within E.P. Thompson's 'counter-theatre of the poor'.[97] As people gazed at macaroni caricatures displayed in print-shop windows, or watched such figures tread the boards, they could not have failed to make the connection with the toffs around them.

The large number of caricatures in which a labouring woman – generally the Billingsgate fishwife or a fruit-seller – harasses and attacks effeminate macaroni (or French tourists) indicates that the theme had a potency that reflected aspects of street life. The theme of the working woman who symbolically castrates the homosexual is also related to descriptions of pilloried sodomites. Pierre-Jean Grosley, in his *A Tour to London*, considered the English public 'haughty and ungovernable' and described attacks on foreigners and even on the English dressed in Parisian clothes, noting that stones were often thrown at Frenchmen in a coach. James Peller Malcolm published a compilation of such anecdotes in 1808, reprinting Thomas Nugent's translation of Grosley of 1772:

> I have already observed, that the English themselves are not secure from the insolence of the London mob. I had a proof of this from the young Surgeon who accompanied me from Paris to Boulogne … at the first visit which he paid me in London, he informed me, that, a few days after his arrival, happening to take a walk through the fields on the Surrey-side of the Thames, dressed in a little green frock which he had brought from Paris, he was attacked by three of those gentlemen of the mobility who, taking him for a Frenchman, not only abused him with the foulest language, but gave him two or three slaps on the face … [98]

Harassment and jesting were part of life for overdressed gentlemen who ventured into many parts of the city, including the street.[99]

Masquerade magic

The masquerade is central to the story of macaroni men – and women. The masquerade complicated the visual logic of dress; it was a real and a fictive event at the same time, at which participants might wear 'costume' – imagined or fancy dress – or 'real' costume: that is, high fashion that nonetheless might be suitable only for the space of this event. Fashion here filled a theatrical role that in turn spilled over into the street, if such clothes were worn in other settings. Writing to Sir William Hamilton, Walpole noted:

> If you were to come over, you would find us a general masquerade. The Macaronies, not content with producing new fashions every day – and who are great reformers, are going to restore the Vandyck dress, in concert with the Macaronesses – As my thighs would not make a figure in breeches from my navel to my instep, I shall wait till the dress of the Druids is revived, which will be more suitable to my age.[100]

Several engravings of masquerade scenes indicate that as well as wearing a domino (an enveloping black silk cape with hood) and fancy dress, many men attended masquerades wearing their own fashionable clothing. Thus, rather than wearing costume, they went as 'themselves', and this is generally how they were caricatured, rather than appearing in a domino or

fancy dress. Many macaroni images place the figures in the context of the masquerade: *From the Haymarket*, by R. Sayer and J. Bennett, for instance, in which a florid-faced fop with extraordinarily high hair lifts his chin back to cope with a massive cravat. Another engraving that is not, strictly speaking, a caricature but rather a hybrid image related to the conversation piece, as well as theatrical scenes, depicts the London Pantheon. It shows particularly high toupees on many of the men, who sport swords and mannered poses (fig. 2.28). The Pantheon was often depicted as a licentious space in which men and women had wan and wasted faces, as in *The Pantheon in Oxford Street* (fig. 2.29). Here male children are neglected and are forced to ride a gilt-topped cane instead of a toy horse.

Caricatures and descriptions of macaroni at these events indicate that combinations of patterns, spots and stripes and clashing colour were favoured. *The Unfortunate Macaroni* (1772) is a clever joke about either an

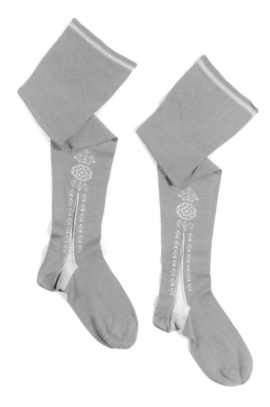

THE UNFORTUNATE MACARONI.

Pub accor to Act Feb V 5 1772 by M Darly Strand

Above left
2.30 **M. Darly, *The Unfortunate Macaroni*, 5 February 1772.** Etching, plate 17.5 × 12.6 cm, sheet 19.4 × 13.4 cm. Courtesy of The Lewis Walpole Library, Yale University

Above right
2.31 **A pair of pinkish-red frame-knitted stockings with gore clocks, English or French, *c.*1730–70, probably mid-century.** Ivory clocks edged with diapered bands and floral motifs, 64 cm. Courtesy of Kerry Taylor

unsuccessful dresser or an unfortunate clashing outfit (fig. 2.30). Coloured silk stockings for the well-to-do had 'clocks' or decorative embroidered seams in colours including green or white, which caricaturists sometimes seized upon (fig. 2.31). The appearance of striped stockings and waistcoats in several macaroni caricatures points to an older cultural understanding of transgressive dress; Michel Pastoureau's study of the history of the stripe indicates that it carried vestiges of diabolical, sinister or ludic overtones, until its use became more common in clothing and furnishing textiles in the 1790s. Medieval Europe expected its 'clowns, musicians, and entertainers, people with no social status', to wear the striped or *mi-partie* clothing (vertical separation by either colour or texture) that young aristocratic fourteenth-century men once wore, as they later represented 'insincerity and falsehood' and even 'disintegration' or 'retrogression'.[101] Striped stockings and banyans were also reminiscent of Oriental aesthetics to European viewers and had been popular since the late seventeenth century. To the admixture of colours and patterns in macaroni fashions can be added the particular ocular effects of vertical and horizontal stripes, particularly when woven with metallic threads, which often have a disconcerting visual potential – that is, they distort our vision slightly and disrupt the natural form of the body (fig. 2.32).

2.32 **Part-waistcoat**, *c.*1770.
Striped silk. Royal Ontario Museum,
Toronto, 942.9.6

Macaroni men were very much associated with new fashionable forms
for 'taking the dust' or fast carriage-driving. Many macaroni men were
satirised on horseback, including the Whig politician Charles James Fox's
(very large) brother Stephen, and a great many images were also made of
young men driving new forms of fashionable carriages. The most modish
vehicle was the phaeton, in which one or two persons could drive, rather
like a sports car today.

A gentleman's visiting card could evoke the elegance of the *manège*. The
fine engraved calling card of 'Colonel Roche', designed by the celebrated
Italian engraver and painter Giovanni Battista Cipriani (founding member
of the Royal Academy, resident in England from 1755), integrated whips and

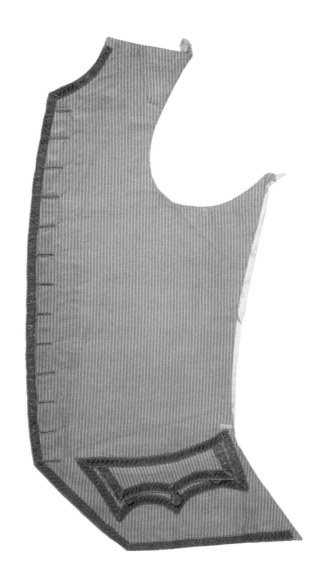

writing (fig. 2.33). It suggests a unified display of elegant calligraphy, as well as a taste for the equestrian fashions that gentlemen spent so much money on in the late eighteenth century. Cipriani was a central figure within the print culture and decorative arts of the day, and having him make a visiting card was the choice of a fashionable connoisseur. The type of swagged decoration associated with neoclassicism was a flexible style that could be applied to many things, from visiting cards to door-knobs, in a way that earlier Palladianism could not.

The issue of social emulation, of which clothing was a central feature, can also be explored in relation to the macaroni and the new confident emergent bourgeois public. E.P. Thompson has set out the historiographical problems in this area. His own work then goes on to support the subsequent approach of John Brewer, that 'middle-class independence was constantly constrained and brought back within the channels of dependency by the powerful controls of clientage'.[102] As Thompson noted, the appearance of the aristocracy had 'the studied self-consciousness of public theatre . . . a studied and elaborate hegemonic style, a theatrical role in which the great were schooled in infancy and which they maintained until death'. He went on to note that to speak of dress as theatre is not to diminish its importance: 'A great part of politics and law is always theatre . . . What one remarks of the eighteenth century is the elaboration of this style and the self-consciousness with which it was deployed.'[103]

The macaroni might have intrigued at the time as they highlighted the artificiality of aristocratic dressing as well as speech and mannerisms. They revealed them to be a theatrical play of artifice rather than part of a natural system: a parody seemed to be emerging that was useful for those who

criticised aristocratic privilege. Thus Hannah Greig says the public focus on outrageous individuals and fascination with scandal literature 'were forerunners to radical attacks on the political infrastructure that emerged in a climate of the European revolution and English political reform from the 1780s and 1790s'.[104] Such a tension had always been part of the training in noble behaviour; the body of the noble was meant to be socially superior, yet it had to be trained in equitation and fencing, and moulded by dance, in order to produce the appropriate bearing; sometimes it was even beaten to ensure it.[105] As acting method made use of aristocratic technologies of the body – poses and gestures – there is a further link to the theatre that emphasised the significance of metaphorical and actual performativity.

'Witty Quibbles': wit and the macaroni

There are other forerunners for the usage of the word 'macaroni' apart from the gastronomic ones already discussed. It may also derive from a pun that only the well-educated eighteenth-century public would have enjoyed – that of the paired meanings of noodle and macaronic poetry, which was a burlesque of Latin forms, designed to be witty. Comments on both types survive in the correspondence of Walpole. The term 'macaronic' was first used in the 1490s to describe Paduan and other Italian poetry in which Latin forms were mixed with the vernacular, the latter being given correct Latin endings. As Siegfried Wenzel notes, Teofilo Folengo (d.1544) 'adopted this practice as a medium for wit, playfulness, and parody' and wrote that 'macaronic poems must have nothing but fat, coarseness, and gross words in them'.[106] It carried within it the sense of 'circumforaneous Wits' (*The Spectator*, 24 April 1711), which creates a nice connection with the jokes later made about South Sea explorers such as Sir Joseph Banks and Dr Daniel Solander. The fifteenth-century use of the term 'macaronic' also referred to the foreign food of gnocchi, pale in colour and requiring sauce or some other addition to make it palatable.[107] The sense of burlesque and admixture, characteristic of the eighteenth-century view of the male macaroni, who seemed to merge masculine and feminine personae in his appearance, as well as the English and the foreign, gave an added resonance to the term. Wenzel notes that the function of macaronic verse in Middle English was in some cases to satirise the true Latin of, for instance, the Vulgate Bible, and to characterise good and evil figures by the language they speak. It also helps to explain the relish that contemporaries took in describing the male macaroni as a type of gender-hybrid. The *Oxford English Dictionary* describes 'macaronic' as 'a burlesque form of verse in which vernacular words are introduced into a Latin context with Latin terminations and in Latin constructions ... Hence of language, style, etc.: Resembling the mixed jargon of macaronic poetry.'[108]

Wit and *jeux d'esprit* were nearly always associated with the macaroni or foppish persona – sometimes attacked as a complete lack thereof – and the word probably entered colloquial English through some combination of these terms in popular culture and the vernacular. The expression was well known to those educated in Latin into the nineteenth century, an anthology of macaronic poetry being published in 1831.[109] *Latham's Dictionary* (1870) recorded the meaning of 'macaroni' as a droll or fool: 'There is a set of merry drolls whom the common people of all countries admire, and seem to love so well, that they could eat them . . . In Holland they are termed "pickled herrings"; in France "Jean potages"; in Italy "*maccaronies*"; and in Great Britain, "jack puddings".'[110] 'M. Darly' (either Matthew or Mary, or perhaps as a team) had in 1763 published *A Book of Caricatures on 59 Copper Plates, with Ye Principles of Designing, in that Droll and pleasing manner, by M. Darly. With Sundry Ancient and Modern Examples and several well known Caricatura*.[111]

Aristocratic macaroni such as Fox were noted for their wit, which was derived from their educational upbringing, urbanity and observations of Paris salon life. Wit was a sign of an urbane and courtly persona; some of Fox's famous responses, with their use of paradox, were taken up in the late nineteenth century by Oscar Wilde. The affected speech of the macaroni circles made extensive use of French and certain pronunciations: *cowcumber* (cucumber), *Jarsey* (Jersey), *charrit* (chariot), *gould* (gold), *bal-cōny* (balcony) and *Lunnon* (London).[112] Pronunciation is a part of the 'lost history' of fashion: Horace Walpole wrote of it thus to Horace Mann in 1782: 'Not only the fashions in dress and manners change, but the ways of thinking, nay, of speaking an pronouncing.'[113] When this taste was played out in the realm of caricature, the macaroni were portrayed as full of facile speech and of little or no substance.

Terry Castle notes that at the masquerade the macaroni made a type of high-pitched squeaking that contemporaries associated with suspect motives and behaviour, similar to that of the castrato.[114] A joke-book set out the macaroni pronunciation and expression, and most newspaper accounts of their conversations tried to convey their speech and expressions. Their talk was peppered with 'Mem', and snuff was generally 'snush'. Such speech and inane discussions were also associated in the eighteenth-century mind with satires of wealthy women; they can be found in a satirical account of a woman's day in *The Spectator* of 1712. When, in 1786, *The Merry Andrew; or, Macaroni Jester. A Choice Collection of Funny Jokes, Merry Stories, Droll Adventures, Frolicksome Tales, Witty Quibbles, Youthful Pranks . . .* was published, macaroni in itself must have meant something comical, for this text contains no other reference to the macaroni apart from a poem in which a monkey was transformed into a Beau.[115] As late as the 1930s a novel, *If I*

Were Dictator: The Pronouncements of the Grand Macaroni, used the notion of macaroni as a type of nonsense to mock regulation.[116]

The term 'macaroni', although often used interchangeably with words such as fop, coxcomb or *petit-maître*, meant something more nuanced and specific. The foreign nature of his behaviour and the macaroni's allegiance to continental (as opposed to national) fashions were also emphasised by the association with Italian pasta as opposed to that national symbol, the roast beef of England. Those less socially insecure than Richard Cosway, such as Charles James Fox and Joseph Banks, may have felt less threatened about the charge; caricatured himself, Banks owned macaroni caricatures and may have enjoyed the association. These contradictions are the subject of the following chapter.

CHAPTER 3

Fact and Fiction:
The Macaroni Caricature,
Personality and Portraiture

I received three packets from England with your letter . . . That of the former date and many others anterior to it confirm me in the opinion that in all stations of life our country produces more extravagant characters and more madmen than any other we know or have heard of. I am unwilling to attribute this to our liberty, though I fear that it is the effect of it.

Horace Mann to Horace Walpole, 11 March 1780[1]

The macaroni are best known through caricature, but the public understanding of this type was also negotiated through a range of media and sites, including the theatre, masquerade, the press, popular songs and jokes, even textile prints and porcelain. Caricature prints had multifaceted meanings, and it is from this position that this chapter approaches the relationship of the macaroni caricature, personality and portraiture. Rather than viewing the genre as stable and reflective of something always pre-existing, a study of the prints indicates that a wide range of meanings was possible within the genre. The historian of credit and Freemasonry, John Money, argues that the rise of the 'middle-class mentality' in the eighteenth century was connected to an understanding that civil society was 'a human artifice' and that 'collective imitation and communication of human example' were more important than divine providence.[2] Hence the significance of the rise of the printed caricature, with its function that exceeded entertainment or instruction.

Matthew and Mary Darly: caricature and the print-shop

The expansion of printmaking in the second half of the century benefited from the mixture of nativism and foreign influences present in a metropolis such as London. Hogarth derived much of his compositional virtuosity from a study of French rococo fashion drawing and prints by the Frenchmen Boitard, Cochin, Coypel, Watteau and Hubert-François Bourguignon, known as Gravelot, who is claimed to have said: 'De English may be very clever in deir own opinions, but dey do not draw de draw.'[3] The French contribution to the advent of richly illustrated English periodicals should be emphasised. Well before the rise of the first fashion magazines in the 1760s they had created the *figure de mode*, situated in a simple landscape or against an architectural backdrop by great artists, including Watteau.

Two of the principal print creators and sellers who benefited from new techniques and markets developing in England in the 1760s and 1770s were the Darlys. Matthew and Mary Darly were the first to capitalise on the macaroni phenomenon; in fact they actively helped to create it. The extensive commentary regarding macaroni in the popular press followed rather than preceded the publication of their macaroni suites. Matthew Darly began his career as a designer and printer of wallpapers, a paper-stainer and an engraver. During the Seven Years War he began to etch the political caricatures by George Townshend, which attacked Charles James Fox, amongst others.[4] Matthew was a noted drawing-master who specialised in publishing the work of amateurs, engraving most of them himself; Mary Darly published a book on caricature drawing around 1762. The Darlys were therefore probably on personal terms with some members of the *beau monde*. Their shops were in the court end of town, at 39 Strand and Leicester Fields. Darly advertised that at his premises:

> Gentlemen and Ladies may have Copper plates prepared and Varnished for etching. Ladies to whom the fumes of the Aqua Fortis are Noxious may have their Plates carefully Bit, and proved, and may be attended at their own Houses . . . Ladies & Gentlemen sending their Designs may have them neatly etch'd and printed for their own private Amusement at the most reasonable rates, or if for Publication, shall have evry grateful return and acknowledgement.[5]

As print-sellers and entrepreneurs, the Darlys traded on the association with aristocratic amateur sketchers when they produced their macaroni suites from 1771. By 1773 the Darlys held exhibitions of up to 300 caricatures, which Diana Donald suggests were a parody of those of the Royal Academy and the Society of Artists. Admission was by catalogue priced at a shilling, which entitled the bearer to one print.[6] Most recently, Joseph Monteyne has argued that the signature 'M Darly' might refer to the collaboration of both Mary and Matthew, and that Mary might have been behind more of the images than has previously been thought.[7]

The Darly issued six sets of 24 caricatures, which were reissued in six volumes, each with a title page, between 1771 and 1773. They were not all of macaroni images, but the fact that they were published together means they have interconnected meanings and relationships. Simultaneously Matthew Darly issued at least two other similar sets of larger-sized prints. Many were reissued in January 1776; the genre thus enjoyed a long circulation and must have had a receptive audience or it would not have been reprinted. Darly's macaroni images tend to be cruder stylistically than the carefully engraved products from competitors such as Bowles, Dawe and Earlom. The Darlys' work became so closely associated with the genre that in July 1772 they published an engraving that played up the circularity of art and life, *The Macaroni Print Shop*, drawn by E. Topham, showing their own store, no. 39 Strand, outside which various ridiculous figures peer at the ridiculous figures engraved within (fig. 3.1). In a reflexive manner, they look at images that had already been published by 'M.' Darly, including an image of Joseph Banks as 'the Fly Catching Macaroni' (see fig. 3.14). The viewers include a wide range of ages, and variously wear a sword, cane, striped

3.1 E. Topham (illustrator), M. Darly (printmaker), *The Macaroni Print Shop*, 14 July 1772. Etching, plate 17.8 × 24.8 cm. Courtesy of The Lewis Walpole Library, Yale University

stockings, large wig-bag and queue. The macaroni to the right with a cane peers at his counterfeit pictured in the window. As a contrast, a John Bull figure is included in a long rustic coat and boots. The size of the prints has been exaggerated for effect; Stephens rightly noted that they were all much smaller than a pane of glass.[8]

Darly's first such suite was entitled *Caricatures by Several Ladies, Gentelmen, Artists &c. Pubd. by M. Darly. Strand* and part of this set was after the well-known caricaturists Bunbury and E. Topham. It included many French references, such as *Monr. le Frizuer* (see fig. 4.17). *My Lord Tip-Toe. Just Arrived from Monkey Land* laughed at the French and fashion at the same time. Darly played here on the stock theme of the poor Frenchman or peasant in patched finery. Darly also included the homosexual joke *Ganymede* in the first set (see fig. 5.12). The most consistent aspect of macaroni dress that recurred was the wig, rather than the court suit. Macaroni wear a powdered wig, caricatured as towering, often with a large wig-bag, queue or clump of hair depending at the rear, or a pigtail in the French manner.

Darly's second suite of caricatures, published in 1772, was entitled *Vol. II of Caricatures, Macaronies & Characters by Sundry Ladies, Gentln. Artists &c.* The very title page announces a parodic intention: elaborate swags of laurel and pompous architectural fragments refer to the exactly contemporary craze for the archaeologically informed neoclassicism of William Chambers, Robert Adam and James 'Athenian' Stuart (fig. 3.2). The frontispiece both announces the contents as topical and pokes fun at yet another fashion, an architectural style that was not universally acclaimed.

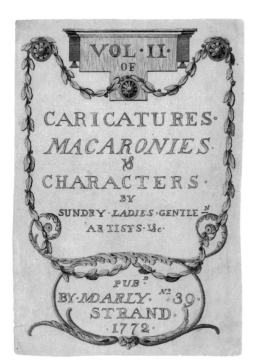

3.2 **M. Darly, *Vol. II of Caricatures, Macaronies & Characters by Sundry Ladies, Gentln, Artists &c*, 1772**. Frontispiece. British Library, London

In a gesture that was typical of Darly's output, the more low-born the person depicted, the more crude the illustrative style. The most ridiculous macaroni, *The Unfortunate Macaroni*, is subhuman in his ugly mask-like features and inelegant posture, and is also given the most absurd outfit, with a patched face and sprigged stockings with clocks (embroidery on the lower inside leg) (see fig. 2.30). M. Dorothy George suggests that he is an unlucky gambler, but he also might be a failed dresser.

No consistent approach was taken with the dress in this series, but nearly all have the high hairstyle of the early 1770s. Several of the plates employ a physiognomy recognised as diabolical, which was also reserved for foreign hairdressers and other members of the appearance trades.[9] It was also visual shorthand for Jewish people at this time. Dress-swords jut out level with the crutch and in varying states of erection that highlight the hilarity and the barbed attack.

Darly's third suite, whose title page reads *1772, Vol. III of Macaronies, Characters, Caricatures &c. Designed by the Greatest Personages, Artists &c. Graved & Pubd. by M. Darly, 39 Strand*, this time in a frame encircled with roses, featured the props and attributes of court dress wielded by the macaroni. One of the caricatures focuses on the bow attached to the wig-bag (*The Bath Macaroni*; fig. 2.2). *The Sleepy Macaroni Ste'-aling a Nap* refers to Stephen Fox, called 'Ste' by the family, who was from the previous generation, also a gambler and known as the lover of Lord Hervey. Artisans and labourers were also mocked in this suite: *The Whale Bone Macaroni* (fig. 5.9), engraved in a self-consciously French manner to underline his distance from English traditions, has the willowy grace and balletic step of the *petit-maître* and a long phallic wig-bag. Such figures also suggest the energy and theatre of commerce and the street.

Volume IV was concerned with the ludicrous spread of macaroni fashions. *The Farmer-Macaroni* carried the verse:

E'en Farmers dress & mount their Ponies,
And all alike, are Macaronies.

Darly kept his suites topical and sensational by including a mixture of fictive and real identities in each set. This suite included the black macaroni, *A Mungo Macaroni*, probably Julius Soubise, whom I discuss below (fig. 3.30). His funniest coup was in calling Richard Cosway *The Miniature Macaroni*. Darly made the image half the size of the rest and also depicted the painter of miniatures as very tiny, overshadowed by his sword and the lady's handkerchief that he holds (fig. 3.3). This must have caused great

3.3 M. Darly, *The Miniature Macaroni*, **24 September 1772.** Etching, plate 17.5 × 12.6 cm. Courtesy of The Lewis Walpole Library, Yale University

hilarity amongst the viewers, for Cosway was both short and burdened by his dress-sword, which he never left off.

In preparing his works, Darly had several older traditions to draw upon, which would have resonated with the viewing public and would have provided the macaroni caricatures with a context. Painted caricatures began on the Grand Tour as painted private jokes shared between young men and their tutors. Italian artists working in Rome inspired the English development of this field. Etchings were made by Anton Maria Zanetti, Pier Leone Ghezzi and Pietro Longhi of other artists and 'people of quality',[10] as a contemporary put it, and were later painted in Rome by English artists including Joshua Reynolds and Thomas Patch (fig. 3.4).[11] Ghezzi produced numerous 'caricatures of personages at the Papal Court at Rome and at the Court of the King of Poland, Elector of Saxony, etched and published at Dresden', which in their style and approach are clearly the forerunners of macaroni prints.[12] French expatriate artists also engaged in this field, and connoisseurs including the marquis de Marigny, *directeur des bâtiments du roi*, wrote himself from Versailles to the Director of the French Academy in Rome when Ghezzi died in 1755, aged 82: 'If among the things in the studio of the Chevalier Ghetzy there are some caricatures of distinction it would give me pleasure to acquire some of them.'[13] Ghezzi was not simply making a mockery of the artists he caricatured, but engaging with them in an intimate fashion. As he wrote under his etching of Jean-François de Troy: 'he will be one of the great sculptors of France', and of Claude Duflos, subject of a vicious caricature: 'Everything from his hand is perfection.'[14] There is a double irony here that may be lost on us now. Caricature might express fondness and a special bond.

The long eighteenth century created its own histories and historiographies regarding the 'invention' of caricatures. There was a wide general awareness amongst the well educated that the caricature tradition drew upon and extended that of the Renaissance physiognomic studies or 'caprices' by Leonardo da Vinci, Giuseppe Arcimboldo and Albrecht Dürer, and the baroque caricatures of Annibale and Agostino Carracci (*Heads*, c.1590) and Gian Lorenzo Bernini.

Eighteenth-century viewers enjoyed examining contrasts of rank, nationality and occupation. The macaroni tradesman-type was drawn from the types that represented ranks and trades via the use of physiognomy, body types, costume and tools. More often than not, the plebeian was 'depicted with ungracious, ill-formed features'.[15] Certain types had particular resonance. The butcher, who was often paired with the macaroni, was

3.4 **Thomas Patch,** *A Punch Party*, 1760. Oil on canvas, 114.3 × 171.5 cm. Dunham Massey, Cheshire

depicted as amorous, thus virile; stout, thus well fed; and nationalistic, for he prepared the roast beef of England. By contrast, the French cook preparing frogs was skinny and miserable (see fig. 4.2). Barbers were depicted with a comb in their hair or carrying a wig-box, a convention that was taken over into the macaroni typology (see fig. 2.4). A French or German hairdresser was indicated with similar tools, but a monstrous visage and scrawny body. The public could thus recognise both trades and nationalities in an instant. Forerunners and variants of John Bull were positioned against the effeminate Frenchman (see fig. 4.5), but also against the 'emaciated and scabrous' Scot in bare legs and a kilt, who was almost as unpopular as the French.

Darly was joined by a number of competitors producing macaroni imagery from 1773. Carington Bowles, map- and print-seller at no. 69 St Paul's Church Yard, London, did not produce overt political themes. His macaroni images included *Docking the Macaroni* (19 January 1773) and *P'sha You Flatter Me* (1773), the latter the companion to *How D'ye Like Me*, probably the best-known and most reproduced macaroni image today (see fig. 5.2). The technical superiority of mezzotint could convey subtle messages about the texture of clothing and the tone of complexion that were more painstaking to achieve in engraving, and Bowles's figures were set in carefully rendered backgrounds such as fashionable and luxurious boudoirs and dressing rooms, which added meaning to the satire. With the addition of wash colours, they stood out from those of his competitors.

John Bowles, whose shop was at no. 13 in Cornhill, entered the fray with *Miss Macaroni and her Gallant at a Print-Shop*, a fine mezzotint by J.R. Smith: 'While Macaroni and his Mistress here, / At other Characters, in Picture, sneer, / To the vain Couple is but little known, / How much deserving Ridicule their own' (fig. 3.5). Various fashionably dressed men examine the prints in a shop window and 'Miss Macaroni' looks modestly away, while a dog fouls the shoe of the man in black. This scatological topos comes from Dutch art and is common in genre painting and work

Miss MACARONI and her GALLANT at a Print-Shop.

While Macaroni and his Mistress here, / To the vain Couple is but little known:
At other Characters in Picture sneer; / How much deserving Ridicule their own.

Printed for John Bowles, at Nº 13 in Cornhill.

underlining the matter of *vanitas*. Several macaroni caricatures that had
already been published appear in the image of the window.

   In the late 1770s Mary Darly resumed production of her husband's
speciality. Her next major set was produced from 1 January 1776, with a
significant dedication to David Garrick (see fig. 6.14). *Darly's Comic-Prints
of Characters, Caricatures, Macaronies &c.* was priced at £4 4s., a substantial
sum. This series, etched in a new economical style that looks almost
modern, referred to that aspect of macaroni dressing which revolved around
accessories. Both women and men secured their shoes with buckles – men's
buckles tending to be square rather than round, although women, too,
adopted square buckles in the early 1780s, before they fell out of fashion.[16]
Such buckles could be set with paste (lead glass) or 'Bristol stones' (chips
of quartz), or diamonds if you were very rich (fig. 3.6). The new macaroni
fashion was for huge silver or plated Artois shoe buckles, which the *Morning
Post* claimed weighed three to eleven ounces. A notice from this newspaper
is pasted on the British Library copy of *Buckles and Buttons. I Am the Thing.
Dem-me* (fig. 3.7), pointing to the difficulty or impossibility of less wealthy
men following this fashion, without resorting to cheaper copies of the dress:

> The macaronies of a certain class are under peculiar circumstances
> of distress, occasioned by the fashion now so prevalent, of wearing
> enormous shoe-buckles, and we are well assured, that the manufactory
> of plated ware was never known to be in so flourishing a condition.[17]

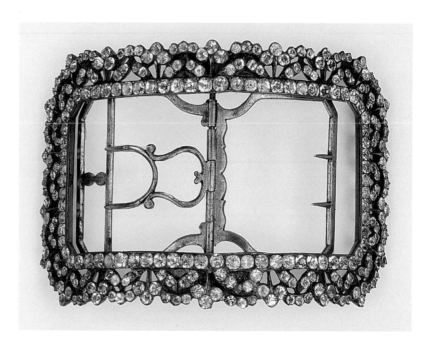

BUCKLES AND BUTTONS
I AM THE THING. DEM-ME.

STEEL BUTTONS I   Coup de Bouton

Above left
3.7 M. Darly, *Buckles and Buttons. I Am the Thing. Dem-me*, 7 February 1777. Etching and engraving, plate 34.8 × 24.4 cm, sheet 38 × 27 cm. Courtesy of The Lewis Walpole Library, Yale University

Above right
3.8 William Humphrey (printmaker), *Steel Buttons I. Coup de Bouton*, 29 April 1777. Etching with roulette, sheet 25 × 30 cm. Courtesy of The Lewis Walpole Library, Yale University

Right
3.9 Folio from a sample-book of buttons, French, *c.*1790. Courtesy of Martin Kamer

The new fashion for huge buttons was satirised in *Modern Shields or the Virtue of Steel Buttons*, in which a man shields himself from his opponent's sword with buttons the size of dinner plates. In similar vein, *Steel Buttons I. Coup de Bouton* (fig. 3.8), published by a competitor, W. Humphrey, features the reflected light from steel buttons dazzling a woman. Steel was a novel status symbol, and many of the best-quality buttons and other steel wares came from England, although the Russian production from Tula was also highly prestigious (part of it consisting of whole pieces of furniture). In French high fashion of the mid-1770s, buttons lost their functional role; the comte d'Artois, who later became Charles X, wore buttons mounted as watches; there were pornographic buttons *à l'Aretin* on sale in the Palais-Royal, as well as rebus and alphabetical buttons.[18] A set *à la Buffon* contained insects imprisoned in glass, or leaves.[19] A surviving French folio of sample buttons numbering in the hundreds includes examples with red and green foils, as well as stamped and engraved pinchbeck (fig. 3.9).

Masculine self-portraits and the macaroni

What is the relationship between the masculine self-portrait and the scurrilous caricature? How does dress work to structure a pictorial dialogue about self-identity? Motives for retaining elaborate dress requisite at court were various, inflected by the social position and personal motivations of the wearers. Macaroni status was attributed to figures as notable as the Whig politician Charles James Fox, sometimes called 'the Original Macaroni'; the botanist and South Sea explorer Sir Joseph Banks – labelled 'the Fly Catching Macaroni'; the renowned miniature-painter Richard Cosway – 'the Miniature Macaroni'; the famed landscape garden-designer Humphry Repton; the St Martin's Lane luxury upholsterer John Cobb; Julius Soubise, the freed slave of the Duchess of Queensberry – 'a Mungo Macaroni'; and the Reverend William Dodd, the extravagantly dressed chaplain to George III. These historical figures provide an opportunity to relate general understandings of fashionability to lived experience. Alleged macaroni status was used to attack the professional credentials of Joseph Banks within the scientific community; Cosway was similarly ridiculed as an absurd-looking *parvenu*. Dodd, 'the Macaroni Parson', in becoming the subject of a forgery trial resulting in his sensational execution, further highlighted the potency of the macaroni label.

Charles James Fox: 'the Original Macaroni'

Matthew Darly's second suite of macaroni caricatures entitled Charles James Fox (1749–1806) 'the Original Macaroni'. The Fox of the later years of his life is probably better known today: a supporter of the Americans and of the French Revolution, rotund, dishevelled and sporting democratic dress.

Fox's shift from youthful macaroni to dishevelled middle age struck all his biographers; 'he was to lead the taste of the town through all stages from coxcombry to slovenliness'.[20]

Charles James Fox is well served by biographers, including in a delightful text by Stella Tillyard.[21] All his biographers discuss his macaroni youth. His mother's family, the Lennoxes, were more French than English, as Charles James's maternal great-grandfather, the 1st Duke of Richmond, Charles Lennox (b.1672), was the illegitimate son of Charles II and Louise de Kéroualle, who had arrived with the diplomats of Louis XIV's court to negotiate the Treaty of Dover. Louise was created Duchess of Portsmouth and was given the Stuart lands in France by Louis XIV. Upon the death of Charles II, the son Charles Lennox was brought up in France, a Catholic, at the Château d'Aubigny. He later renounced his religion and returned to England, where he enjoyed a handsome income from coal dues, granted by his father. The family maintained Francophile links throughout the eighteenth century and this certainly informed Charles James's macaroni identity.

Paris and her products had been inaccessible during the Seven Years War (1756–63); the wearing of French fabrics had been banned during this period, although many were smuggled in nonetheless. The wealthy English who had been deprived of their Grand Tour flocked to Paris after the Treaty of 1763. Fox's family travelled there immediately and regularly, in 1763–4, 1766, 1767 and 1769. Mr and Mrs David Garrick also left for Paris in September 1763. Charles Fox first visited Paris when he was 15 and was seen as a schoolboy 'with his hatt & feather very french & very much improved'.[22] He visited again between April and May 1765 as a 16-year-old with his brother Stephen and his mother; in September 1766 he left for the Grand Tour, returning in August 1768; and was in Paris again in 1769 and 1771. Lord Holland, not at all vexed, noted that the travel was producing the 'petit maître achevè'.[23]

With unlimited funds and the best introductions, the 16-year-old 'CF' delighted in the urbanity of continental Europe and her fashions; 'the fascinating vivacity of French manners, the seduction of Italian luxury, at times enslaved him: he drank large draughts of pleasure,' noted a Regency biographer disapprovingly.[24] In France and Italy, Fox was well placed to absorb the elaborate male fashions of the late 1760s. He is supposed to have made a special trip to Lyons to purchase silk waistcoats, and he began to sport the red heels associated with Versailles and carried a 'little odd French hat'.[25]

Back in London, Fox was 21 in 1770, the period when the macaroni pose was about to peak:

. . . he indulged in all the fashionable elegance of attire, and vied, in point of red heels and Paris cut velvet with the most dashing young men of the age. Indeed there are many still living who recollect Beau Fox strutting up and down St James's street, in a suit of French embroidery, a little silk hat, red-heeled shoes, and a bouquet nearly big enough for a may-pole. These and similar qualifications he displayed in most of the courts of Europe which he visited in the course of his tour, and if he did not return like his maternal ancestor, Charles II, with all the vices of the continent, he at least brought back a wardrobe replete with all its fashions.[26]

Sir N.W. Wraxall recalled, 'At five and twenty I have seen him apparrelled en petit Maitre with a Hat and Feather, even in the House of Commons.'[27] A notorious gambler, Fox became part of the Whig club-land that was notorious for its extravagance, having straw laid in the street to dull the sound of carriages, for instance. Like gambling debts, dress was a very visible part of conspicuous consumption, a lavish dress, like the sumptuous Whig country estates and townhouses – Spencer House was built in the 1760s – indicating that here lay the true power in England. Whigs of two types dominated politics between 1760 and 1790. Fox, along with Rockingham, Portland and Grey, stood for ancient liberties and against the government Whigs, who stood for executive authority and stability – North, Pitt and Liverpool. Fox and the Earl of Carlisle paraded in the Mall 'in a suit of Paris-cut velvet, most fancifully embroidered, and bedecked with a large bouquet; a head-dress cemented into every variety of shape; a little silk hat, curiously ornamented; and a pair of French shoes, with *red-heels*'.[28] An Edwardian biographer of another self-styled macaroni and friend of Fox, Walter Stanhope, made the antipathy explicit when he noted: 'Charles James Fox and young Lord Carlisle, were viewed with displeasure by the King and Queen who endeavoured to maintain a simplicity in manners and attire.'[29] The current king was nicknamed 'Farmer George'; his wife Charlotte was also a foreigner and their court did not match the scintillation of its continental counterparts, although their rusticity has been greatly exaggerated and recently corrected in books and exhibitions. The king was characterised by a preference for plain dressing, in which his orders and decorations indicated rank. For his birthday court in 1791:

> His Majesty Was dressed, as he always is on his own birth-day, very plain. THE PRINCE OF WALES Appeared in a *chocolate* coloured silk tabby coat, richly spangled all over with fine silver spangles, and embroidered on the seams; the waistcoat was of white filé, ornamented in the same manner; his Royal Highness likewise wore his brilliant diamond epaulet, star, George, Sword, and buckles.[30]

Neither the King nor the Queen approved of extreme sartorial fashion.

The clothes also sent out messages: the King was allied with the sober Tory Pitt, whereas the flashier Prince of Wales was allied with Fox and the Whigs. As the Whig forebears had opposed absolutism, there was an irony in this re-importation of French court dress, wit and manners as a style detached from its original premise. The Whigs wore aristocratic dress without the autocratic agenda inherent in the French original. Fox loved Paris and her society, but hated the Bourbon autocracy. Thus his adoption of macaroni dress was not a tribute to monarchy, but a statement of a cosmopolitan outlook and Whig confidence; later he applauded the beginning of the French Revolution and compared it to 1688. There may also have been an element of outdoing the court followers, who included a large number of non-noble sycophants, such as Richard Cosway.

Many contemporaries interpreted macaroni behaviour as deliberately provocative. Lord Bolingbroke wrote, probably in a jesting manner, requesting a Paris suit:

> A small pattern seems to be the reigning taste amongst the Macaronis at Almack's, and is, therefore, what Lord B. chooses . . . As to the smallness of the sleeves, and length of the waist, Lord B. desires them to be outré, that he may exceed any Macaronis now about town, and become the object of their envy.[31]

An element of resisting authority was also present. French silks were considered to be desirable for their colour and quality of weaving, cheaper than that which was available in England, and fashionable for both men and women. In 1749 an Act of Parliament banned 'the importation and wear of foreign embroidery and brocade, and of gold and silver thread, lace, or other work made of gold or silver wire manufactured in foreign parts'; there were public burnings of seized goods.[32] This was in part the result of pressure exerted by the Anti-Gallican Society, established in 1745. Foreign embroidery was considered superior in terms of its design; the seizure in 1764 of Lord and Lady Holderness's baggage, full of 200 prohibited examples, was widely publicised.[33] Other customs seizures included materials for the embroidery of elaborate men's silk waistcoats. From 1765 to 1826 there was a complete prohibition of foreign silk fabrics; smuggling was common, however, and such textiles continued to be available. Ambassadors and foreign ministers were frequently suspected of smuggling goods, but private houses were not permitted to be searched. The fabrics that such figures wore must have appeared doubly alluring. There was contraction in the English silk industry from 1763 to 1773, blamed on French imports and the new printed cotton fabrics.[34] The new fashion for both sexes was for a silk with much smaller pattern repeats. Men's silks, too, created an appearance of smaller and lighter scale. In late 1770 Fox visited

Paris again, to purchase the new clothes that it was customary to wear for the king's birthday, a Regency biographer writing that:

> it was an undoubted fact that the sole intention of his journey was to purchase clothes for the approaching birth-day, in defiance of the laws of his country, by which a penalty of two hundred pounds was attached to the wearing of apparel of French manufacture. Purchasing suits and lace for others, the Customs House impounded those that had not been worn and burned them.[35]

French clothing was thus illicit, but still clearly preferred by some men at this date. In 1763 Lord Riverstone paid £27 10s. 3d. for a Paris scarlet un-cut velvet suit, for which he paid an extra £2 5s. 6d. to someone for 'bringing them from Paris and landing them duty-free'.[36] In today's money this is approximately £3,600 ($5,000), with £360 ($500) paid in duties. As a comparison, in the mid-1760s Gainsborough was charging between 16 and 40 guineas for a half-length portrait and 60 guineas for a whole-length.[37] Walter Stanhope's diary records the seizure of plum-coloured silk breeches from Paris, part of a suit that was to be embroidered in silver; no similar silk could be found in England to match the top, and the suit was wasted.[38] The case of Lord Villiers in 1773, for bringing French-made clothes back through Dover, was lost for the prosecution, and the principle was established that from this date a gentleman could not be 'stripped' at the border or prosecuted for bringing textiles in for his own use. William Hickey's *Memoir* suggested that 'the master of the vessel' conducting passengers by ferry sometimes speculated in selling on men's fashions from France, including the popular *nivernois* hat and new French outfits of preposterous cut and colour, which some clients later took with them to Bengal in order to shock the locals.[39]

The allure of continental finery must have been irresistible to those who loved fashion. The royal wedding of the future Louis XVI and the Archduchess Maria-Antonia (Marie-Antoinette) was held in Paris on 16 May 1770, and English macaroni – including Stanhope – witnessed the remarkable splendour of the celebration and clothing; the duc de Croÿ noted, 'all that one saw was a solid amphitheatre of fine clothes'.[40] B.C. Walpole remarked that at the 1771 birthday of the English king the noblemen and gentlemen wore French suits, but the ladies honoured English dress.[41] By 'French suits' he probably meant suits of a French cut, rather than French textile.

Young fops such as Fox, who had just had a taste of cosmopolitan living at first hand, may also have been resisting the general thrust of English dress. The court-style dress, or *habit à la française*, which they wore in the London streets, was not requisite for the respectable classes. A good example of this contrast is found in Fanny Burney's reaction upon meeting the Tahitian Omai, who was present at a dinner with Joseph Banks and Dr

Solander: 'As he had been to Court, he was very fine. He had on a suit of Manchester velvet, Lined with white satten, a Bag, lace Ruffles, & a very handsome sword which the King had given him.' Omai, she concluded, had more natural grace than the European courtiers: '& appears in a new world like a man [who] had all his life studied the Graces'.[42] Her Rousseau-esque comment indicates the disfavour into which the more artificial modes of court life based on the French model were falling. (Omai appears to have been very handsome, if images of the period can be believed.)

The description of manners found in the travel genre is unsatisfactory in assessing matters such as when men stopped wearing the sword; when Garrick read Pierre-Jean Grosley's 1770 analysis of London, *Londres*, which was written after a six-week visit and with no functional English, he sent a list of mistakes to a friend:

Charles-James Cub Esq.

By little Actions striving to be Great,
And proud to be, and to be thought a Cheat.
Jenyns.

> ... what I have read is Error from beginning to ye End ...
> He says none of ye English wear Swords except ye Physicians,
> & they are always dress'd in black. I never saw a Gentleman
> dress'd in London Without his Sword, & the Physicians wear
> Cloaths of all Colours, like other People ... [43]

Garrick was very alert to sartorial nuance and there is no reason to doubt his account.

Fox does not appear to have used the word 'macaroni' to describe himself, but preferred the term *petit-maître*, which was affectionate within salon society. He was the subject of a large number of caricatures, most of which characterised his appearance as a macaroni in his youth. This imagery resonates with public disapproval of Fox and his father, Lord Holland. *Charles-James Cub Esq.* – an engraved portrait of Charles Fox with a fox's head in place of his own, in a plain wainscoted English room – was published in *The London Museum* in May 1771 (fig. 3.10). Fox is richly dressed in *habit à la française*; on the ground lies a copy of a *Treatise on French Dress*. The plate is accompanied by the following text by Soame Jenyns: 'By little Actions striving to be Great, / And proud to be, and to be thought a Cheat.' In another version of this print, Fox's hair is being curled with torn-up strips of the Magna Carta.

The text refers to the 'Grand Defaulter', the first Lord Holland. A similar theme informs the description of 'The Public Defaulter of unaccounted millions', published in *The Macaroni, . . . and Theatrical Magazine* of January 1773 and accompanied by the plate *The Young Cub* [Charles James Fox], in which he carries a muff – not a general part of English male attire – and wears an embroidered coat and breeches with a lace-trimmed vest. Some viewers may have recalled the older imagery regarding his father, such as *Renard Stating his Accounts*. Imagery relating to Charles James Fox was thus part of an older tradition.

Part of the joke of the caricatures of Fox must have been that he did not fit the bodily ideal of the young courtier; rather than having well-turned legs and a slender form, he tended to the plump, like his brother Stephen. Fox's appearance as a young macaroni can be imagined from a respectful portrait engraving of him at around 21 years of age (fig. 3.11). The profile here is perfectly suited to display the silhouette of the typical high wig with side-curls and a large wig-bag, which appears to weave around the front of the throat *en solitaire*. Fox wears a frock coat with tasselled frogging, and a quilted waistcoat; this may represent him dressed for the country, or it may represent the more informal modes of dressing that were also penetrating metropolitan life. The particular association of macaroni dress with a hairstyle is evident here. The face also displays an insouciance that accords with *petit-maître* stereotypes. Fox does not appear to have had himself

London Mag. Nov. 1779.

The Hon.ble Cha.s James Fox.

Above left
3.11 Unknown artist,
The Hon.ble Chas. Fox Esq.,
*c.*1770. Line engraving, dimensions
unknown. National Portrait Gallery,
London, NPG D2363. Given by
Henry Witte Martin, 1861

Above right
**3.12 'The Hon.ble Chas. James
Fox',** in *London Magazine*,
November 1779. Etching with
engraving, plate 20.5 × 12 cm, sheet
22.2 × 14 cm. Courtesy of The Lewis
Walpole Library, Yale University.
L. Reed Portrait files. LWL Portrait
Prints, box 36

painted in oils in macaroni dress, but an engraving of him in fashionable but
more moderate dress appeared in the *London Magazine* in 1779 (fig. 3.12).

Dress became significant in Fox's later parliamentary career. In 1795,
when Fox opposed Pitt's Sedition and Treason Bills, as threats to English
liberty, he appeared at a large public meeting at which estimates range from
two thousand to thirty thousand people. Wordsworth wrote to Coleridge:

> A little after 12 the Hustings being prepared, the Duke of Bradford &c.
> came upon it. Much hallooing & clapping on their appearance. The
> Duke was dressed in a Blue Coat & a Buff waistcoat with a round Hat.
> His hair cropped and without powder – Fox also cropped, and without
> powder. His hair grisly grey . . . [44]

Wraxall noted that Fox wore his frock coat and waistcoat into the House
of Commons; 'neither of which seemed in general new, and sometimes
appeared to be thread-bare'.[45] His dress was designed to appeal to popular
feeling; Fox wrote that Foxites had 'the popularity, and I suspect we shall
have it universally among the lower classes'.[46] His female supporters, such

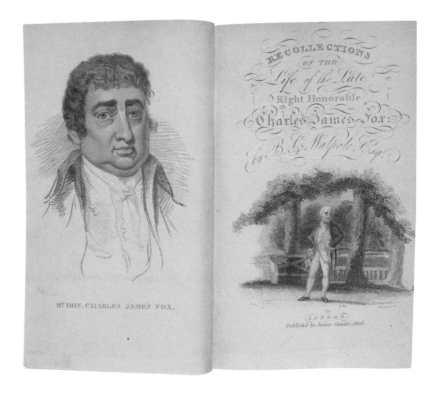

3.13 B.C. Walpole, *Recollections
of the Life of the Late Right
Honorable Charles James Fox*
(London: James Cundee, 1806).
Frontispiece. British Library,
London

RT HON. CHARLES JAMES FOX.

as Georgiana, Duchess of Devonshire, 'adopted a dress in compliment to
him, composed of a mixture of garter-blue and buff'.[47] These were also the
colours of Washington's army. John Brewer argues that Fox and his circle
'were more responsible than any other group for the demise of elaborate,
courtly dressing'. This is not at all the stream related to the dandy; the dandy
is not the 'opposite' of the courtier, as is sometimes suggested; 'his sartorial
precision gave way to a studied neglect of his appearance'.[48]

By the early nineteenth century Fox's gambling and macaroni phase, his
'dissipation and extravagance' were read disapprovingly as a youthful flaw
in 'this distinguished senator and states-man'.[49] The Whiggish behaviour
of Fox and his set was demonised. The frontispiece to B.C. Walpole's
*Recollections of the Life of the Late Right Honorable Charles James Fox;
exhibiting a faithful account of the most remarkable events of his political
career, and a delineation of his character as a statesman, senator, and man of
fashion . . .* (1806) illustrated the contrast: the jowly Fox with unpowered hair
on the left; the macaroni on the right, arms akimbo, dress-sword in place,
trimmed suit (fig. 3.13). The Regency illustrator does not appear to have
understood macaroni hair, which he omitted from the illustration.

Sir Joseph Banks: 'the Fly Catching Macaroni'

Also present in the club-land of Fox's youth was another famous macaroni, the botanist Sir Joseph Banks (1743–1820), who was knighted for his expedition to the South Seas and created President of the Royal Society. Banks was in his early thirties in the early 1770s. He had inherited a considerable estate and travelled with Captain James Cook on the *Endeavour* between 1768 and 1771. Banks considered his trip – alarming to his family – as the ultimate Grand Tour. As to why he did not simply go to the continent, he is supposed to have said: 'Every blockhead does that;

Whyncord del.

The FLY CATCHING MACARONI.

I rove from Pole to Pole, you ask me why,
I tell you Truth, to catch a _____ Fly.

Pub by DDarly accor to Act July 12.ᵗ 1772 /39/. Strand.

my Grand Tour shall be one round the whole globe.'[50] He visited Labrador,
the South Seas, Iceland and Holland. In the South Pacific he collected
an extraordinary range of specimens and artefacts and engaged with
indigenous peoples. On his return, he housed the more 'feminine' aspect
of his collection (cloaks, jewellery, feathered costumes) in one room of his
Soho residence (another room called 'The Armoury' was devoted to the
topic of the warrior, and included clubs, weapons and the like).[51] Darly's
third volume included Sir Joseph Banks as *The Fly Catching Macaroni*:
Banks stands on two globes, one inscribed 'Antartick Circle', the other
'Artick Circle' (fig. 3.14). The accompanying text reads, 'I rove from Pole to
Pole, you ask me why, / I tell you Truth, to catch a --- Fly.' With a fly-catcher
he attempts to catch a multicoloured moth or butterfly. Banks is depicted
with ass's ears (surely negative), a large ostrich plume in his hat such as
were worn by women, and a macaroni club of hair. He is dressed simply in
broadcloth. This was a topical print, as Banks and the Swedish naturalist Dr
Daniel Solander were also social figures *du jour*. Lady Mary Coke recorded
in her diary for 1771 that 'the people who are most talk'd of at present are Mr
Banks & Doctor Solander'.[52] Darly included this print in the background of
The Macaroni Print Shop (see fig. 3.1). James Gillray referred to the earlier
Darly image when he caricatured Banks as *The great South Sea Caterpillar,
transform'd into a Bath Butterfly* (etching of 1795).

Darly's fifth volume included *The Botanic Macaroni*, another likely image
of Banks, who had recently returned from Iceland with Dr Solander. And
Banks might appear in an untitled print by Collier and Sanderson (fig. 3.15)
that closely resembles an undated engraving showing a finely dressed man,
entitled *Mr. Bankes* (fig. 3.16). In July 1772 Darly published *The Simpling
Macaroni*, a jibe at Banks's botanist companion, Dr Solander FRS: 'Like
Soland-Goose from frozen Zone I wander, / On shallow Bank's grow's fat

3.17 M. Darly, *The Simpling Macaroni*, 13 July 1772. Hand-coloured etching, plate 17.7 × 12.6 cm. Courtesy of The Lewis Walpole Library, Yale University

The SIMPLING MACARONI.

Like Soland-Goose from frozen Zone I wander,
On shallow Banks's grows fat, Sol · · · · ·.

Pub accor to act by MDarly Strand July 13.ᵗ 1772

Sol-----' (fig. 3.17). Solander later became Banks's librarian in London and gained a slightly dissolute reputation.

The virtuoso Banks was regarded by contemporary society as combining the cult of dilettante study of antiquities or natural history (which were not necessarily regarded as separate studies) with that of being a traveller; the virtuoso meshed well with the idea of the macaroni, who sought inspiration abroad rather than at home. The macaroni nuance of Banks thus operated on several levels. The term was part of the tensions in

3.18 **George Dance**, *Portrait of Sir Joseph Banks*, *c.*1800. Pencil, 21.7 × 19.7 cm. National Library of Australia, Canberra, Rex Nan Kivell Collection

the Royal Society in 1783–4, when Banks's opponents portrayed themselves as men of science rather than 'the Macaroni's of the Society' – as professional men rather than as dilettantes. Banks had made enemies in the scientific community for rewarding rank and favouring natural history. In the text *Philosophical Puppet Show* (1785), he was addressed as 'A Celebrated Connoisseur in Chickweed, Caterpillars, Black Beetle, Butterflies, and Cockle-Shells'.[53] Banks's reaction to being caricatured is unknown but, like Fox, his social status ensured his confidence and he may have enjoyed the notoriety. His library included a number of macaroni caricatures and other satires relating to fashion, as well as many of the periodical sources that described the macaroni. His sister, Sarah Sophia Banks (1744–1818), a virtuoso collector like Fox but of ephemera rather than natural history, owned a large annotated collection of macaroni images, including one of him.

Sir Joseph Banks retained an aspect of his macaroni youth in old age. In a quiet portrait of him reading, sketched by George Dance, in around 1800, his macaroni tail and side-curls, minus the toupee, are conspicuous in the profile format (fig. 3.18).

Richard Cosway: 'the Macaroni Painter'

English society was particularly alert to those whom it felt were using clothes to achieve a social status they did not merit, but it was also a society that came to welcome talented and entrepreneurial people, as well as being a place that sometimes embraced the outré and the eccentric – something that continues to this day. The miniature-painter Richard Cosway (1742–1821) provides us with a famous example of a macaroni from a modest background. Cosway was a remarkable success story. The talented son of a Devonshire headmaster, he was sent to London to study painting before he was 12. He won first prize in a competition conducted by the Society of Arts in 1755. He had ambitions to paint large-format pictures, but was most successful with the miniature, providing his male and female sitters with the fashionable long necks, almond eyes and soft wispy hair they preferred. As Aileen Ribeiro has argued in her work on Cosway's role as an artist of taste and fashion, he provided rather more detail of their fashionable clothing than many other painters, perhaps an indication of his sartorial leanings.[54]

Cosway grew rich and successful from the patronage of the Prince of Wales (later George IV) and Whig circles in the 1780s, providing the Prince with fashionable portraits of himself and his circle, and with advice on his art collection. Cosway began to sign his miniatures in Latin from at least 1787, and for this pretension he was caricatured as 'Dicky Causeway in Plain English' in 1786. In 1781 he married the painter Maria Hadfield. Maria's father was the innkeeper for wealthy English gentlemen on the Grand Tour in Florence and she had been brought up on the continent. She was quite a character herself, being a painter and famous for her affair with Thomas Jefferson in Paris.

As a married couple, they had lived in considerable splendour in Berkeley Street, and from 1784 in part of the handsomely designed Schomberg House in Pall Mall. The latter was notable for having previously housed the studio and residence of Gainsborough and for a luxury textiles shop in another wing.[55] The Cosways' standard of living caused envy amongst other painters, and Cosway dressed with an image to match his status as court painter to one of the most vain and sartorially extravagant English princes in history.

Luxuriousness, generally, was a characteristic associated with Cosway. His famous gilded sitter's chair made by Locke (which survives) was emblematic of the twinning of fashion and furnishings in his life and work. He interacted with the French diplomatic community, and even the French king, at a high

level. The Cosways' social agility therefore probably caused envy; Cosway's wealth at death was £12,000, about US $1.3 million today.

At the time of the macaroni craze, Cosway was in his early thirties and had just become the first miniaturist to become a full member of the Royal Academy, in 1771. As Graham Reynolds notes, 'Cosway achieved in his life many of the social ambitions which Sir Joshua Reynolds had staked out for the artist.'[56] Fine clothing was an essential part of that persona for Cosway. His *Self-portrait* of *c.*1770–75 shows him dressed in the height of Parisian elegance, in fabrics possibly purchased from Paris (fig. 3.19). This portrait is probably the finest representation of a macaroni man, in terms of both artistic skill and the detail of the stylistics of the dressing. The height of his powdered wig, the delicate rose brocade of his waistcoat and French needle-lace provide the strongest indication of what a wealthy London macaroni looked like. The ermine lining of the brocaded blue coat, once a prerogative of nobility, is a particular conceit. The toupee of the wig is not far removed from the types seen in caricature. Cosway paints his clothing in exquisite detail: the solitaire, or bow, has pinked (cut) edges; the blue-and-mauve brocaded silk is a diaper pattern, with sprays of tiny roses at the lapels. The distinctly studied pose

can be compared with that of Jean-Baptiste Perroneau's *Portrait of Jacques Cazotte*, who wears a similar wig-bag with black satin ribbons and inserts his hand in his coat in a pose of studied nonchalance (fig. 3.20). This type is the 'hand-in-waistcoat' portrait, which carried within it the iconography of august nobility. Cosway's most prominent hand is therefore self-affirming, yet the other delicate and open glimpse of fingers, combined with the gaze, suggests attention beyond the frame. He looks at something, as if discerningly. He sees himself as others see him, but also as the figure on a coin, albeit slightly distended by fashionable coiffure into the form of an oval.[57] There is a knowing tension about the face; it is not the completely relaxed *esprit* of a French courtier by Perroneau. Caricatures perpetuate his new standing no less readily, if not more respectfully, than his own self-portrait, a masterpiece of tender painting. He himself was his greatest work of art.

Cosway also posed for Zoffany's commemorative painting *The Academicians of the Royal Academy* (1771–2), with the hat and cane of the courtier or macaroni at his side (fig. 3.21, far right of the painting). He wore a green silk or velvet suit and a gold brocade waistcoat, and held a gold-braided *chapeau bras*. Only he and Sir Joshua Reynolds have swords.

The pose is redolent of the swaggering posture conferred by Van Dyck on the likes of Charles I, as well as that prototype, the Apollo Belvedere. This pretension must have grated with Reynolds, for in dressing in such a superior fashion, Cosway suggested that he was inherently superior. He wore this get-up everywhere, not merely in the presence of the Prince, and for this he was mercilessly lampooned. J.T. Smith referred to Cosway thus, in *Nollekens and his Times* (1828):

> He rose from one of the dirtiest boys, to one of the smartest of men. Indeed so ridiculously foppish did he become that Mat Darly, the famous caricature print-seller, introduced an etching of him in his window, in the Strand, as 'The Macaroni Miniature-Painter' . . . I have often seen Mr Cosway at the Elder Christie's Picture-sales, full-dressed in his sword and bag; with a small three cornered hat on the top of his powdered toupée, and a mulberry silk coat, profusely embroidered with scarlet strawberries.[58]

The currency of Cosway's reputation was also indicated by the appearance in 1772 of two prints satirising him, one by Dighton, the other by Darly. As the miniature-painter was short in stature, the joke was doubly strong. *The Macaroni Painter, or Billy Dimple sitting for his Picture* (fig. 3.22) has traditionally been held to represent Cosway. Engraved by R. Earlom after a drawing by Dighton, it is a hand-coloured mezzotint published by Bowles and Carver in *c.*1770. In one coloured example, Cosway wears a cinnamon-coloured coat, blue breeches and white stockings; the sitter wears a red coat, light blue waistcoat, brown breeches and white stockings. It was topical enough to be included in the background of *Miss Macaroni and her Gallant at a Print-Shop* (see fig. 3.5).

The Paintress of Maccaroni's (fig. 3.23) was published in 1772 as a companion to *The Macaroni Painter*; in the nineteenth century this was believed to be the famous woman painter Angelica Kauffmann; Dorothy George states it is more likely to be Maria Hadfield, later Cosway, but the Cosways were not married at this date and there is no reason why it may not represent the fashionable painter Kauffmann. The artist is depicted in a fine striped silk dress and trimmed cap, hardly practical for such work and underscoring her gender and exceptional status as a woman artist. Significantly, she paints portraits of caricature-like macaroni men, not women, which makes the image somewhat licentious, as well as suggesting that her art is unseemly or lacking in fine aesthetics. Kauffmann's art was frequently self-reflexive, such as the tondo (circular) self-portrait *Alexander Leaves his Mistress Campaspe to Apelles* (1783), in which she painted herself as an assertive Campaspe, becoming model and artist simultaneously.[59]

The MACARONI PAINTER, or BILLY DIMPLE fitting for his PICTURE.

Printed for Bowles & Carver, Map & Printsellers Nº 69 in St Pauls Church Yard, London

The PAINTRESS of MACCARONI'S.

The MACARONI PAINTER, or BILLY DIMPLE sitting for his PICTURE.

Opposite
3.22 R. Earlom after Robert Dighton, Bowles and Carver (publisher), *The Macaroni Painter, or Billy Dimple sitting for his Picture*, 25 September 1772. Coloured mezzotint, 35.2 × 25.2 cm. British Museum, London

Above left
3.23 Carington Bowles, *The Paintress of Maccaroni's*, 13 April 1772. Hand-coloured mezzotint, plate 35.4 × 25.2 cm, sheet 41 × 30 cm. Courtesy of The Lewis Walpole Library, Yale University

Above right
3.24 R. Earlom after Robert Dighton, Bowles and Carver (publisher), *The Macaroni Painter, or Billy Dimple sitting for his Picture*, 25 September 1772. Mezzotint, plate 35.4 × 25.2 cm. Courtesy of The Lewis Walpole Library, Yale University

Right
3.25 W. Humphrey, *The Paintress. 'The proper Study of Mankind is Man'*, 15 May 1772. Mezzotint, plate 35.2 × 25 cm, sheet 42 × 27 cm. Courtesy of The Lewis Walpole Library, Yale University

The PAINTRESS.
'The proper Study of Mankind is Man'.

Cosway continued to be the butt of caricatures in the 1780s. *A Smuggling Machine or a Convenient Cos.auway for a Man in Miniature* (published by H. Humphrey in January 1782) depicts him standing under the petticoats of his tall wife, Maria; the image was topical as Cosway was newly married. In the background is a picture of a little man in wig-bag and sword, climbing a ladder that rests on the breast of a woman. George notes that this represents Cosway climbing to fame, on either Angelica Kauffmann or the Duchess of Devonshire. Beneath is engraved a quotation from Julius Caesar that begins:

> Lowliness is Young Ambitions Ladder,
> Whereto the climber upward turns his Face
> But when he once attains the upmost round
> He then unto the Ladder turns his back,
> Looks unto the clouds – scornin the base degrees
> By which he did ascend.

Pretty clear what they thought of him.

The painting in Bowles's caricature of *The Paintress* includes, to the left, a man who is cross-eyed or whose eyes cannot focus. This droll image includes the same treatment of a circular mirror or a blank painting, as in *Billy Dimple sitting for his Picture*. The mirror here is significant; mirrors are, as Eirwen Nicolson noted, revelatory devices within print culture, as they are motifs of unmasking, uncloaking and uncovering.[60] Closer inspection of the uncoloured version of this print reveals the mirror in fact to be 'smeared' and therefore neither blank nor reflecting (fig. 3.24). The framed mirror in the centre of the room does not seem to be a mirror at all – it reflects nothing – although it gives the impression of one. The man in the painted portrait on the wall above looks down on the sitter in a bemused manner. The way that the British Museum's coloured version of the print is rendered is relevant.[61] The colourist has used a different colour on each item of the sitter's suit. It seems to be a self-conscious comment about the act of painting. The curtain drawn back, but not fully, is a device that also relates to time and to truth.

In W. Humphrey's *The Paintress* (15 May 1772), a female artist in a finely trimmed silk dress, who might be Kauffmann, paints a grotesque ruffian boy, a street sweeper or chimney sweep (fig. 3.25). His blackened face is a contrast to her white skin. The print is subtitled 'The proper Study of Mankind is Man', the famous line from Alexander Pope's poem *An Essay on Man* of 1734. There is a painting or print (also smeared) on the upper-centre wall of a dark-skinned people, on an equally dark ground, dancing, which is sure to refer to the contemporary interest in natives of the South Pacific, who also feature in contemporary women's periodicals such as *Bon Ton* magazine. The scene appears, in fact, to be an Australian Aboriginal corroboree. The work refers to the eighteenth-century attraction to the contrast of nature and artifice, which, as Diana Donald argues, derives both from William Hogarth's art practice and philosophy and from John Bulwer's earlier work, *Anthropometamorphosis*.[62] The woman artist – who is by her very nature exceptional at this date – sits on a chair whose design is absurd, and abuts an equally vulgar and rich carpet. By having painted such a scene she also shows that she is 'up to date' with New World discoveries, even though she has never been there; the irony here is that 'natives' were already produced as images before they were 'brought back' to Europe as individuals. The subsidiary aspects of the image are jokes about nature and culture, feeling and artifice, primitivism and scientific 'advancement'. The satire also centres on mimesis: she paints what she sees, but she is unable to 'improve' his appearance; is she therefore a failure as a portrait painter, as her choice of subject is so inappropriate, even careless? Her persona as she paints is naïve.

Caricature images such as *Billy Dimple sitting for his Picture* play with the notion of the fashionable observing and then crafting copies of the equally fashionable; who is sitting to whom, and which is the greater work of art? As a joke-book quipped of the macaroni type and his cosmetic rouge and whitener: 'Why is he like a Picture? Because he is painted.'[63] This elision of wearing/appearing and creating/painting was used again in the nineteenth century by the brilliant critic William Hazlitt, who wrote of Cosway's technique that it was:

> not easily expressed in words. It consists in the fact that the portrait is so lightly laid upon the ivory as to appear almost as though it had been blown into position, and was an aerial thing of graceful lightness, that, like a bit of gossamer, had rested upon the ivory and had become fixed there . . . Brilliantly flippant it is, of course, but at the same time exquisite in taste and perfect in finish. The want of apparent labour in the playful grace of many of Cosway's conceptions is apt to deceive the observer into neglecting to give to the artist a proper need of appreciation, such as he deserves. The effect appears too easy, too showy, and even too tricky to be considered great, but it is not so, and the closer Cosway's miniatures are scrutinized, the stronger will be the opinion that, although flippant, and even tricky, they are marked by very high artistic character, and by a skill in brush-work of exceeding rarity.[64]

Readers of Hazlitt might have been aware of Giorgio Vasari's positive comment about women and miniature-painting in the Renaissance, nonetheless framed within a hierarchy in which a miniature could never equal the status of history painting.

The contemporary writer Henry Angelo claimed that George III was amused by Cosway's manners and looks, the royal family enjoying a laugh at his appearance. Frederick B. Daniell, in his catalogue of Cosway's work, notes: 'It is said that George III, when speaking of the artists employed by himself and his son, observed with reference to Cosway, "Among my painters there are no fops"'.[65] On one unfortunate occasion Cosway, finely dressed in a silver-embroidered dove-grey court dress, tripped on his sword and fell over in the mud in front of the Prince of Wales's carriage and a large crowd. These tales were related almost in glee: 'My old friend Cosway, though a distinguished artist, and a very intelligent, loquacious, entertaining little man, was certainly a mighty macaroni . . .'[66]

Reverend William Dodd: 'the Macaroni Parson'

Amongst the macaroni landscape walked a man of the Church. The Reverend William Dodd (1729–1777) was a fashionable court preacher, Freemason and charitable leader, who became infamous for what some historians have considered the beginning of 'white-collar crime'. At one point Chaplain-in-Ordinary to George III, he was known as 'the Macaroni Parson', caricatured as such, and came to the unfortunate end of being executed for fraud, hanged at Tyburn on 27 June 1777. Dodd, an entrepreneurial figure who published popular versions of Shakespeare, amongst other activities, lived too well and was in serious financial trouble. In order to bridge his finances, he had forged the signature via a third party on the bond of a former pupil, Philip, godson of the Earl of Chesterfield and later 5th Earl (whose illegitimate son was subject of the justly famous *Letters*). The deal was found out when a solicitor questioned an ink-blot on the document and, despite Dodd repaying most of the money immediately, through a circuitous route that many read as malicious, he ended up on trial and condemned.

Like Cosway, Reverend Dodd was a court follower who dressed to match the ambience of that milieu, wearing make-up, silks and perfume when attending the court of St James. His modern biographer suggests that he used cosmetics as a prop to decrease the visible signs of sweat and effort, and to improve his demeanour during his preaching performances. These were considered papist and Francophile, but they were also fashionable and appealing; large numbers of women attended them. He opened the Margaret Chapel in Bath, for example. Like Cosway, Dodd would descend from an expensive coach and enter the Chapel Royal with a reek of scent, 'which shocked the conservative altar dressers and Sergeants of the VESTRY'. A contemporary noted that 'he walked with his head erect and with a lofty gait, like a man conscious of his own importance'.[67] A caricature suggestive of Dodd shows such a pose and trailing ecclesiastical drapery, almost coquettish (fig. 3.26). Certain churches were becoming prominent for the display of fine clothing amongst the worshippers as well, where

The Macaroni Parson.

Left
3.26 'The Macaroni Parson',
The Macaroni and Theatrical Magazine, December 1772, p.97.
Courtesy of The Lewis Walpole Library, Yale University

Below left
3.27 A. Hamilton, *The Revd. Dr. Dodd. Taken from the Life in Newgate the Morning of his Execution*, 1 August 1777. Etching and engraving, plate 18 × 10.8 cm, sheet 21.1 × 12.5 cm. Courtesy of The Lewis Walpole Library, Yale University

Below right
3.28 'Doctor Dodd', *Walker's Hibernian Magazine*, 7 July 1777. Courtesy of The Lewis Walpole Library, Yale University

Nº XXI.

THE REVᴰ Dᴿ DODD.
Taken from the Life in Newgate the Morning of his Execution.
Published as the Act directs by A.Hamilton Junr near St John's Gate Aug.1.1777.

Doctor Dodd

A Macaroni Family returning from Church.

3.29 *A Macaroni Family returning from Church*, June
1773. Date inferred from companion
plate *The Old Political Macaroni
with his wise Family at Breakfast*.
Hand-coloured etching, sheet 12 × 17
cm. Courtesy of The Lewis Walpole
Library, Yale University

A Macaroni Family was also issued as
*The English Frenchifyed Macaroney,
his lady and French Footman Comeing
From Church* (Private collection).

women wore particularly extravagant versions of fashion. John Money reads
the significance of the Dodd episode as connected with the 'changing place
of the middling orders in the moral and political life of the nation'. Dodd's
trial for forgery highlighted anxiety surrounding the rise of credit; failures
had increased dramatically after 1765, being nearly three times greater
than those at the time of the South Sea Bubble, yet credit underpinned the
nation's success in war, when it was able to raise funds more easily than
other nations.[68] Dodd was depicted in an engraving dressed in a rich banyan
or dressing gown as 'Doctor Dodd' in *Walker's Hibernian Magazine* (fig.
3.28), as well as in plain dress for the gallows (fig. 3.27). Attending church
in a papist fashion with Francophile attendants and unnecessary
accoutrements such as snuff-boxes and muffs carries the satire of *A
Macaroni Family returning from Church* (fig. 3.29). Dodd's macaroni status
may have represented the impugned side of sensibility, the disingenuous
and merely fashionable display of sentiment. Charity was developing as the
set of good works that emerged from the activation of Adam Smith's 'mutual
sympathy' at this time, but the Dodd equation was too narcissistic and did
not add up.

David Garrick: celebrity actor

Registers of meaning and address assumed in the comedy of manners relate
to macaroni caricature prints, and vice versa. David Garrick (1717–1779),
for instance, owned a large collection of prints, including 106 plates by
Hogarth and a parcel sent by his friend Charles Bunbury.[69] The imagery of
the macaroni type may have informed the way in which he performed these
roles on stage. Matthew Darly dedicated one of his 1772 suites of *Macaronies,*
Characters, Caricatures to Garrick. George Winchester Stone Jr and George
Kahrl state that this dedication was 'In recognition of Garrick's patronage of
engravers and print sellers', and it was also a witty and topical comment on
the importance of Garrick in popularising the fop as a stage character and
his many references to such prints in the text of his plays.[70]

   Flashy dressing was not universal amongst all socially sophisticated men.
Garrick, often under attack for his relations with social superiors and his
comfortable lifestyle, dressed conservatively in the 1770s, perhaps to counter
the charge from snobs like Horace Walpole that he was an upstart. Perhaps
he also associated the styles of the macaroni with the dress of the very young,
as did the latter. Garrick did not lack an interest in clothes, and had been
commissioned by the Duke of Devonshire in 1753, 1757 and 1758 to design and
purchase fabric for his annual king's birthday suit.[71] In the 1740s Garrick had
been represented in the height of elaborate French fashion by Jean-Baptiste
van Loo, in a suit trimmed with gold frogging and a contrasting long-waisted
waistcoat with a rich and deep border of brocade. Thomas Patch had painted
a caricature of David Garrick, Sir Horace Mann and other English tourists
abroad in 1763. Garrick forms the centre of the composition and is lavishly
dressed in court dress, with sword and diamond- or paste-buckle shoes.
He is believed to have purchased a new suit of Italian velvet on his Grand
Tour, commemorated in his portrait by Pompeo Batoni (fig. 6.3).[72] The suit
is a rare survival with provenance; it is a colour known as 'carmelite', a dark
purplish-brown velvet (fig. 6.2). He projected a more sober image at home
in his portraits by Gainsborough (fig. 6.1) and Reynolds (1773), the time of
macaroni fashions. In the former painting, Garrick wears a simple suit that
appears to be broadcloth, a waistcoat trimmed simply with galloon, and
neatly powdered but not affected hair. Reynolds's portrait of Garrick reading
to his wife places him in plain velvet, whereas she is in furbelows (puffed
trimmings). It was thus a study in gender contrasts. Despite having the
latest neoclassical and *chinoiserie* furniture styles by Thomas Chippendale
in his London house and Hampton villa, in sartorial fashions Garrick was
conservative in the 1770s.[73] This was probably advisable for the man who
satirised 'fribbles' and macaroni so effectively in his stage roles and plays,
and who was falsely accused of being the lover of Isaac Bickerstaffe.

A MUNGO MACARONI.

Publish'd according to Act by M.Darly 39. Strand, Sept.r 10 1772.

3.30 **M. Darly**, *A Mungo Macaroni*,
10 September 1772. Etching, plate
17.6 × 12.7 cm. Courtesy of The Lewis
Walpole Library, Yale University

Julius Soubise: 'a Mungo Macaroni'

London also had a macaroni of colour, Julius Soubise
(1754–1798). He was an extravagantly dressed macaroni who
seemed to enjoy an active and varied social life. He had been
brought as a slave from the West Indies to England, where
Catherine Hyde, the eccentric Duchess of Queensberry,
convinced the captain to part with him. She gave him a
leisured childhood, in which he was taught to fence and
attended Mr Angelo's fashionable riding school, or *manège*,
for young men. Soubise played the violin, composed and
learned oration from Garrick.[74] He began to pass himself off
as the son of an African prince, hence the Duchess called
him 'Master Soubise'. This was also an act of ownership
and condescension; other famous black men of the period,
such as Ignatius Sancho, were named by aristocrats 'on the
strength of a comic resemblance to a fictional character'.[75]
After a scandal involving a servant girl, Soubise was hustled
off to Bengal, where he established a riding school.

Macaroni caricatures of Soubise parodied a foppish
upstart whose outfits and entertainments, financed by the
Duchess, affronted both racial and social expectations of an African male.
Soubise was 'expensive in perfume; [and] wore nosegays'.[76] He became
'a Mungo Macaroni' in caricature, an offensive term meaning a rude or
forward black man. 'Mungo', 'Marianne' and 'Sambo' were names given to
blacks on the stage, comic black people being stock figures of fun who were
'ridiculous but affectionate versions of the eighteenth century servant'.[77]
Soubise thus also overlapped with the image of the servant dressed beyond
his means. The presence of the well-clothed refined black servant caused
consternation and was used in plays and prints by those who demanded that
the importation of black servants be curtailed.

Soubise occupied an ambiguous position. There were about 20,000
people of colour living in London in the eighteenth century. Life for such
people was full of contradiction. Soubise was a friend of Ignatius Sancho,
the grocer and correspondent to the famous, whose letters were published
in 1782. Just as Soubise paraded the streets in expensive finery, the protégé
of a wealthy woman, so Ignatius Sancho, as a shop-owner, could vote, was a
friend of Charles James Fox and voted for him in the 1780 election.[78] Sancho
circulated drawings and caricatures amongst his friends, indicating the
significance of portrait and personality as channels of communication.

Many black children in the eighteenth century were used as ornaments
themselves. As fashionable pages, they carried trains, parrots and lapdogs;
some were given classical names like 'Pompey' and dressed in precious

silks, as a contrast to their black skins. Soubise inverted this order by setting up an independent lifestyle and establishment, and by assimilating the ornamental to his person. The reaction to Soubise seems to have found him not so much absurd as remarkable – the exception which proved the rule that blacks were not as urbane and civilised as whites. The fabulously dressed Soubise would also have meshed in people's minds with the fascination with the African prince, wrongly captured, enslaved and freed. There were real examples of this figure, who provided a popular plot for plays.

Darly included *A Mungo Macaroni* in the fourth volume of his macaroni suite (fig. 3.30). There has been some debate as to whether this represents Soubise. The other option is the MP Jeremiah Dyson, called 'Mungo' in a debate by Colonel Barré in January 1769. The figure of 'Mungo' was a black slave in the comic opera *The Padlock* (1768) by Isaac Bickerstaffe and Charles Dibdin, the name suggesting that Dyson was kept at dirty jobs by the government.[79] The caricature parodies the subject, whoever he is, for reasons of style, but it is one of the few macaroni images in which the face,

body and dress are not subject to exaggeration or caricature. The dress is that of a respectful fashion plate of the time. Clearly the fact that a black man had adopted a macaroni persona was enough to mark the image as a caricature. Mungo Dyson's speech tended to be exaggerated; in another image (not illustrated) he remarks, 'Massters Massters' in speech bubbles. Here, the irony of a black man adopting the (white) courtier's *esprit* is sufficient for the image to function as a caricature.

As Soubise had concrete means of support, he became an exceptional and visible example of a low-born non-white macaroni who took his place in fashionable society, at the theatre and other diversions. He was topical, and the identification is supported by another image. A caricature entitled *The D------ of [. . .]-- playing at Foils with her favorite Lap Dog Mungo after Expending near £10000 to make him a---------* * represents the Duchess of Queensberry and Soubise fencing (fig. 3.31). The Duchess had apprenticed her 'page-slave' to Angelo, the fencing-school master; on the ground is a book entitled *Les Ecole des Armes Avec Les Attudes est Positions Par Angelo*; Angelo had produced a famous folio on fencing. Two account books, one marked 'Vol. 5', seem to hold the 'Mungo Bills'. Soubise is depicted in fashionable dress and he has removed his large nosegay to the ground. His face is carefully drawn, with some exaggeration. He wears his own slightly greying frizzy hair moulded in the front, in the macaroni manner. He challenges the Duchess as his sword touches her chest: 'Mungo here, Mungo dere, Mungo Ev'ry where above & below / Hah! Vat you Gracy tink of me Now'. Soubise's macaroni pose resulted in the paradox that he was both in and out; 'There was among these pioneering black Britons a sense of both belonging and not belonging, a sense of being part of the nation and being outside of it.'[80]

The macaroni thus began as something of an aristocratic youth formation. Their affectations were adopted by courtier followers and retainers who were not high-born, but were able to afford examples of expensive fashions. This was a period, after all, of a new '"public" increasingly defined as an aggregation of private individuals rather than an elite of patricians'.[81] What these historical figures have in common is a recognition and exploitation of the power of dress. All these figures were popular subjects in the field of caricature. Underlying this insight is a more or less self-conscious understanding of the performance of identity. Dress is constructed as a costume that creates a reality, rather than as a straightforward expression of some inherent character. The power this construction afforded was put to diverse ends by different personages, and was practised with varying degrees of self-consciousness. Charles James Fox made an explicit statement of cultural alignment with French culture, in order to annex an authority of taste in opposition to the Tories. All the other macaroni mentioned here

3.32 **Tea canister (front and back), Prattware English pottery, decorated with macaroni figures and their parents in relief,** *c.*1790–1800. Pearlware, polychrome paint, 12.7 × 8.3 × 5.1 cm. Courtesy of Paul Vandekar and Earle D. Vandekar of Knightsbridge, Inc.

might be said to have exploited different versions of this cosmopolitan authority to their own ends: Banks, for example, to assert the dilettantism of the aristocracy; Cosway to celebrate and perpetuate his new socially esteemed self. Over the course of the nineteenth century these types became romanticised within a generalised 'Georgian past'. Yet the dress of such figures was not simply a matter of folly or fun for the young.

This chapter has examined the dyad of 'macaroni' and 'caricature' as genres or types. There is the possibility of further mixed genres, as in the caricature crossed with the portrait or the conversation piece (a type of portrait in an indoors or outdoors setting), as well as low and high art – as, for example, in the macaroni either depicted on or made of ceramic, which continued to be produced into the early nineteenth century (fig. 3.32). Caricature is not simply a reflection of social reality, distorted for comic effect, but can be said to have created the site in which the macaroni identity was consolidated. The caricatures of the caricatured figures consuming visual caricatures depict this very process occurring. In this sense, the macaroni's representation in caricature is always that medium's portrait of its own potential fascination and power.

CHAPTER 4

'French knavery' and Fashion: The Macaroni and Nationhood

*F*or God's sake return home. Nature never meant you for a Frenchman.
Burn your formal bag-wig, and put on your far more agreeable scratch.
Viscount Bolingbroke to George Selwyn[1]

*I*l n'y a point de Pays dans l'univers où la mode régne avec autant
d'autorité qu'en France.

François-Charles Gaudet,
Bibliotheque des Petits-Maitres, 1762[2]

Many texts and images of macaroni commented on the relationship
between fashion, luxury and gender at a time when those terms were also
the subject of political, social and economic debate.[3] Both men and women
of means were voracious purchasers of sartorial fashions. This enthusiasm
was frequently noted in the context of the Grand Tour, when the novelty
and glamour of new fashion goods generated excited responses to Lyons
silk waistcoats, Italian velvets and fur-lined suits. There was a well-
established tradition of wealthy men acquiring clothing on the continent
and then having themselves painted in them, either in Italy or back in
England. Reynolds's portrait of *Frances Hastings, 10th Earl of Huntingdon*
(1754, collection of The Huntington), wearing a blue suit with full skirts and
elaborate frogging, is one such example, probably the choice of the sitter.

Fashion at the time was virtually synonymous with the French, whose
ability to create ingenious trifles of all kinds simultaneously fascinated
and repelled the English observer. The concept of fashion as an abstracted
force acting on the body politic and influencing behaviour and morals was
generally personified as French, and also as feminine. This accounts for
part of the invective directed at the macaroni. But France was not the only
driver of fashion, and the macaroni's intrinsic connection with Italy further
coloured the trenchant critique. French and Italian goods and manners had
added appeal because travel to the continent had not been possible, and the
importation of French textiles was banned, during the Seven Years War.
The lure of the high quality and striking design of continental textiles was
unabated in England, however, and the macaroni association with such goods
must also be placed in the context of eighteenth-century political economy,
in which there was a contested view of how to manage imperial production
and consumption.[4]

Satirical attacks on the macaroni were part of a wider Francophobic
discourse by which the English partly defined themselves. The matter of
'Frenchness' provided a convenient stereotype and opposition that could
be extended to comment on every facet of national difference, from the
parliamentary system to the rearing of children. The amused suspicion

of the English towards the follower of fashion was a much older hostility. In the late seventeenth century this censure had been more strongly directed at women. The 'macaroni years' shifted much of the diatribe towards men.

The notion that the English character was being compromised by the spread of fashion was more than an amusing word-play; it was part of the process by which the relationship of national identity and manhood was modulated at a time of global geopolitical change. Although men were eager and active consumers of fashion goods during the period, eighteenth-century English culture was constructing new models of gendered consumption in which women were more strongly connected with spending. The macaroni have relevance here for Victoria de Grazia's argument that 'sexualised metaphors applied to the circulation and consumption of goods may be taken to stand for elusive social relations' – that is, she argues that from the eighteenth century onwards, goods were transformed 'from being relatively static symbols around which hierarchies were ordered to being more directly constitutive of class, social status, and personal identity'.[5] The macaroni might certainly be identified in this way, and were often represented in visual and verbal culture as synonymous with foreign goods; they were read by and through what they consumed. Indeed, they let themselves be read in this way, upsetting cultural preconceptions about gender and spending; thus their contemporaries joked that they seemed to move more within the realm of women than that of men.

Despite the specific political and social nuance of the macaroni at the time of their appearance, they are part of a longer lineage of ideas concerning the relationship of fashionability to English nationhood and gender. This chapter examines this relationship through two main sources. The first is the genre of travel literature, which played an important role in defining and describing the French and other continentals, such as Italians, as different in character from the English. As well as acting as guidebooks for tourists, these travel books were consumed by those who stayed at home, thus playing a broader role in defining types and manners. Many journals, letters and diaries comment on the excitement and challenges of travel. Caution must be exercised in treating the contents of such works as an unproblematised source for fashion history, but, like the theatrical stage, they played a significant role in defining nationhood. Yet these so-called 'ego-documents', to use Jacob Presser's term, are a useful counterpoint to more abstract economic, demographic and social theories.

The second source to be considered here is the long-running debate on the relationship between fashion and luxury. For people of the time, this was in part about understanding the classical authors. As Jane Bridgeman notes of Renaissance art, the classical tradition taught that clothing should be appropriate and not necessarily beautiful. Leon Battista Alberti had

written, 'You, then, must respect your clothes.' Giovanni Della Casa's
Galateo: The Rules of Polite Behaviour (Venice, 1558, much reprinted) and
the humanist Baldassare Castiglione's *The Courtier* (1528) demanded 'clean
well cut and appropriate' dress.[6] Young men could be 'vivacious and elegant',
but gaudy clothes were the province of 'mercenaries, itinerant musicians
and homosexuals', or at the very least of men who spent too much labour
and time on self-adornment.[7] Being well educated and well bred might be
French-inflected. It therefore had to be managed, as in the protocol for the
usage of dancing masters. *The Spectator* recorded in 1711:

> It is the proper Business of a Dancing Master to regulate these Matters;
> tho' I take it to be a just Observation, that unless you add something of
> our own to what these fine Gentlemen teach you, and which they are
> wholly ignorant of themselves, you will much sooner get the Character
> of an Affected Fop, than a Well-bred Man.[8]

Travel literature: fashion as French

France was an extremely popular destination for the English traveller in
the eighteenth century, and for many young men it represented their first
foreign destination when embarking upon the Grand Tour. The fashionable
and curious, such as Horace Walpole, also visited for tourism and shopping,
and the wealthy ordered fabrics, furniture, silver, porcelain and *bibelots* from
Paris boutiques and had them shipped home.[9]

   English guidebooks for the traveller to France fell into two genres.
There were straightforward guides that listed towns, places of interest,

VIEW ON THE PONT NEUF AT PARIS.

distances and inns. There were also detailed commentaries, written as
much to entertain the armchair traveller as for the young man embarking on
the Grand Tour. These were undoubtedly read by large numbers of women,
for whom travel opportunities were more limited, and played an important
part in forming stereotypes of national difference. The caricatures of
French life by Henry Bunbury referred to many of the ideas contained in
such guides, and caricaturists may well have consulted their contents before
commencing a design (fig. 4.1).

The clothing, manners and food of France and England were often
the subject of contrast. As Linda Colley notes, attempts to form notions of
Britishness from the very diverse countries of England, Wales and Scotland
were less about common ground than about defining Britons in terms of this
other great power.[10] The sirloin, ham and capon of England were compared
by printmaker Brandoin with the scanty food (skate or dogfish, even a meagre
bone) served by the French, and the appearance of the hearty, self-confident
English butcher dressed in gaiters contrasted with a scrawny long-haired
Frenchman in stockings and small-sword, who strings up cats, onions and
frogs (fig. 4.2). The English enjoy a keg of beer; the French a fountain of
wine. Such a satire fails to recognise how much the English enjoyed French,
Hungarian and Spanish beverages and commented on the delights of French
cuisine when they travelled there.

John Andrews, who wrote three commentaries on French mores over
a 20-year period, crafted his works entirely around a set of oppositions
that contrasted English vigour, manliness and 'liberty of discourse' with

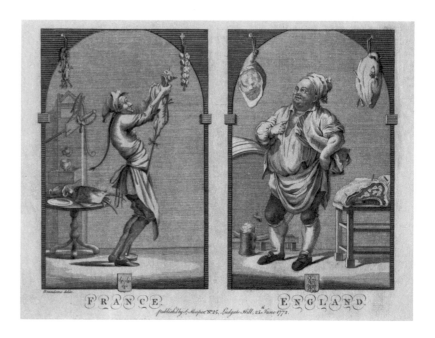

French flattery, vanity and excess. Frenchmen wear court dress when inappropriate, spend more time with ladies than the English normally do, and preside at feminine spaces and practices such as the *toilette*. The French, we are told, are a people obsessed with the trivial, with 'what dresses were worn on such a day', their minds 'warped from any freedom of exertion'.[11] There are echoes here of the common macaroni stereotype of the empty-headed man, taken up by the mannequin character 'blockhead' from George Stevens's *A Lecture on Heads* (c.1765), discussed later in this book. Another writer of travel manuals, Tobias Smollett, wrote in 1766: 'France is the general reservoir from which all the absurdities of false taste, luxury, and extravagance have overflowed the different kingdoms and states of Europe. The springs that fill this reservoir, are no other than vanity and ignorance.'[12]

Philip Thicknesse's rebuttal of Smollett's sensationalist text describing a visit to France nonetheless agreed:

> I am apt to think the taking of snuff, the powdering of the hair, and the great attention shewn by all degrees of people in France, to adorn their persons, is a piece of state policy to prevent their employing their intellectual faculties.[13]

English travel manuals commented on the different appearance of the Frenchman, and the necessity of acquiring a new wardrobe on arrival in Paris:

> when an Englishman comes to Paris, he cannot appear until he has undergone a total metamorphosis. At his first arrival he finds it necessary to send for the taylor, peruquier, hatter, shoemaker, and every other tradesman concerned in the equipment of the human body.[14]

Walter Stanhope wrote from Paris in 1769: 'an innumerable swarm of those blood-sucking insects called tradesmen were summoned, or came without summons to equip us in the French taste'.[15] Fashionable but expensive conventions suggested that gentlemen should wear suits trimmed with silver for spring and autumn, silk clothes for summer, cloth laced with gold and preferably velvet for winter. Even the detail of the embroidery was specified in French fashion prints – usually botanical in inspiration. This clothing was generally considered too elaborate for the London street, although a macaroni might not have agreed:

> On his return to his own country, all this frippery is useless. He cannot appear in London until he has undergone another metamorphosis; so that he will have some reason to think, that the tradesmen of Paris and London have combined to lay him under contribution: and they, no doubt, are the directors who regulate the fashions in both capitals . . .[16]

4.3 M. Darly, *An English Macaroni at Paris changeing English Guineas for Silver*, 17 March 1774. Etching, plate 17.9 × 24.7 cm, sheet 19 × 26 cm. Courtesy of The Lewis Walpole Library, Yale University

Some visitors got themselves into serious financial trouble with the necessity of acquiring such wardrobes. Dominic Janes has pointed out the significance of the caricature attributed to Horace Walpole himself of Clotworthy Skeffington, as an early example of direct observation of the effeminate English fop abroad.[17] Skeffington was 7th Viscount and 2nd Earl of Massereene. He visited Paris around 1765 and signed bills for a sum between 15,000 and 20,000 livres. One version of his downfall has it that he was cheated at cards; another that he refused to pay his debts. He was relegated to a debtors' prison, where he spent £4,000 a year living in luxury until he was released in 1789 at the onset of the Revolution.[18]

The more Francophobic guidebooks claimed the French were a nation who cheated the English in their currency exchange, as in *An English Macaroni at Paris changeing English Guineas for Silver* (fig. 4.3). Several guides were written to assist the English tourist after the war ended in 1763. Smollett's guide of 1766, referring to French innkeepers and shopkeepers, noted, 'One could imagine the French were still at war with the English, for they pillage them without mercy.'[19] Warnings were made regarding the substitution of poor-quality lace and trim for the fine goods inspected. The very title of an anonymous guide of *c.*1766, a study of 'French knavery', indicated the distaste many Englishmen felt for their near-neighbours: *The Gentleman's Guide, in His Tour through France. Wrote by an Officer in the Royal-Navy, who lately travelled on a principle, which he most sincerely recommends to his Countrymen, viz. Not to spend more money in the Country of our natural enemy, than is requisite to support with decency the character of an Englishman.*[20]

AN ENGLISH MACARONI AT PARIS
changeing English Guineas for Silver

4.4 François-Louis-Joseph Watteau (designer), A.B. Duhamel (engraver), 'Petit-Maître vetu d'un Habit à large revers et double collet à l'Anglaise...', *Gallerie des Modes et Costumes Français, 55e Cahier des Costumes Français, 49e Suite d'Habillemens à la mode en 1787*, Paris, 1787. Hand-coloured engraving, 28.9 × 20.6 cm. Museum of Fine Arts, Boston, The Elizabeth Day McCormick Collection 44.1679. © 2018 Museum of Fine Arts, Boston

The elaborate appearance of much of the Paris populace amused and puzzled some of the English tourists. It can still be a striking contrast today. As historians such as Daniel Roche have indicated, the taste for novelty and luxury accelerated in that great metropolis during the consumer revolution of the mid- to late eighteenth century in France as well as in England, when second-hand and cheaper versions of the suits, dresses, laces and ribbons of the rich were added to merchants' own wardrobes, and even to those of servants, artisans and shopkeepers. The English were particularly startled by the use of parasols and muffs by Frenchmen, which had feminine connotations after the seventeenth century in England and were rarely depicted in eighteenth-century portrait painting.[21] When the émigré family of the marquis de Falaiseau arrived in London, they could not understand why people were laughing, until they realised it was because of the immense muff the father carried.[22] Even the *abbés* of Paris were stylish and well dressed and sometimes carried such accessories, as did stylish Italian men. As Kimberly Chrisman-Campbell describes, there were nonetheless gendered conventions related to muffs: French women preferring sable and soft furs, and French and Italian men carrying muffs made from predatory animals such as fox, wolf, lynx, dog and even bearskin, worn right up until the years before the Revolution (fig. 4.4).[23] Bunbury included the muffs and a parasol in *View on the Pont Neuf at Paris* (published by Darly in 1771), in which a lemonade-seller, shoe-blacks, a *perruquier* (wig-maker) and an *abbé* pass under a series of Catholic edifices in the background (fig. 4.1).

The street was often disorderly and this was a trap for finely dressed people without a carriage. Harassment was suffered in the street by those considered overdressed in England. Numerous caricatures depict the Frenchman being accosted in the street by the good English butcher, having his queue or pigtail cut from behind by a working woman or boy in a symbolic act of castration, or even having mice deposited in his wig-bag (figs 4.5, 4.6). Others were attacked by a Billingsgate fishwife – women sold fish, and men the meat, in the streets of London. *Sal Dab givin Monsieur a*

Right

4.5 Adam Smith, *The Frenchman at Market, Intended as a Companion to the Frenchman in London, by Collett*, engraved for the *Oxford Magazine*, 1770. Etching, plate 11.3 × 18.2 cm, sheet 13 × 21 cm. Courtesy of The Lewis Walpole Library, Yale University

Below

4.6 John Collett (illustrator), *The Frenchman in London / Le Francois a Londres*, 10 November 1770. Hand-coloured etching and engraving, plate 35.7 × 25.8 cm, sheet 44 × 29 cm. Courtesy of The Lewis Walpole Library, Yale University

Receipt in full depicts a woman holding a lobster over the bottomless breeches of a shirtless but 'laced' Frenchman, worthy of a 1930s surrealistic episode (fig. 4.7). The English also remarked that Frenchmen would not wear their hats outdoors, no matter how cold, for fear of disturbing their coiffures, nor for passing gallantries (fig. 4.8). This practice was taken up by the macaroni and was viewed as an index of the silliness and impracticality of both the English macaroni and the French.

The pretentiousness of the poorer French classes was also a standard English jibe. Some of these understandings were derived from the travel genre; others from Hogarthian painting and print culture. The stage undoubtedly borrowed much of this imagery from Hogarth, whose painting *Roast Beef at Calais* and print *O the Roast-Beef of Old England* (published in March 1749) contrasted English plenty and freedoms with French misery and autocracy.

Lord Hervey had commented on the sartorial innovations of Parisian women in 1728, writing to his mother thus: 'where fashions are come to that extravagance that unless they wear their Pettycoats over their Heads as often in publick as they do in private I can't comprehend what they can invent

next to make people stare'.[24] It was claimed within the travel literature – almost certainly incorrectly – that silk stockings were the fashion in France 'even among the meanest mechanics'.[25] Of the more lowly French it was also said, 'you will rarely see him without his lac'd coat, silk stockings, powder'd hair, and lac'd ruffles, which are often tack'd upon either false sleeves, or a shirt as course as a hop-sack'.[26] In Samuel Foote's play *A Trip to Calais* (1778) the English tourists Minnikin and Margery observe French shoe-blacks who take snuff with the manners of the high-born: 'See how politely they offer their snuff to each other . . .'[27]

French hair, like macaroni hairstyles in the 1770s, was the source of particular consternation to foreign observers. G.F.R. Molé's account of the history of French hairstyles noted in 1773 that all heads in France were dressed, powdered and pomaded or puttied (*mastiquées*), except those of the monks and peasants.[28] Smollett claimed that the women's hair had been copied from that of Hottentots: 'the vilest piece of sophistication that art ever produced'.[29] In French caricatures, high women's hairstyles are sometimes described as *à l'anglaise*, which tells us much about cultural chauvinism and the function of caricature as a mirror to another place or state of being.[30] The ridiculous fondness for hair was held to derive from the first race of French kings, who were distinguished by their long hair; 'even the peasant who drives an ass loaded with dung, wears his hair en queue, though, perhaps, he has neither shirt nor breeches'.[31] In something of an irony, elaborate male hairstyles featuring the queue (when the end of the wig was not placed in a bag) were often described as *à l'anglaise*, possibly with reference to macaroni men, but also demonstrating the growing power of England as a nation that generated fashionable looks of its own (figs 4.9, 4.10).

As David Garrioch has noted, the salon, like the *petit-maître*, was the link between the court and polite society.[32] The 'little master' or French fop was a richly dressed and effeminate figure who surrounded himself with feminine accoutrements and *mondaine* society. Men wore the *habit habillé* (which

Dessiné par Le Clerc   Gravé par Voysard

Jeune elegant en habit moucheté avec une veste blanche garnie de bandes d'indiene et coeffé d'un chapeau à la Suisse et une queue à l'Angloise.

A Paris chez Esnautz et Rapilly rue St Jacques, à la Ville de Coutances. A.P.D.R.

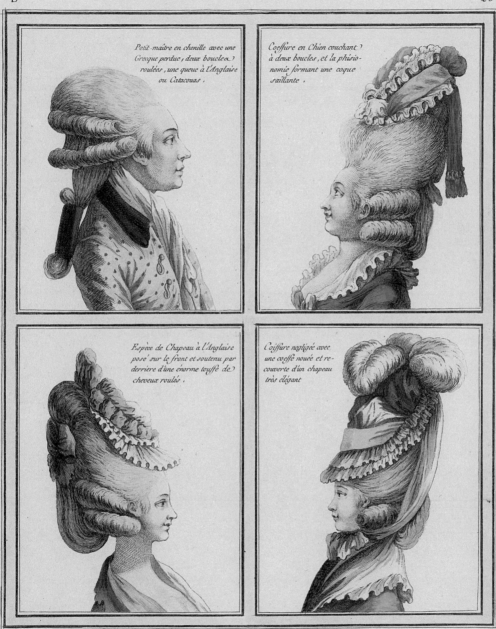

Petit-maître en chenille avec une
Grecque perdue, deux boucles
roulées, une queue à l'Anglaise
ou Catacouas.

Coeffure en Chien couchant
à deux boucles, et la phisio-
nomie formant une coque
saillante.

Espèce de Chapeau à l'Anglaise
posé sur le front et soutenu par
derriere d'une enorme touffe de
cheveux roulés.

Coiffure negligée avec
une coeffe nouée et re-
couverte d'un chapeau
très elégant

A Paris chez Esnauts et Rapilly, rue St Jacques a la Ville de Coutances. A. P. D. R.

can be translated as 'dress suit'), better known as the *habit à la française*. Court dress was more widely adopted in Paris than in London, and the syntax of French court dress was complex. Very few people could be presented at the French court, but others could watch, so long as they were appropriately attired. The royal couple dressed finely in special wardrobes for court, which was sometimes operated as a more informal 'half court', when informal modes were permitted for women. The preferred textiles were silk and velvet: Chrisman-Campbell recounts that even late in the century a woollen suit adorned with diamond buttons was sniffed at by one snobbish observer.[33] Different colours were expected to be worn at different French palaces by the men, who were also required to wear hunting clothes dyed in particular shades. The court wardrobe was visually splendid, costly and consisted of a harmony of parts and gracefulness. Embroidery was generally floral in inspiration, underlining seasonally appropriate dress. Lighter-weight silks were worn in summer. Rich cloth of silver and gold was imperative for the finest court dress, which shimmered in candlelight (fig. 4.11). *Gallerie des Modes* published a summer suit in that great rarity, printed cotton or linen (*toile peinte*), of a vermicelli pattern with bands of printed *indienne* or cotton (or an imitation thereof) instead of braid or galloon (fig. 4.12).

Winter demanded different clothes for the aristocracy. French and Italian men were noted for their very fine winter coats lined with furs (fig. 4.13). A well-executed dated portrait extant from the beginning of the macaroni episode is Jean-Baptiste Greuze's *Charles-Claude de Flahaut de la Billarderie (1730–1809), comte d'Angiviller* (fig. 4.14). The count, who was in charge of the sons of the dauphin and hence had the important role of tending the heirs to the throne, is depicted by Greuze as both intelligent and finely dressed. As James Thompson notes in his subtle reading of the painting, the slight suggestion of speech in the face accords perfectly with the animation of the clothing, which also reveals a continuation of rococo aesthetics from the reign of Louis XV. A pale-plum silk jacket is lined with brown fur, probably sable, and trimmed with the elaborate 'frogging' that

characterises much macaroni dress. Such *passementerie* sat on the surface of the coat and had little practical purpose. As a contrast with the large expanse of the monochrome silk jacket, the waistcoat bursts forth above the waist, the top buttons undone, suggesting a certain easy negligence in the sitter as he awaits the result of his portrait. The waistcoat is a splendid brocaded silk, probably Lyons-made, with meandering ribbons of gold thread and red roses, which pick up the red ribbon appending his Order of St Louis. Such textiles do not necessarily include embroidered flowers, as is sometimes stated, but the most luxurious textiles included ones in which the floral motifs and meandering sections were integral to the extremely complicated woven structures of the silks. The gold thread is carefully rendered in paint by the artist and sits on the surface of the canvas. The ground of the waistcoat is powder-blue and, like the jacket, it is fur-lined, but in this case with a white fur. The sitter's wig-bag is a grey-blue, with the stitches clearly delineated. As Aileen Ribeiro has noted, artists made quite self-conscious decisions as to how they chose to render sartorial fashions, and with what particular detail and effect.[34] In this case, Thompson reminds us that the Goncourts, those great chroniclers of eighteenth-century life for the nineteenth century, wrote of Greuze that he himself was 'fond of personal adornment and flashy clothes'.[35]

By the early 1780s, new fashions for men arose. The French, in emulation of the English, began to wear long informal *fraques*, or sometimes 'frock coats' (the word was used in eighteenth-century sources, before its better-known use in the nineteenth century), sometimes crossing in the front and called *en Lévite* (fig. 4.15); the name also accorded to a loose informal garment for women. They also copied the riding coat, the *redingote*, some examples of which had three fallen collars. The French seemed to retain their tricorn hats longer than the English, although the *petits-maîtres* who are so vividly portrayed in the first fashion periodical, the *Gallerie des Modes*, are also illustrated wearing soft outdoor hats (fig. 4.16), either round or sometimes with a very wide upturned brim and large matching rosettes.

Rédingotte à trois colets et Croisée par devant, dite Rédingotte en Lévite .

A Paris chez Esnauts et Rapilly rue S.t Jacques à la Ville de Coutances A.P.D.R.

Petit Maitre en Chenille Fraque de couleur à la mode Veste de soie à bordure en broderie de soie de di verses couleurs, les Boutons du Fraque d'argent à jour ileil coeffé d'un Chapeau à la Pensilvanie .

A Paris chez Esnauts et Rapilly rue S.t Jacques à la Ville de Coutances . A . P . D . R .

MON.^R LE FRIZUER.

4.17 **Henry William Bunbury,**
Monr. le Frizuer, 12 May 1771.
Etching and engraving, early state,
reissued, plate 15.5 × 10.7 cm, sheet
18 × 13 cm. Courtesy of The Lewis
Walpole Library, Yale University

Some members of the French luxury trades advertised
their wares and displayed the patronage of the aristocratic
and financial elite by wearing rich dress such as the latter
enjoyed. The appearance industry was a very large sector
of the Parisian economy, with 40 per cent of all trades, or
about 12,000 masters, dealing in clothing and the crafting
of hair, make-up and wigs.[36] Some of this sector designed
themselves as walking advertisements and amazed the
English visitor to Paris. *Monr. le Frizuer* [*sic*] by Darly
shows an absurdly dressed hairdresser carrying the tools
of his trade, with a number of combs stuck in his hair (fig.
4.17). A pair of English porcelain figure groups by Derby,
known as *The Hairdresser* and *The Shoemaker*, were based
on French designs by François Boucher (fig. 4.18). They
show a near-impossible elegance for a tradesman, as well
as proximity to the bodies of women, as corset-makers and
hairdressers tended directly to them.

A Friday night out in Paris continues to amaze
today. John Andrews wrote in 1770: 'nothing is still more
common than to see numbers of people sauntering in the streets of Paris, as
completely and magnificently apparelled as if they were going to court.'[37] He
described the French as enslaved to fashion for political and social reasons.
The French, he argued, have little chance of a role in government and thus
few options to pursue but voluptuousness and gallantry, 'an intercourse
whereof vanity is the real basis'.[38] The cultivation of French-derived
manners was to be avoided, for more than reasons of common sense: 'what
we might gain in delicacy and refinement, we might lose in Manliness of
behaviour and liberty of discourse; the two pillars on which the edifice of
our national character is mainly supported'.[39]

Fashion became an emblem for enslavement and absolutism, and
the language used to deride France's fashionability parallels that used to
diminish the French political system. The French, Andrews recounted,
tamely submit 'to the guidance of the Mode', whereas of all nationals, the
English act 'from pure, native, unrestrained impulse'.[40] And the English,
he noted, need look no further than the period before the Restoration and
the [Glorious] Revolution for the consequences of such folly.[41] This claim
sits rather uncomfortably with what is known of the growth of English
fashionability over the course of the eighteenth century.

The English were also struck by the very different French political
and social system, with classes ranging from an autocratic nobility to the
peasantry. The French nobility was ten times more numerous than the
English one, although the population was only three times larger. French

4.18 *The Hairdresser* (from a pair with *The Shoemaker*), English, Derby porcelain factory, *c.*1780. After figures modelled by Étienne-Maurice Falconet, after designs by François Boucher, for Sèvres. Porcelain (unglazed), 17.7 × 18.5 cm. The Johnston Collection, Melbourne (A1191-1998)

salon society, which appeared to be run by and for women, produced an urban aristocratic culture that made French culture look feminine.

The prodigious spending of the French nobility on fashion was not a myth; Mme de Montmorin's tailor was owed 180,000 livres, and Mme de Matignon paid her hairdresser 24,000 livres to style her hair in a different manner every day of the year.[42] Frenchwomen wore considerably more make-up than their English counterparts: Lord Hervey had been shocked by the painted faces on his Grand Tour visit in 1716, and David Garrick commented in Paris in 1751: 'In our walk [31 May] we saw two very pretty French women unpainted, wch was a greater curiosity than any I have yet seen in Paris.'[43] Hervey was even more surprised by the Parisian men 'who paint themselves white and look paler than poor *Banquo*' (a character in *Macbeth* who returns as a ghost).[44]

The English were also struck by different social conventions in Paris. At some point in the early eighteenth century the English had given up the practice of men kissing men as a greeting. John Carr wrote in 1803: 'In different directions of my eye I saw about thirty men kissing each other. The women in France never think their prerogatives infringed by this anti-anglo mode of salutation.'[45] As with the macaroni, this homosocial behaviour was seen as an affront to women rather than as a threat to men, an issue explored further in the following chapters. Some writers used references to Juvenal's concept of a debauched Rome in order to chastise the French nation: 'It would therefore seem, that Paris approaches fast to its end, if what an Ancient says be true, that unbounded Expence is an evident sign of a dying city.'[46] This text is obviously a spoof, possibly by the great satirist Louis-Antoine de Caraccioli, the title punning on the notion of 'impartial critique'; but these ideas drawn from the 'Romans of the Decadence' frequently recurred.

That Smollett's account was part of an anti-French industry is indicated in the title of the 1766 rebuttal by Philip Thicknesse, *Observations on the Customs and Manners of the French Nation, in a series of letters, in which that nation is vindicated from the misrepresentations of some late writers*. He nonetheless agreed, regarding the universal habit of dressing the head in France:

> It is astonishing how universal the fashion is in France to dress the head; scarce a man, woman, or child, above the degree of the meanest peasants, but have their hair dressed and powdered in the highest taste of the country.[47]

A Regency travel guide described a statue of the Virgin and Child, with the Queen of Heaven dressed in the latest French mode, the Christ Child in court fashion with a neatly powdered wig:

> In the church of Notre Dame at Caen was an altar piece with a statue of the virgin dressed in a white muslin gown, spotted with silver; a little bouquet of artificial flowers graced her bosom, and her wig was finely curled, and powdered. The figure in her arms, which was intended to represent the infant Jesus, was dressed in a style equally unsuitable; his hair was also curled, and powdered, and a small cocked hat placed upon his head. Our delighted guide, whose eyes sparkled with self-complacency, asked if we had ever seen a prettier Virgin Mary, or one dressed more handsomely.[48]

The image of a fashionable Frenchman as a monkey was very common and provides a further link with the macaroni, who was frequently satirised in this way. The level of invective was astonishing: Smollett claimed that the common French people resembled 'large baboons walking upright'.[49] There was a long tradition that furnished this iconography. A late seventeenth-century poem entitled *The French dancing-master and the English soldier: or, the difference betwixt fidling and fighting, displayed in a dialogue betwixt an Englishman and a Frenchman* described the French as 'like puppets in a play': 'To act the Mimick, fidle, prate and dance, / And cringe like Apes, is a le mode France'.[50] An early eighteenth-century text, the anonymous poem *The Baboon A-la-Mode: A Satyr against the French, by a Gentleman*, sustained a mockery of artifice in the following manner for 22 pages:

> Their modes so strangely alter human shape,
> What nature made a man they make an ape:
> The faults of her which they pretend to cure,
> Burlesque GOD's image with their garniture.
> 'Tis to that foppish nation that we owe
> Those Antick dresses that equip a beau:
> So many sorts of rigging dress the elf,
> Himself sometimes does hardly know himself . . .
> In English, fops and knaves; in French, they're beaus
> In short, they are an ill-contriv'd lampoon;
> And to conclude, a French-man's a baboon.[51]

In this poem, the French take civilisation too far and reduce man to a state of bestial nature. Also in this vein is Garrick's *The Sick Monkey* of 1765, a parable in verse about a monkey who is a player in a court of other animals. The monkey has fallen ill with an attack of the nerves, after other animals have castigated him for his imitations of them.[52] This might have been read by contemporaries as a spoof on the vain pursuit of fashionable clothing and manners. The joke is the monkey's perceived attempt to act humanly, and his failure to do the same; as well as the suggestion that all humans are base creatures putting on airs.

The English were particularly fond of recounting how, after the Glorious Revolution of 1688, they were slaves to no one, unlike their neighbours the French, who lived under the spectre of absolutist rule. Nonetheless, William III, vanquisher of the French, continued to order his luxury goods from Paris, and French craftsmen were used to build Blenheim Palace for his general, the Duke of Marlborough.[53] Despite the efforts of the Anti-Gallican Society, which directly criticised the importation of French luxury goods, the English continued to be enamoured with French fashionable life, architecture and the 'useful' arts, including fashion, as well as etiquette. This anomaly fired trenchant and amusing critiques of the new tyrant Fashion. Engravings such as *Pantin à la Mode*, in which an ape dressed in a tricorn hat plays with the tail of a Frenchman's wig – the man a puppet of fashion, like the toys the women hold – provide the backdrop for the macaroni stereotypes of the following decades. For those who purchased English goods, Linda Colley has argued, the English inflection of the rococo and other French styles was an attempt to market native products as being as stylish and cosmopolitan as those of France, and thus reduce the demand for imports.[54]

Fashion and the luxury debate

Luxury was blamed for the threat that appeared to be posed to the social orders; it threatened to dissolve 'several ranks'.[55] This was very much the case after the Seven Years War, when Britons were faced with the anomalous situation that they had just vanquished the French, destroying their position in North America, and established themselves as the leading European imperial power, yet their nationals were rushing to Paris to inspect the latest novelties and import them, at great cost to the British balance of trade. Things French had extra allure as the English traveller had been unable to visit Paris for close to a decade; Charles James Fox, David Garrick and Horace Walpole were amongst those who travelled there immediately, enjoying the wide variety of fashionable goods sold in Paris, from buckles to sword cutlery and waistcoats (fig. 4.19). Despite any amount of satire, Paris was certainly the centre of European fashion in the eighteenth century. Horace Walpole wrote to Conway in October 1758 regarding the cessation of war: 'In the meantime we have several collateral emoluments from the pacification; all our milliners, tailors, tavern-keepers, and young gentlemen are riding to France for our improvement and luxury.'[56] This included fashion in the broadest sense of clothing, textiles and decorative arts, including porcelain and furniture. The quality of French manufactures, the specialisation of France's guilds and the centralisation under Colbert in the late seventeenth century of the textile and tapestry trades resulted in a pool of expertise unparalleled in Europe, although Italy equalled France in the splendour of its textile culture, and objects made of porcelain, metals, ivory and the like were notable in many other European centres.

The 1760s and early 1770s were still a time of great emulation of things French; but the Anglomania developing in this period would reverse the pattern of influence considerably, creating a new fashion pendulum, though the quality of many French goods continued to render them desirable. Despite the fact that England and France were at war nearly every second decade, fashion dolls that set the modes for women found their way through trade embargoes, and French goods were smuggled across blockades.

Within the nationalist framework, the supremacy of French fashions, whether in waistcoats or snuff-boxes, perturbed the English mind, as it undermined mercantile theory. Mercantilism, prevalent from the

mid-sixteenth century, encouraged government intervention in regulating the economy. Mercantilists were concerned with the generation of a surplus of exports in the balance of trade and the maintenance of high levels of bullion. The English spoke in horror of their coin flowing across the Channel, filling the coffers of merchants who were shifty and unscrupulous.

French court dress and manners were also associated with Jacobitism. There was turmoil in England between 1742 and 1746; and Bonnie Prince Charlie landed in 1745. The slight vestigial threat of a French-sponsored Jacobite invasion to restore the Catholic Stuarts lingered until after mid-century, further fuelling hostility about French neighbours and their attributes. Many writers argued that the pursuit of fashion was also a menace to British manhood and military strength. The issue of nationalism, masculinity and Francophobia is of particular relevance in understanding reactions to the macaroni. In the print *What is this my Son Tom* (1774), a Frenchified macaroni meets his father, the sober John Bull. 'The honest farmer, come to town, can scarce believe his son his own, / If thus the taste continues here, what will it be another year?' (see also fig. 3.32). In the 1740s, when anti-Jacobitism was at its peak, Garrick wrote several prologues that were designed to amuse the audience in their anti-Gallican sentiment. His prologue to James Ralph's *The Astrologer* (1744) proclaimed:

> A modish frenzy so corrupts the town,
> That naught but Alamode de France goes down:
> We all submit to this fantastic yoke;
> Like them we dress, we dance, we eat, we joke;
> From top to toe they change us at their will;
> All but our hearts – and those are British still.[57]

This is an assertion of inherent character or 'heart', a state of being that macaroni behaviour contradicted. In 1754 Garrick's epilogue to *Barbarossa* noted:

> An English gentlemen should never think –
> The reason's plain, which every soul might hit on –
> Who trims a Frenchman, oversets a Briton . . .

And Garrick's character of the fine gentleman in *Lethe* declared: 'In short, I have skim'd the Cream of every Nation, and have the Consolation to declare, I never was in any Country in my Life, but I had Taste enough thoroughly to despise my own.'[58] The anonymous work *The Devil upon Crutches in England, or Night Scenes in London: A Satirical Work by a Gentleman of Oxford* (1755) recorded: 'I never yet knew a Man that was fond of foreign Manners and Fashions, but had a weak Head, or a bad Heart. – But by what unaccountable Fatality I know not the once brave, rough, and victorious

English, are entirely Frenchified . . .'[59] The banter concerning macaroni, their inanity, inconsistency and treacherous Francophilia thus worked within an older, fairly continuous lineage and circulation of ideas and genres.

Caricatures that revolved around the contrast between the unfashionable English and the fashionable French were part of a humorous trade that also produced poems cheaply for the amusement of the public. *Fashion: or, a Trip to a Foreign C-t. A Poem* (1777) encapsulates neatly the notion that fashion was a foreign entity, not native to England, with the added elaboration of a country and city opposition. The poem, which sold for one shilling and sixpence, concerns an Englishman who decides to leave his 'moss-rooft old barn' for the city, and calls upon the tailor and hairdresser to transform his appearance. His suit is pulled from a chest and sent for retrimming:

> For many a year undisturb'd had it laid,
> E'er since the Pretender did England invade.

The barber-hairdresser, mocked as a grimacing foreigner, makes up the country-man's face and produces a macaroni hairstyle:

> Mon friseur avançant en air et grimace,
> Avec rasoir aiguisé, smoothed my face.
> With powder of orris, pomatum, a compound
> Of hog's lard, and dog's lard, and tallow a pound; . . .
> The horse-tail behind, such a monstrous huge pack,
> He cram'd in a bourse, or a bag, or a sack.

To complete the metropolitan effect, the country-man adds a sword and a *chapeau de bras*. A series of hilarious incidents then follow, as he is carried by chair into the city, a mode of transport that was mocked as particularly French; they refused to walk anywhere in Paris, it was claimed. The satire culminates when he witnesses a woman's hair-piece fall off:

> From their covert dislodg'd by the shock of the fall,
> Fleas and bugs march'd in companies o'er the hall:
> Quite puny, and faint, they all limped about, And hobbled along like old age in the gout: . . .[60]

In this scenario, even the vermin are debilitated.

Conduct books and the English gentleman
Conduct books were also a repository of attitudes towards models of appropriate masculine dress and national ideals. Most were based on the model of Baldassare Castiglione's *The Courtier* (1528), which advocated a restraint that appears to have been absent from the eighteenth-century

French court. Castiglione explains that grace is 'very agreeable and pleasant to all', but argues against excess and feminine modifications:

> I don't want him to appear soft and feminine as so many try to do, when they not only curl their hair and pluck their eyebrows but also preen themselves like the most wanton and dissolute creatures imaginable. Indeed, they appear so effeminate and languid in the way they walk, or stand, or do anything at all, that their limbs look as if they are about to fall apart; and they pronounce their words in such a drawling way that it seems as if they are about to expire on the spot . . . Since Nature has not in fact made them the ladies they want to seem and be, they should be treated not as honest women but as common whores, and be driven out from all gentlemanly society, let alone the Courts of great lords.[61]

Following the Glorious Revolution, the English took the moderate precepts of Castiglione to heart. Instruction manuals for the young English gentleman demanded neat and modest moderation in dressing, with due consideration to social status:

> Be neat without gawdiness, gentile without affectation: In fine, the Taylor must take measure of both your purse and of your quality, as well as of your person: For a sute that fits the character, is more a la mode than that which fits well on the body . . . I have seen some Fops over-shoot extravagance; . . . a man of war might be rigged up with less noise, and some-times at less expense . . . [62]

This approach was entirely repudiated by macaroni practice, wherein there was no character other than that fitted along with the 'sute'. In the view of this guidebook, it was equally damning to adopt a slovenly air – 'this is to sacrifice one vice to another, to attone for vanity with nastiness', exactly the type of precept advocated by Lord Chesterfield later in his *Letters*.[63] Many contemporary readers were unimpressed with the publication of this collection. Fanny Burney noted in her journal in 1774:

> We had a good deal of conversation upon Lord Chesterfield's *Letters* which have lately been published. I had the satisfaction to find that our opinions exactly coincided – that they were extremely well written, contained some excellent *hints* for Education – but were written with a tendency to make his son a man wholly unprincipled; inculcating immorality; countenancing all *Gentlemanlike* vices; *advising* deceit; & *exhorting* to Inconstancy. 'It pleased me much' said Mr Hutton, 'in speaking to the King about these Letters, to hear him say – "For my part, I like more streight forward work".'[64]

Comparing the young man to Omai, newly arrived from Polynesia, Burney concluded that the former was a 'meer *pedantic Booby* . . . I think this shews how much more *Nature* can do without *art*, than *art* with all her refinement, unassisted by *Nature*.'[65]

As Michèle Cohen notes, Chesterfield, who believed in a continental education for his illegitimate son, can be contrasted with David Fordyce, whose *Dialogues Concerning Education* of 1745–8 argued that young British men should be trained 'free from the gilded chains of French politeness'.[66] The line between slovenliness and vanity was fine, regionally and temporally arbitrary, and specific. In the early 1700s terms such as 'fop', 'beau' and 'coxcomb' were used to describe the fashionably dressed man; the suggestion was that they were an unnatural hybrid, mingling male and female attributes – the prototype of the 'unsexed male misses', fribbles and macaroni, discussed later in relationship to theatre. Thus the anonymous author of *A Gentleman Instructed in the Conduct of a Virtuous and Happy Life. Written for the Instruction of a Young Nobleman* noted of the fop and beau:

> had their mothers made a voyage to the Indies, I should suspect they had some relation to an Ape: For certainly they are of a mixt species, and often the beast predominates, but always the coxcomb . . . [67]

Similarly, *The Gentleman's Library, Containing rules for conduct in all parts of life, written by a Gentleman* preached restraint and moderation, describing fashion as 'a spreading contagion, and epidemical foolery of the age'. In a model that would be taken up and applied to the macaroni, the most fashionable were described as empty-headed: 'the greatest pride and affectation in apparel, are lodg'd with persons of the most substantial ignorance. The souls of idiots are actuated merely by frail sense, their eyes are made their principal directors.'[68] This text used Ciceronian exemplars to chastise both rusticity and foppery, and to advocate a medium between the two extremes.

The conditions of eighteenth-century life, with increased travel and dislocation, contributed to new meanings of fashion:

> . . . Handsome Apparel is a main Point, and People, where they are not known, are generall honoured according to their Cloaths; because from the Richnesse of them we judge o their Wealth; . . . but who ever pretends to dazzle Men of Sense into Respect, merely with Scarlet and Gold-lace, will fall short of his Pretensions.[69]

Samuel Johnson wrote observantly on the matter of arbitrary cultural conventions in 1775, when he was attempting to convince his country mother of the harmlessness of his up-to-date fashions worn in London: 'where there is no real good or evil in the act itself [I] would willingly comply with the custom of the place'.[70] He may have underestimated the power of dress to undermine the notion of inherent good or evil.

The macaroni consumer

Public morality, social hierarchy and government control provide part of the motivation for critiques of fashion and luxury.[71] Until the macaroni period, the majority of English diatribes against fashion took the form of attacks on women for their worship of fashion, and naturalised women's identification with vanity and fashion. Fashion's critics were vocal in the 1740s and 1750s when the anti-Gallican movement was launched, and this continued as an important cultural theme at the same time as the macaroni, during the 1760s and 1770s. Fashion, like Nature, was generally personified as female. *Modern Refinement, a Satire* (1777), 'By the author of the Register of Folly', put it thus:

> Such is refinement! – but I blush to own
> Its portrait to GREAT-BRITAIN's sons is known!
> Were it to FRANCE and ITALY confin'd,
> From whence it came to taint the ENGLISH mind, . . .
> Send back the Siren to her native shore,
> And make each BRITON great, as heretofore;
> No longer slaves to FASHION let them be,
> But like their fathers, generous, bold, and free. – [72]

Fashion was alarming, viewed not only as the tool of France but as an instrument of female dominance. Suggesting that Salic law (excluding female succession to thrones and fiefs) encouraged French women to take revenge on their men, John Andrews noted that a lady's *toilette* 'is, in truth, the shrine at which all men of genteel rank offer up their daily services'; 'no people being more the dupes and subjects of their women than the French'.[73] In a later text Andrews claimed 'the French are more than any other people, subject and subservient to the government and controul of their women'. French men's fondness for fashion was often characterised by the French themselves as providing an opportunity to gain access to women.[74] This was an older view of 'effeminacy' that had also pertained in England, but whose persuasion seemed to be seriously eroded by the 1770s.

All things French tended to be conflated with the female sphere. In England, periods of menstruation were called the 'French lady's visit' or 'being the French Lady'.[75] The study of the French language was also being re-gendered at this time; by the late eighteenth century, French became viewed as a feminine accomplishment rather than as primarily a language of civility.[76] Ralph Schomberg's *Fashion. A Poem* (1778) merged the racial and gendered concepts in order to describe the reign of 'giddy Fashion' in France, who in England also 'sought new slaves to honour her command':

> Why to the grand Pantheon press the throng?
> Say, Muse! for ev'ry thing to thee is known –

'Tis FASHION there maintains her painted throne.[77]

The themes reiterate those of the 1740s: 'O France, whose Edicts govern dress and meat, / Thy victor Britain bends beneath thy feet!'[78]

From the early eighteenth century it had been noted that women held a peculiar fondness for dress. As G.J. Barker-Benfield notes, the 3rd Earl of Shaftesbury's 'sensational psychology' – derived from Locke – argued that there was a physical basis for differences between men and women.[79] To the Whig Shaftesbury, modern manners should be polite and 'harmonious', a fashionable but not foppish 'manly liberty' working with 'the goodly order of the universe'. The rise of commercial culture, urban leisure and fashion culture could be embraced, but must be managed via discipline, erudition and moderation.[80] England had a long tradition of discussing women as being particularly addicted to finery: 'womankind, who are carried away with everything that is showy, and with what delights the eye, more than any one species of living creature whatsoever . . . ' noted the *Tatler* in the early eighteenth century.[81] The behaviour of the macaroni was disturbing, for it upset the cultural preconception – backed up by the educational observations of Locke and Rousseau – that men should be immune to an enslavement to fashion, being, as they were held to be, such different creatures from women. To this conjunction can be added the popular understandings of the gendered consumer, to which the macaroni stereotype provided both ammunition and a challenge.

The macaroni, on the one hand, bolstered the gendering of fashion consumption as feminine by their perceived 'effeminacy', silliness and whimsicality. They were therefore also contributing to the consolidation of the gender binaries that shaped men's relationship to fashion for the next 200 years. Their pursuit of things continental disrupted the notion of an inherent English national character, although fashion and design generally always operate through an interrelationship with other places, times and situations. This leads to the next discussion about the macaroni inflections of gender and sexuality, its relationship to the state and social settings – even to health and psychology.

CHAPTER 5

'Pretty Gentleman': Macaroni Dress and Male Sexualities

*E*legance is the Absence or Debilitation of Masculine Strength
and Vigor.

[Philautus], *The Pretty Gentleman*, 1747[1]

*T*he ruling manners of our women are essentially the same with those of
the men ... The sexes have now little other apparent distinction beyond
that of person and dress. Their peculiar and characteristic manners are
confounded and lost, the one sex having advanced into boldness, as the other
have sunk into effeminacy.

London Chronicle, April 1757[2]

*B*uggery: the English say, both the word and things came to them from
Italy, and are strangers to England. Indeed they love the fair sex too
well to fall into such an abomination.

Henri Misson, *M. Misson's Memoirs and
observations in his travels over England*, 1719[3]

Within the burgeoning field of gay and queer studies there remains
considerable disagreement as to how to analyse the motives, moods and
feelings of 'men loving men' in the past.[4] A general conclusion is that by at
least the early eighteenth century, 'queer' subcultures or groups existed in
many towns and cities of Europe. Sexual behaviours were not the same as
sexual preferences, although clearly the latter influence the former.

This chapter examines the sexual charge of macaroni men, with a focus
on their dress, manners and places of resort. It considers the profound shift
that reconfigured connections between the seductive allure of English
male dress and sexual desire over the course of the eighteenth century.
Whereas in the early years of the century the foppish paraphernalia of
court dress was held to attract women and enhance 'heterosexual' allure,
by the era of the macaroni, such dress was frequently interpreted as an
irritation to women, which could also connote a lack of interest or ability
in heterosexual desire and performance. As was emphasised in Chapter 3,
many well-known macaroni such as Charles James Fox were never accused
of being homosexual. Nonetheless, macaroni dress was connected with the
sodomite in a substantial number of popular visual and verbal sources. It
began to be associated with an English variant of the 'homosexual' or same-
sex subcultures that were emerging in urbanised western Europe by the late
seventeenth century. These subcultures (or, at the very least, groupings of
men) exploited the same spaces in which fashion was often displayed and
disseminated: the Royal Exchange in London, the piazzas and parks, and the
modish masquerade venues. Whether this dress was a cause or a symptom
of homosexuality varied in the accounts.

The eighteenth century saw the development of the notion of a 'third gender' to describe a nascent 'homosexuality', a cultural ideal that would remain current until challenged in gay politics of the 1960s to 1970s. This third state was sometimes positioned as that either of the hermaphrodite or the eunuch. Horace Walpole, changing the words of Lady Mary Wortley Montagu slightly and referring to the courtier and politician John, Lord Hervey, noted that 'there were three sexes: men, women and Herveys'.[5] Alexander Pope had characterised Hervey in the *Epistle to Dr Arbuthnot* (1735) and *The Dunciad* as 'Sporus', Nero's male favourite, aligning him with Roman eunuchs – a particular idea of the 'three sexes' that continued to be popular in the nineteenth century, being used by the opera composer Gioachino Rossini, no less.

A significant number of sodomites were arrested in the years following 1700 in London and Utrecht, and the relevant court proceedings document the existence of what appeared to contemporaries as a new grouping of passive, effeminate men who desired only men, whether adult or adolescent. They were classified as a third, deviant gender, combining aspects of male and female behaviour. This was not named at the time, but terms such as 'neuter' or 'amphibious' evoked the state. 'Amphibious' means 'leading two lives' and is a term used by Pope in *The Dunciad* to characterise Lord Hervey as Sporus:

> Amphibious thing!, that acting either part . . .
> Now *trips* a Lady, and now struts a Lord.[6]

These expressions – 'neuter' and 'amphibious' – were precisely those used later to describe the macaroni.

A more sober model of English dress and behaviour was noted by foreign visitors in 1722: 'The dress of the English is like the French but not so gaudy; they generally go plain but in the best cloths and stuffs . . . not but that they wear embroidery and laces on their cloathes on solemn days, but they don't make it their daily wear, as the French do.'[7] The hedonic macaroni emerged after the Seven Years War. Criticisms were made of English military officers and militia that they had become foppish and feminised during the period of the French and Indian Wars (Revolutionary Wars) in North America, and numerous prints were made of them as macaroni men. As Matthew McCormack notes, the insinuation was not necessarily that they were homosexual, but rather that they had become 'culturally distant from the people'.[8]

By the 1760s, too much attention to fashion on the part of a man was read as evidence of a lack of interest in women, and as potentially unattractive to women. In 1774 Fanny Burney had little patience with coxcombs 'full of affectation & airs', 'the Conceit, the half witted liveliness', preferring 'the

5.1 John Raphael Smith,
The Promenade at Carlisle House,
1781. Mezzotint after his own design,
dimensions unknown. Private
collection

manly manners, solid sense & entertaining Humours' of a Scottish visitor.[9]
Contemporary joke-books also rehearsed the theme:

> A Macaroni who was fond of a girl of the town, catched her lately in bed
> with a carman; on which he charged her with her scandalous want of
> taste. The girl coolly replied, 'You used to sleep with me for the credit
> of lying with a woman; and I sleep with this carman; for the pleasure of
> lying with a man.'[10]

A mezzotint of 1781 by the internationally successful John Raphael
Smith entitled *The Promenade at Carlisle House* illustrates the tension in the
attraction of fine clothes (fig. 5.1). Ellen G. D'Oench has demonstrated that
the women who appear in this image are 'light girls' or ladies of the night,
and notes that this print, which is related to the genre of the conversation
piece, commanded a high price (£3 6s. at the end of the century), as it
was believed that the women were identifiable demi-monde portraits.[11]

The coloured example illustrated here shows two competing clothing systems for men operating at the same time. To the left by the tea-table is an attractive young man in short dove-grey woollen broadcloth, high boots and a soft riding hat, leaning forward with a negligent posture, surrounded by a bevy of attractive women; he looks as if he has just walked in from the street and slumps forward on the richly upholstered armchair. To the right appears a fop with a cane, tricorn hat and buckled shoes, who surveys the scene, observing two finely dressed women who appear as if they will sail past him out of the picture plane; to his right an elderly fop converses with a plain woman in the background. The rich range of clothes harmonises with the elaborate mirrors, candle-arms and the suggestion of wallpaper; even the printed decorative surround of the print is in the fashionable neoclassical style. The youth is cast in the light of the composition; the fop in relative darkness. The extravagantly dressed lady-killer was now in decline, and the desirable male is the one wearing modern sporting dress, accentuated by his apparent and natural youth.

Masquerade and travesty

The macaroni and the masquerade were closely linked in the popular imagination. Both held suggestions that were richly subversive of normative gender and sexual roles. Attendance at the masquerade had been a fashionable diversion since the 1720s and continued to be very popular into the 1770s.[12] London's masquerade venues were the perfect site for the display of fashionable dress as well as 'costume' and thus were an ideal vehicle for the unveiling of a new macaroni outfit.

Contemporaries recognised the ancient roots and modern form of the entertainment:

> This pretended entertainment forms, perhaps, one of the most insipid, unmeaning mummeries, that ever, with its barbarous attempts at wit and humour, insulted taste and common sense ... The origin, indeed, of Masquerades is extremely ancient, and took its rise from the drunken mirth at the vintages in the southern climes ... it made also a considerable part of religious processions, long before Christianity, as well as both the Pagan and Popish carnivals. We have retained all the folly, without a particle either of the meaning, or the spirit of it.[13]

In 1724 the Bishop of London claimed that these diversions were a French plot to enslave men in 'Licentiousness and Effeminacy'.[14] The events permitted a social licence that was perhaps unprecedented in English public entertainments. Although Amanda Vickery has been gently critical of this idea of the masquerade as liminal space – noting, for example, that they were not as demotic as has been suggested – masquerades were by definition antinatural, permitting erotic release.[15] The mask on the face connoted physical and moral detachment; participants at a masquerade were also called 'masks' themselves. Within caricature conventions, masks stood in for duplicity. Some masqueraders wore the dress of characters from plays and novels, emphasising the interplay between the 'real' and the fictive.

Reports regarding the entertainments, decorations and dress of the participants at masquerades were extremely common in the periodical press directed at the 'middling sort', and particularly at the women readers within this social group. Masquerades were criticised by the Church and by moralising commentators for their promotion of luxury, vanity and sexual licence and game-playing, as well as for their dangerous social levelling, as anyone who could afford the price of the ticket was admitted. When the Pantheon opened in early 1772, Mrs Harris noted the appearance there of 'most of the gay ladies [i.e. prostitutes] in town and ladies of the first rank and character; and by appearance some very low people'.[16] Perhaps because of this prurient disapproval, magazine hacks penned witty and detailed accounts of the occurrences of the previous evening's entertainments. The presence of foppish men was regularly noticed. A Regency writer reminisced upon the height of the hair at these popular entertainments:

> It will scarcely be credited now, that the fops and macaronis of this date actually wore their hair frizzled out on each side [of] the head to more than the breadth of the visage, and that a solid pound of hair powder was wasted in dressing a fool's head ... Ranelagh [pleasure garden] was the élite of fashion. The gentlemen wore powder, frills, ruffles, and had gold headed canes, etc., etc., forming a great contrast to the dandyism of the present day ... [17]

Extravagantly dressed macaroni are nearly always present in engravings of crowd scenes at masquerades. It is worth noting again that striped stockings and waistcoats in some macaroni caricatures reinforced possibly transgressive overtones: Michel Pastoureau's cultural history of the stripe, already cited, suggests that diabolical, sinister or ludic overtones might still have attached to the stripe until its use became more common in textiles of the 1790s, although it had also been a popular fashion in the seventeenth century, in reference to 'Siamese' and other exotic foreign dress.[18]

Contrary to the popular conception that men's dress changes little over time, the fashionable suit of the 1760s was shorter than in earlier periods. More of the man's body was therefore revealed. *The Cold Rump or Taste Alamode* refers both to the short coat-tails preferred by the macaroni, which accordingly showed off more rump, and to sodomitical taste – the fire being a fairly obvious aside to sinful states (fig. 2.24). The fire-tools stand erect by the figure's side, like the cane and sword of the macaroni. The face is what Dorothy George's generation called the 'Semitic' type, with a huge powdered wig and pigtail, which flares out like the coat and legs and stands in for the phallus. This is a particularly flamboyant and vigorous image of a macaroni, certainly not one in which he is presented as wan. Perhaps the joke here is that he might be manly, but he still risks his rump for fashion.

In May 1772 *Town and Country Magazine* published an intriguing report regarding the latest masquerade. In the course of this report, entitled 'Characters of the Pantheon masquerade described', the journal noted:

> A great many of the ladies of rank and beauty chose to adapt the male dress in domino [cloaked disguise], and appeared as masculine as many of the delicate Maccarony things we see swarming every where, to the disgrace of our noble patient British race. There was this difference, that they looked lovely and charming, and were justly admired, while every person of sense despises the ridiculous Billy Whiffles of the present age … the fictitious duchess of Y--k's sister was a very smart little fellow in appearance, and several more that might be added, looked better than the effeminate beings, their dress justly burlesqued.[19]

Whether the account is apocryphal or not is impossible to ascertain; its effects, however, are clear. This passage attributes the macaroni to the realm of the sexually dubious. 'Whiffle' was slang for penis, and 'Billy Whiffle' appears as an effeminate epithet in other contexts discussed below. Did this episode really take place? Did a group of cross-dressed women lampoon the exaggerated appearance of the macaroni present? The influence of the theatre is the first consideration. 'Breeches' roles for women were amongst the most popular performances; engravings of the Irish actress Peg Woffington in the 1740s and of the Anglo-Irish Dorothy Jordan in the 1780s in cross-dressed roles played on their fine legs, delicate hands and gestures and fashionable male costumes. The theatrical convention would have sanctioned a female performance of the macaroni behaviour at the masquerade; it was not inconceivable that women might rent or borrow such costumes and wear them to the event. Other images and accounts contribute to a slightly different understanding of the episode. Women were frequently characterised by an attitude in which they took revenge on, and attacked signs of, homosexuality as an affront to women, not to other men. As Madeleine Kahn notes of the conundrum of cross-dressing: 'The problem was double edged: men masquerading as women might find themselves trapped in the devalued realm of the feminine; and women, by masquerading as men, might usurp male power and prerogatives.'[20]

How D'ye Like Me, a mezzotint of 1772, could almost have been drawn to illustrate the story carried by *Town and Country* (fig. 5.2). The image is the very incarnation of the macaroni persona, and is frequently reproduced

HOW D'YE LIKE ME.

Printed for Carington Bowles, Map & Printseller, N°69 in S¹ Pauls Church Yard, London. Publish'd as the Act directs

in dress histories to illustrate the type. It is a brilliant caricature that fuses the real and the fictive, suggesting that the viewer has just come across the macaroni in his dressing room. It is also one of the clearer examples of the sodomitical overtones of the macaroni. The subject stands in the feminised space of the boudoir or dressing room, framed by a mirror, the symbol of vanity. The dressing room was often associated with the masquerade; thus, even without the title, a connection to vanity, luxury and the masquerade is made. As Stephens noted in the British Museum catalogue, with one hand the macaroni 'trifles' at his chin, the other 'being in his breeches pocket, while he is tripping, as if about to dance. Smiling, he asks the question of the title.'[21] He in fact thrusts his chin forward with his finger. He sports an enormously tall club-wig, with side-curls and huge solitaire. Tucked under his arm is a tiny hat; as in Paris, the macaroni's hat was often held, rather than worn, and thus functioned as an affront to English practicality. He wears the tiny high-heeled shoes, light silk stockings and dress-sword associated with macaroni dressing. The femininity of this macaroni is reinforced in the simpering pose, dainty feet and suggestion of a vulva in the folds of his breeches. His phallus is transformed into a mere decoration – the sword-knot and tassel at his side. This particular print raises the important point of whether 'over the top' but authentic fashions worn by men at a masquerade might have registered at the time as a 'costume' and whether the figure on view might be a 'character' at a masquerade. *P'sha You Flatter Me* is the companion to *How D'ye Like Me*. A lady wears equally extravagant clothing with a very high toupee wig. As the companion print creates the impression that the figures address each other, the images work to suggest that the macaroni inhabit a feminised world of complementary fashion, flattery and vanity.

The following year a similar image was produced: Philip Dawe's *The Macaroni. A real character at the late Masquerade*, which also survives with a different title as *Pantheon Macaroni* (fig. 5.3). The Pantheon was a newly opened masquerade venue in central London, built in 1770–72 as 'a winter Ranelagh'. Walpole described it as 'the most beautiful edifice in England'. Designed by James Wyatt, the Pantheon had a domed hall with double-storeyed aisles and rounded ends, evoking the Hagia Sophia. Friezes and niches were lit with green and purple, a fire burned in a neoclassical grate and the dome was illuminated from gilt vases.[22] 'Multicoloured' macaroni took their place within this novel fairyland, which was appropriate to their tendency for display. Several macaroni with particularly high hair and affected manners address fashionable ladies in the illustration *The Inside of the Pantheon in Oxford Road* (fig. 2.28). They can also be seen walking across the floor or 'stage', as it were, in the anonymous pocket-book engravings *A View of the Company at the Pantheon, Oxford Street* and *A View of the Company at Ranelagh*, which Barbara Johnson pasted into her album of fabrics and fashion prints, now in the Victoria and Albert Museum. Macaroni also populate the image *Bagnigge Wells*, which was considered a more modest resort than the Pantheon; the company drink tea from fashionable china services, and macaroni men fawn over women under artificial light (fig. 5.4).

Dawe's print played on the disjunction between the 'real' character of the macaroni who appeared amongst the 'fancy' dress of the other revellers; its subtitle, 'A real character at the late Masquerade', was significant. Like the earlier print *How D'ye Like Me*, this cleverly suggested that the

macaroni was a figure so ludicrous that his clothing became a type of
disguise or costume. That two such prints appeared suggests that the
joke was worth repeating. The viewer knew, of course, that the garments
exhibited here were exactly the ones sported by macaroni on a daily basis.
They include a hugely tall wig with side-curls, an elaborately trimmed coat,
striped stockings, dotted breeches, large paste buckles, a huge corsage of
flowers and a painted and patched face. As the Pantheon was more elite
than Vauxhall and Ranelagh pleasure gardens, the print possibly mocked
aristocratic pretensions. When caricaturists derided men of lesser social
standing as macaroni, they generally presented them as lumpish, deformed

PANTHEON MACARONI.

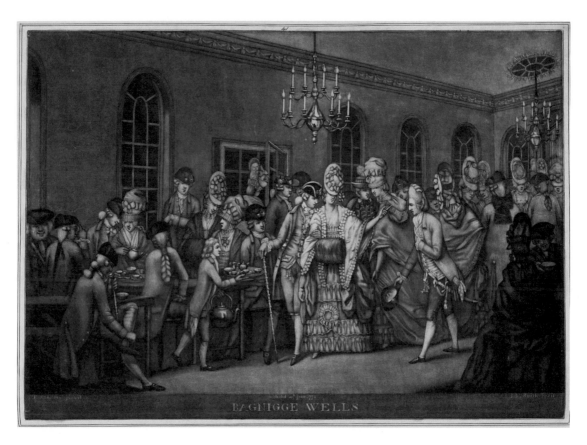

BAGNIGGE WELLS

5.4 J. Sanders, *Bagnigge Wells,* **25 June 1772**. Mezzotint, 35.3 × 50.2 cm. British Museum, London

or wearing an odd mixture of everyday and court dress. Here the dress, although exaggerated, is consistent with descriptions of fashionable dress, as worn by the painter Richard Cosway, for example.

Dawe's *Macaroni*, encrusted with make-up, smiles with a grimace, the wrinkles around his lips suggesting an attempt to mask his age. The notion of a painted mask of the face meshes with the papier-mâché masks commonly held by participants at these events to conceal true identity. His fluttering hands, one of which sports a large ring, resemble the joints of a puppet, doll or artist's lay figure. Placing him in an enclosed feminised space reinforces the effeminate subject matter. A dressing table swagged in gauze and lace, similar to the ones in contemporary prints of ladies dressing, topped by a dressing set of make-up pots, is evidence of his complete feminisation. Jars are named 'essence' and 'Rose'. The mirror and four gilded frames that surround him underline the theme of vanity; the empty frame is a common motif in caricatures of fashion. The cat's head on the crest of a chair – ignored by the Victorian cataloguer of the image – is emblematic, implying the catamite (from the Latin *catimatus*, 'kept boy' or 'minion').[23] It makes overt that which the other signs and symbols more subtly suggest.

THE MASQUERADE DANCE.

In 1771 Darly published *The Masquerade Dance*, a remarkable image of homosociality that the nineteenth-century cataloguer of the British Library collection provided with a scant explication (fig. 5.5). Stephens notes, 'An engraving of characters in a masquerade ... The costumes include that of a bishop, who is dancing with a Turk; a Greek monk dances with a quaker, and a Jew with a monk. The Devil plays on a pipe.'[24] He neglected to mention that there are no women present; this is an all-male assembly. Terry Castle used the image as part of her argument that there was a homosocial potential to masquerade activity that was understood by contemporaries. The events were liberating for women, she argued, as they might escape their chaperones; cross-dressed, they exulted in the freedom of divided garments and adopted male airs, cursing and swearing, for example. Men might also step outside normal social roles. Cross-dressed men were present; sodomy was commonly believed to follow from transvestism: 'These Sallies of Gallantry, I fear, will soon metamorphose the Kingdom into a Sodom for Lewdness.'[25]

Grown Gentlemen taught to Dance, on one level a satire of awkward social climbers and fashionable pastimes at assemblies, might also have been read in this context (fig. 5.6). One of the men has a copy of a pamphlet entitled 'The Blunderer' in his pocket; the print is also possibly a joke about the socially awkward, homosocial and misogynistic nature of parts of British society.

Contemporaries reported a peculiar speech pattern adopted by some men at the masquerade events, a falsetto squeaking. Falsetto was connected in people's minds with Italian opera – a foreign introduction of a genre of music that was of major concern to moralists (it was often sung by castrati

GROWN GENTLEMEN taught to DANCE.

Engraved after an Original Picture of Mr. John Collett, in the Possession of Mr. Smith.

Printed for Jno. Smith, No. 35, in Cheapside, & Robt. Sayer, No. 53, in Fleet Street, as the Act directs 20th. Augt. 1768.

and was considered to be sensual).[26] Castle suggests that the use of such tones by men denoted comic emasculation; the figure of the castrato may have been parodied here. These descriptions can be compared with reports of macaroni speech patterns, with peculiar pronunciations and unusual words, to suggest that the macaroni may have projected an alternative identity through speech as well as dress. 'Nothing is now heard, but sweet Chit-chat, and tender prattle-Prattle, Shreds of Sentiments, and *Cuttings* of Sentences, – all soft and charming, elegant and polite,' complained the text attacking the 'pretty gentleman' in 1747. Examples of reported Frenchified speech include 'Oh! Pard'n me, mi Dear! I ke'n't possibly be of that Apinion'; 'you would grow enamoured of his Address, and admire the enchanting Beauties of refined Elocution. *O! fie! Ye filt-hy Creter!'*[27] The use of camp parody, documented earlier in the century in the molly-house 'gay bar' scandals, unsettled social norms in a simple way, through the mechanism of the throat.

Broadcloth, broad shoulders

Macaroni men did not only engage with a form of continental court dressing premised on the silk suit. Many images of them survive that indicate the term 'macaroni' was synonymous with 'fashion' more generally, and fashion changed rapidly in the period 1760–80. The cut of the clothes should be considered carefully. Macaroni men were associated with tight clothes with narrow sleeves – styles that suit the very young. A character in the play *The Pantheonites* of 1773 complained that his new suit was so tight that 'I have no more use of arms than an Egyptian mummy.'[28] In the 1770s finely cut suits of broadcloth in monotone colours were also chic. This is the attire that can be seen in that rare thing, an eighteenth-century painting depicting a young man of fashion who was connected to a queer scandal. Daniel Gardner painted a group portrait now entitled *The Hon. Edward Onslow (1758–1829), John FitzWilliam, 8th Viscount FitzWilliam (1752–1830) and George Augustus Herbert, 11th Earl of Pembroke (1759–1827) Playing Chess*, a delightful pastel set into a neoclassical gilt overmantel mirror, of a date that accords with the age of the sitters, about 1775, at Clandon Park (fig. 5.7).[29] Onslow and John, or possibly Thomas, future Viscounts FitzWilliam, are playing chess together (the board incorrectly set, as the cataloguer notes). Herbert, the future 11th Earl of Pembroke, is standing with his arm across the shoulders of Onslow, who wears light blue and has finely dressed hair. Behind them is a black pageboy holding a basket of fruit, for whose services it was once said they were playing. The picture forms an integral part of a chimney-piece mirror in a drawing room that was elegantly redecorated by the famous mid-twentieth-century decorator John Fowler. The whole *mise en scène* was, alas, lost with the fire that destroyed most of Clandon in 2015.

5.7 Daniel Gardner, *The Hon. Edward Onslow (1758–1829), John FitzWilliam, 8th Viscount FitzWilliam (1752–1830) and George Augustus Herbert, 11th Earl of Pembroke (1759–1827) Playing Chess, c.1775*. Pastel set into a gilt overmantel mirror, 69 × 86.5 cm. Clandon Park, Surrey

Edward Onslow has the quintessential appearance of a young macaroni man. He was the second son of George Onslow of Imber Court, later 4th Baron and 1st Earl of Onslow. The son went into exile at Clermont-Ferrand in 1781 because of a homosexual incident at the Royal Academy's Annual Exhibition, involving himself and one 'Phelim Macarty'. He then married a French woman and created a French Onslow family. In a letter to his son, the 10th Earl of Pembroke wrote, 'in the name of wonder, My dear George, what is this Mindening [maddening?] story of our cousin Ned Onslow, & Phelim Macarty Esq . . . I should hope that no kinsman of ours *donne dans le sexe masculine . . .*' (a word-play that means 'gives in/it? to the masculine sex'). The picture was not removed for some reason; nor was Onslow disowned, but was visited in France later by the family.[30] A portrait

5.8 *The Hon. Edward Onslow,*
possibly French, *c.*1800. Pastel,
61 × 50.2 cm. Clandon Park, Surrey

purporting to be him in older age shows the fashion change that took place in the space of 30 years, to more practical, masculine-looking clothing; thinning, long hair that is probably his own; and a sombre post-revolutionary subjectivity (fig. 5.8).

The 'she-he gentry'

From the early years of the eighteenth century the appearance and layout of shops improved in London and the people who worked in them were equally fine. James Peller Malcolm cited in 1808 the *Female Tatler* of 1709, describing Ludgate Hill thus:

> The shops are perfect gilded theatres, the variety of wrought silks so many changes of fine scenes and the Mercers are the performers in the Opera; and instead of *vivitur ingenio* you have in gold capitals, 'No trust by retail'. They are the sweetest, fairest, nicest, dished-out creatures; and by their elegant address and soft speeches, you would guess them to be Italians. As people glance within their doors, they salute them with – Garden-silks, ladies Italian silks, brocades, tissues, cloth of silver, or cloth of gold, very fine mantua silks, any right Geneva velvet, English velvet, velvet embossed. And to the meaner sort – Fine thread satins both striped and plain, fine mohair silk, satinnets, burdets … Gentlemen's nightgowns ready made … The fellows are positively the greatest fops in the Kingdom, they have their toilets and their fine night-gowns, their *chocolate in the morning* and their *green tea two hours after*; Turkey polts for their dinners, and their perfumes, washes, and clean linen equip them for the Parade … It is not improbable that many of these effeminate drivellers composed part at least of the various clubs held at different Taverns.[31]

This passage indicates several things. It shows the range of goods available and the language used to describe them; it suggests the theatre of the street and the cacophony of selling; and it links the mercers and man-milliners to the shadowy taverns we have learned of previously.

Men in the appearance industries were frequently singled out as sexually compromised or dubious, in the eyes of hostile audiences. Malcolm wrote of 'man-milliners':

> The impropriety and folly of employing young and vigorous men to serve female customers with articles of dress, and those silly catch-pennies idly supposed ornaments to the person now so prevalent, is by no means a new trait in our customs; that it should be continued,

though severely reprehended even so long since as 1765, is astonishing ... but now what head of hair can be dressed for to be seen without the assistance of a smart male hair-dresser?[32]

Fanny Burney found male mercers more 'entertaining' than the clothes. As she wrote in *Evelina* (1778), 'At the milliners ... we were more frequently served by men than by women; and such men! So finical, so affected! They seemed to understand every part of a woman's dress better than we do ourselves; and they recommended caps and ribbons with an air of so much importance, that I wished to ask them how long they had left off wearing them!'[33] Their extreme elegance and thinness were emphasised by Darly, as in *The Whale Bone Macaroni* (fig. 5.9) and *The Macaroni Haberdasher*. By the 1790s it was claimed that such men took work from women, who had to become servants or prostitutes instead. *Bon Ton* magazine reported in 1791:

> It is supposed that there are, within the cities of London and Westminster, at least 30,000 men-milliners, haberdashers, artificial flower-makers, and other *insects*, who usurp the proper occupations of women. In the present unexampled demand for recruits, it would be a most popular measure to put all such *beings* into a state of requisition for foreign service. They would make a charming 'food for powder'.[34]

Mary Hays called the group the 'she-he gentry'.[35]

The macaroni hairdresser type, with excessive hair and equally absurd clients, was translated into a variety of interrelated media, including caricature prints and porcelain figurines (see fig. 4.18). In Isaac Cruikshank's print *The Man Milliner* of 1793, the lady customer remarks to the fashionably dressed young man: 'Indeed, Mr Fribble, I am not to be done in this manner ... Your yard is to short by an inch.' The reference to his yardstick for measuring ribbons concerns his virility, or lack thereof.

That something to do with sexuality was at stake in part of the macaroni repertoire was noted more than a century ago in the section of the *Catalogue of Prints and Drawings in the British Museum* compiled by Frederic George Stephens. Although the catalogue is astonishing in its detail, Stephens became discreet when it came to the matter of homosexuality. The more suggestive queer prints are provided with scant, sometimes embarrassed explication, and he declined to print the bawdy retort of a woman appended to an engraving, which he notes referred to the 'alleged vice of the macaronies'.[36] In describing another

The WHALE BONE MACARONI.

Publish'd according to Act Oct. 22. 1772. for M. Darly. 39. Strand.

macaroni as 'evidently of a feeble habit of body', he resorted to the topical notion of degeneration that was applied to the newly pathologised figure of the homosexual-criminal in the late nineteenth century by Max Nordau and Cesare Lombroso.[37] Amidst the fine detail of the catalogue, Stephens was forced to confront the obscenity of the macaroni; however, for the more vulgar images he neglected to spell out the precise information provided for most other prints. He was, after all, writing in the 1880s, around the time of mounting speculation that aestheticism was both generating and being taken over by homosexual interest groups from the arts and the theatre.

Stephens ventured the following interesting thesis regarding the macaroni, which is partly incorrect, but extremely revealing in its emphasis:

> The Macaronies were much disliked by the popular party, and therefore they became obnoxious within the attacks of satirical draughtsmen, because they belonged to the wealthier orders of society, were somewhat demonstratively affected and refined in their costume and manners, and, above all, because they were, politically, on the side of the Court. Horace Walpole and the Earl of March, George Selwyn's friend, the afterwards notorious 'Old Q.' or Duke of Queensberry, and Selwyn himself, were leading Macaronies.[38]

This is an intriguing paragraph as it masks what Stephens was really describing. All the figures that he names were either libertine or homosexual in their tastes, and comprised a well-known coterie formed at Eton.[39] The well-informed reader could read between the lines; it was no secret that Horace Walpole was homosexual in outlook. However, none of these men were considered macaroni in their day. Walpole was never caricatured as a macaroni (although he was sometimes mocked as a sodomite), and apart from a great devotion to masquerade balls, he neither dressed nor affiliated himself with macaroni taste; he was too old, at any rate, to engage properly with the style. Nonetheless, Walpole was always considered very 'queer' by observers. He was characterised by an odd style of walking, 'like a peewit', his legs splayed and stepping 'on tip-toe as if afraid of a wet floor'.[40] As a youngster he was very stylish; on his Grand Tour he chose to be drawn by Rosalba Carriera in a gorgeous waistcoat, but that was 20 years earlier, when such elaborate clothing was *de rigueur*. Walpole also made a great many comments about the artist Thomas Patch, who was accused of sodomy after a confession by his footman in the 1750s.[41]

In the 1760s and 1770s Walpole enjoyed describing the more excessive macaroni affectations in London, fashions that he associated with the very young. What Stephens seems to be proposing is that, for him, the concept of the macaroni had become synonymous with some version of 'queer' by the time he was writing his compilation of the British Museum collection of satirical prints.

FRONTISPIECE

Behold a Monster bursting to the view,
Nor Turk, nor Christian, Pagan he, nor Jew;
No Sawney Scot, Welch Taff, or Irish Honey,
But Manhood's Jest! — à London MACARONI.

5.10 *The Macaroni Jester, and*
Pantheon of Wit (London:
J. Cooke et al., n.d. [1773]).
Frontispiece. British Museum,
London

In the 1930s M. Dorothy George's contribution to this extraordinarily detailed catalogue used words more appropriate to her period, such as 'simpering', to suggest politely rather than to state overtly what appears in some of these images. She described *The Oxford Macaroni* as 'walking with mincing steps' as he strides forward, arms akimbo. Perhaps here she refers in a coded way to some of the eighteenth-century sexual scandals involving sodomy at Oxford, or perhaps to the 'corseted' tight shoes (Oxford brogues) that young men wore there in the nineteenth century.

The eighteenth-century literary and visual representations of the macaroni used the language and concepts available at the time to describe the sodomite and same-sex desire. Themes of emasculation and unsexing featured prominently. The alleged impotence of the macaroni is indicated in a contemporary magazine cutting attached to a caricature entitled *The Scavoir Vivre* of 1772, a portrait of a macaroni coloured in red, blue and buff. Consider the candid sexual nature of the following:

A Correspondent who dates from the Star and Garter, Pall-mall, informs us, that a Club of a new order of Maccaronies is just instituted there, under the title of The Scavoir Vivre. These gentlemen have thought fit to decorate themselves with a Uniform of scarlet Cloth, with Velvet Collar and Sleeves of Bleu Celeste. This Society applied one Day last Week to the College of Heralds for a Set of Arms to be made out for them, but received for Answer, that they must first be erected into a Corporation. It is feared they will not be able to carry their Point.[42]

The notion that the macaroni represented an indeterminate, neutral or ambiguous gender was also very common:

I am going to speak of that wretched thing, called a Macaroni. To the Naturalists I leave it to determine, whether it is masculine, feminine, or neuter – whether it belongs to the species of beasts, or – whether it is of the reptile kind . . . it is neither a Christian, nor an ass, nor a four-footed beast, nor a woman. Perhaps it is a species of the butterfly . . . I have more sense than to call it masculine: But I shall call it he for my own convenience.[43]

The Macaroni Jester, and Pantheon of Wit was issued in 1773 with a frontispiece engraving of a macaroni bursting from an egg (fig. 5.10).

The following text was appended:

> Behold a Monster bursting to the view,
> Nor Turk, nor Christian, Pagan he, nor Jew;
> No Sawney Scot, Welch Taff, or Irish Honey,
> But Manhood's Jest! – a London MACARONI.

Similarly, 'A new description of a macaroni', asked:

> Is it a man? 'Tis hard to say –A woman then
>   – A moment pray –
> So doubtful is the thing, that no man
> Can say if 'tis a man or woman:
> Unknown as yet by sex or feature,
> It moves – a mere amphibious creature.[44]

This text was drawn in part from David Garrick's play *The Fribbleriad* of 1761 (see Chapter 6). The image of the egg is pertinent. Eggs relate to Eros, but they also relate to folklore and superstition; witches were meant to fly in egg-shells.[45] The egg is empty, once birthing takes place; empty-headed like the fashionable figure who bursts forth in his glorious costume.

How widespread the macaroni appearance and persona were in eighteenth-century England is difficult to conclude. The lives of the aristocracy were chronicled in much more detail than the 'middling' and 'lower sorts'. Contemporary barbs in the newspapers suggested that macaronism had spread, from the circles of the court to the artisanal classes. A periodical article provided the following detailed description:

> The infection of St James's was soon caught in the city, and we now have Macaronies of every denomination, from the colonel of the Train'd-Bands down to the errand-boy. They indeed make a most ridiculous figure, with hats of an inch in the brim, that do not cover, but lie upon the head, with about two pounds of fictitious hair, formed into what is called a club, hanging down their shoulders as white as a baker's sack: the end of the skirt of their coat reaches the first button of their breeches, which are either brown striped, or white, as wide as a Dutchman's; their coat-sleeves are so tight, they can with much difficulty get their arms through their cuffs, which are about an inch deep; and their shirt-sleeve, without plaits, is pulled over a bit of Trolly lace. Their legs are at times covered with all the colours of the rainbow; even flesh-coloured and green silk stockings are not excluded. Their shoes are scarce slippers, and their buckles are within an inch of the toe. Such a figure, essenced and perfumed, with a bunch of lace sticking out under its chin, puzzles the common passenger to determine the thing's sex; and many a time an

5.11 'Character of a Macaroni. Illustrated with the polite Macaroni, cut in wood', *Town and Country Magazine*, vol. 4 (May 1772), p.242. Woodcut. British Library, London

honest labouring porter has said, by your leave, madam, without intending to give offence.[46]

The article was supported by a crude, unsigned woodcut, in which the macaroni is depicted with a cane and hanger-sword (fig. 5.11). His sullen frown belies the title 'the polite Macaroni', clearly a reference to contemporary debates regarding manners and sensibility. In his catalogue entry for this plate Stephens quoted a long section of the much-cited text above, but did not print the final section, which sounds like a salacious nineteenth-century newspaper report or a joke by a cab-driver directed at the camp figure 'Bunny' Neil Rogers. It is perhaps for this reason that subsequent historians of costume and manners neglected to explore the dimension of queer and the macaroni for many years. If they relied on the generally very detailed and comprehensive entries of Stephens and George in their magisterial catalogues of the British Museum print collection, they would have been unaware of some of the nuance.

Macaroni also played into the very old figure of the Antipodean world; of gender and natural law usurped. *The Macaroni Jester, and Pantheon of Wit* includes bon mots such as:

> The following articles of News are such as may appear in the News-papers fifty years hence, if the present Macaroni taste should prevail; as, in that Case, the Women will become the best Men.
>
> ... Yesterday the Rev. Mrs K----- preached before their Majesties at St James's, the Archbishop, her Husband, being violently afflicted with a Fit of the spleen. – The sword of State was carried to and from Chapel by the Honourable Lady Charlotte G ...
>
> Sir Richard P--- is dangerously ill of a fright, occasioned by the sight of a mouse, which casually ran into the room, while he was drinking coffee with Counsellor Fribble ...
>
> Yesterday died of a Consumption, occasioned by the use of paint, Sir William Whiffle, who has long been deemed the first-rate Macaroni of the Age.[47]

'Fribble' and 'whiffle' were older terms interchangeable with 'macaroni', and refer to effeminate men with delicate sensibilities. *Bon Ton* magazine reported in 1791 of the former word:

> Fribble: This word signifies one of these ambiguous animals, who are neither male nor female; disclaimed by his own sex, and the scorn of both. There is however a silly simper in their countenances. Without

any of the good qualities of their own sex, they affect all the bad ones, all the impertinencies, and follies of the other; whilst what is no more than ridiculous, and sometimes even a grace in the women, is nauseous and shocking in them. A wretch of this species loves mightily the company of the ladies . . . He even endeavours to make himself necessary to them: combs their lap-dogs, fancies their ribbons, recommends the best scented powder, and loves to be consulted in the cut of their cap, their tea, and the placing their china baubles: helps them in their notting, ringing, embroidering, or shell-work; understands pastry, preserving, pickling and the like. They are as fond withal of scandal and all the tittle-tattle of the tea table as the veriest woman. They are great critics of dress, and the assortment of colours; can tell which will suit a complexion, and which not . . . Nor is their own dress neglected; the muff, the ermine facing, a cluster ring, the stone buckle, and now and then a patch, that on them does not always suppose a pimple, are the plague spots in which the folly of these less than butter-flies break out. Even their swords hang at their sides garnished with a tawdry sword-knot, purely for ornament, like bobs at a lady's ear . . . they disfigure the graces, caricature the faults, and have none of the virtues of that amiable sex.[48]

The term 'whiffle' is also apposite. Whiffle is an effeminate sea-captain in Tobias Smollett's *The Adventures of Roderick Random* (1748). He is described thus:

a tall, thin, young man, dressed in this manner; a white hat garnished with a red feather, adorned his head, from whence his hair flowed down upon his shoulders, in ringlets tied behind with a ribbon. – His coat, consisting of pink-coloured silk, lined with white, by the elegance of the cut retired backward, as it were, to discover a white sattin waistcoat embroidered with gold, unbuttoned at the upper part, to display a broch set with garnets, that glittered in the breast of his shirt, which was of the finest cambrick, edged with right mechlin [i.e. genuine lace from Mechlin, now Belgium]. The knees of his crimson velvet breeches scarce descended so low as to meet his silk stockings, which rose without spot or wrinkle on his meagre legs, from shoes of bue Meroquin [morocco leather], studded with diamond buckles, that flamed forth rivals to the sun! A steel-hilted sword, inlaid with figures of gold, and decked with a knot of ribbon which fell down in a rich tossle, equipped his side; and an amber-headed cane hung dangling from his wrist: – But the most remarkable parts of his furniture were, a mask on his face, and white gloves on his hands, which did not seem to be put on with an intention to be pulled off occasionally, but were fixed with a ring set with a ruby on the little finger of one hand, and by one set with a topaz on that of the other

…surrounded with a crowd of attendants, all of whom, in their different degrees, seemed to be of their patron's disposition; and the air was so impregnated with perfumes, that one may venture to affirm the clime of Arabia Foelix was not half so sweet-scented.[49]

The ship's surgeon, a dirty and dishevelled man, declares of Whiffle: 'for I will proclaim it before the world, that he is disguised and transfigured, and transmographied with affectation and whimsies; and that he is more like a papoon than one of the human race'.[50] Smollett portrays Whiffle as fickle and sodomitical, along with Strutwell in the same novel; he had attacked homosexuality in the poem *Advice* (1746) and an Italian marquis and a German baron were also portrayed as sodomitical in *The Adventures of Peregrine Pickle* (1751).[51]

'Fribble' was a common expression, used at the time to denote a type of fop, that people recognised from song and stage in the 1760s and 1770s. In the humorous song 'The Queen's Ass' of *c.*1760 the 'fribbles' feign hysterical shock at the sight of the queen's new pet zebra or 'ass' grazing near Buckingham Palace:

> The Fribbles cry out, "Tis a Sin and a Shame
> To Suffer a Sight with so filthy a Name':
> Though they rail, yet will each take a Peep thro' his Glass,
> For who wou'd not peep at her M------'s A--?

The novelty of a newly imported animal was taken up in the following passage in *Walker's Hibernian Magazine*, in describing the arrival 'from France and Italy [of] a very strange animal, of the doubtful gender, in shape somewhat between a man and a monkey … Its dress is neither in the habit of a man or a woman, but peculiar to itself, and varying with the day.' The author went on to note of the current American wars: 'Alas! They are as harmless in the field, as they are in the chamber, but they may stand as faggots to cover the loss of real men.'[52]

Joke-books also contained numerous comments concerning the lack of potency of such men or, indeed, their lack of interest in women:

> Lord H --- one day signifying his suspicions to his lady that her children were not his, she replied, 'Indeed, my Lord, you make yourself easy on that head, for I vow to Heaven I never injured your bed – till after I was pregnant.'[53]

The most telling jest that suggests the macaroni was a type of gender joke is as follows: 'A Macaroni being told that none of his Franity could keep a secret; "yes (cried he) but we can for no one yet knows whether we are Male or Female."'[54]

Other caricatures and accounts in the popular press are quite specific regarding the issue of what we now call 'homosexuality'. In his first suite of macaroni images, Darly included an image entitled *Ganymede*, which Dorothy George argued refers to Samuel Drybutter, a bookseller convicted of unnatural offences in 1771 and possibly placed in the pillory that year (fig. 5.12). Drybutter was a 'toyman' or dealer in small luxuries who was regularly in trouble with the law. He was thought to have written the only sodomitical passage in *Fanny Hill*, although this is unclear: he may have been a friend of Cleland.[55] The press claimed that Drybutter was conducting a type of sodomites' resort in a rented house in Pall Mall, and his notoriety was linked with the infamous case of Captain Robert Jones, who was convicted for sodomy in 1772 and labelled a macaroni, although there does not seem to be any evidence that he resembled one. Drybutter continued to come to the attention of the authorities and the public, and he was killed by injuries inflicted by a mob in 1777.[56] In the engraving he is represented as a pretentious man, with his hand placed in his jacket (once a sign of nobility), a fashionable flared suit coat, ruffled shirt and cane. George noted that his 'shoulders are round, almost to deformity'.[57]

Darly spelled out the crime in another crudely designed print entitled *Ganymede & Jack-Catch*, which refers to the act of sodomy and its subsequent punishment (fig. 5.13).[58] Jack-Catch states, 'Dammee Sammy you'r a sweet pretty creature & I long to have you at the end of my String.' Ganymede replies, 'You don't love me Jacky.' Jack-Catch is soberly dressed; his name means the hangman; Ganymede's dress is distinguished by lace ruffles at the shirt front and a neatly styled wig. The association between the two engravings is strengthened in that Ganymede has the same physiognomy in each case. Relevant also are *Ho He, the Blackguard Macaroni* (published by T. Pether on 22 June 1773) and its companion print, *Stephen Stru Ye Tallow Macaroni*. Accompanied by text that referred to the folly 'such as Jack Catch [Ketch] and the Devil hath reservd for their Own private purposes', these prints undoubtedly referred to a sodomitical practice; it was considered a great sport to attack sodomites in the pillory.

Ketch was notorious as the bungling London executioner under Charles II, but was also well known via Dryden's reference to him in 'A Discourse Concerning Satire' of 1694, a work that 'has been read as an illustration of the wit that elevates satire above mere abuse'.[59] J.R. Wood notes: 'by invoking the historical Jack Ketch, who cruelly mutilated his victims, Dryden covertly suggests that behind even the most elegant and witty satire there lurks the impulse to wound one's enemies and to see them suffer'.[60] Consider also *Refin'd Taste* by Richard St George Mansergh-St George for Robert Sayer of May 1773, a reissue of a plate by Darly. A fashionably dressed civilian gazes through a glass at a soldier in uniform. The following verse is etched:

Eternal Infamy, that Wretch Confound,
Who Planted first this Vice on English Ground
A Crime that spite of Sense & Nature reigns,
And Poisons Genial Love & Manhood stains.
Vide Rod. Random.[61]

Also relevant to readings of macaroni sexuality is the captivating story of Billy Dimple and his valet, published in *The Macaroni, Scavoir Vivre, and Theatrical Magazine* in 1773. The recirculation of eighteenth-century text is indicated in that the engraving illustrating this story appeared several years later in the *Oxford Magazine* of January 1776. My Young Lord Dimple, alias Toupee, decides to visit his uncle in the West Country, taking with him his valet de chamber, 'a most exquisite French frizeur, being afraid that his delicate locks would suffer grievously from the rude hands of country hairdressers'. The pair suffer many affronts and jokes along the way, but continue to dress in their best macaroni clothes. 'In this gallant trim' they ride on, 'but they had not gone far before two young lads, standing at the door of a little alehouse, hallowed out, there are two French bougres going by'. As *bougre* was a colloquial expression for sodomite, there is nothing ambiguous about this text; Frenchness adds extra piquancy to the barb. Enraged at so grievous and horrible an affront, the master horsewhipped the boys. Hearing their screams, their companions arrived and unhorsed the foppish pair. In retribution they were tied back to back and lowered into a coal pit where men were at work. Here they terrified the miners: 'They all stood aghast for some minutes, not knowing what species of animals to take them for, and still less what gender they belonged to.' One declared they were two cockney barbers, as he had been to London and 'zeen zuch like varmin there'. On calming down, the colliers offered them a glass of gin, and Monsieur cried out, 'Begar, me lord, it burns my guts out' – further innuendo that would hardly have been lost on the eighteenth-century reader. The imagery of a black pit, a passage to sodomitical hell, is apparent elsewhere in this journal:

> Were you to see a group of them together, you would swear, that the sepulchres had disgorged their nauseous contents – Such a stench! and such figures! lean, disjointed carcases, with shrill and dying voices![62]

The accompanying engraving, *Lord Dimple & his Man in the Coal Pit*, shows the moment Lord Dimple and his hairdresser are lowered into the pit to be met by the miners (fig. 5.14). Dimple splays his fingers in fright, and his man has one of the more hideous noses invented in the period. One group of miners gesture in shock or surprise, others smile, point and smirk, with the coarse faces beloved of Darly.

Other prints survive that support this sodomitical reading of the macaroni. The London-based Swiss illustrator Brandoin created a finely drawn composition for *A French Petit Maitre and His Valet*, carefully engraved in turn by Charles Grignion, a contemporary of Gainsborough (fig. 5.15). A grotesque and elderly fop shuffles down the Rue d'Enfer, the Street of Hell, in Paris, bedecked with a huge corsage and wig-bag and tightly fitting court dress, the coat brocaded with hearts. Underlining his depravity, the face is also poxed. The formal elements of this enigmatic print, politely ignored by early cataloguers, suggest a 'cock and balls' leaning against the wall in the centre; the drain or sewer to the left connotes the back-passage, a common analogy in eighteenth-century texts. Although the setting is Paris, the mood is macaroni.

Theorists and promoters of homosexual rights in the early twentieth century, including Edward Carpenter, noticed 'a marked tendency to nervous developments in the [homosexual] subject, not infrequently associated with nervous maladies'.[63] The model of the hysteric, so common in late nineteenth-century definitions of the pathology of the homosexual, was present in many macaroni caricatures. Men were demonised for projecting the characteristics associated with women. *Certain City Macaronies drinking Asses Milk*, an illustration in the *Oxford Magazine* of 1772, showed men being handed asses' milk by a fat, old woman. The accompanying text described the advantages of drinking this milk 'in nervous cases, and even in hysterics', by 'delicate men such as we – beings of superior clay, whose fine feelings are sensible of the slightest pressure'. One was 'terrified for fear it should rain'; another noted 'a shower of rain would be the death of me'; a third carried an umbrella (then considered a French affectation), 'for fear of the worst'. Asses' milk was used to great effect by Pope in his *Epistle* of 1735, which called 'Sporus! That mere white curd of ass's milk . . .'[64] Asses' milk carries two further contrasting suggestions. The first is the practice of bathing in it in Antiquity, by famed women such as Cleopatra and various Roman empresses, to preserve their looks; hence, when consumed by males, its use was highly effeminate. Second, the male ass since Antiquity has, from the size of its genitals, figured as a symbol of hyper-virility (as in Apuleius' *Golden Ass* and the anonymous Greek

Lord Dimple & his Man, in the Coal Pit.

A FRENCH PETIT MAITRE and HIS VALET.

predecessor *Lucius, or the Ass*). Hence drinking asses' milk might have been a tonic to restore virility, and therefore might be consumed by invalid or delicate males.[65] The lavish expenditure of the English on the Grand Tour can also be raised here: Lady Mary Wortley Montagu wrote to the Countess of Bute from Padua, in 1758: 'All the others [young Englishmen] now living here (however dignified and distinguished), by herding together, and throwing away their money on worthless objects, have only acquired the glorious title of Golden Asses.'[66] Asses' milk was sold by the bankrupt 'nightclub trader' Mrs Cornelys in Knightsbridge in the 1790s, shortly before she died.[67] References to that animal, the ass, are extremely common in the macaroni prints.

Macaroni might also be martyred. *The Maccaroni Sacrifice* referred to the traditional practice of burning convicted sodomites at the stake. The engraving was a frontispiece to *An Appendix to the Vauxhall Affray or Macaronies Defeated . . .* of 1773. Subtitled 'This incence shall revive degraded Manhood', the caricature depicted Parson Henry Bate, 'the fighting parson' (also editor of the *Morning Post*, and afterwards Sir Henry Bate Dudley), sacrificing three macaroni before the classical building inscribed 'Temp. of Virtue'. He points a feather at them, possibly referring to the taste for feathered hats, as well as feebleness. The fire is being stoked by a near-nude man. The print refers to an incident that took place in Hyde Park on 23 July 1773 when three men of fashion threw insults at a woman. They were the Hon. Thomas Lyttelton, known as 'the wicked Lord Lyttelton'; George Robert Fitzgerald, 'Fighting Fitzgerald'; and Captain Crofts. The incident concerned a quarrel, in which Bate resented the attentions paid to his companion, Mrs Hartley, the actress. Bate accused Fitzgerald of meddling in the initial dispute and of being leader of a second attack upon him in Vauxhall Gardens. This was followed by a fight between Bate and 'Captain Miles', who was really the footman of Fitzgerald dressed up. The incident generated many reports and squibs in journals such as the *Morning Post*, competing versions of which were collected into the book *The Vauxhall Affray; or, The Macaronies Defeated*, a substantial 120-page text.[68] The macaroni in the caricature are shown linked together; one is chained around the leg to the sword of the other, and by extension to the third, who is part consumed by fire. They say, in turn: 'I owe this infamy to you two'; 'If I had been advised by Mother D--n I had not got in this damned Scrape'; 'Oh! Save my Miniature Picture.' This suggests that the third one is the guilty party who led the others astray; one is a mother's boy, the third cares only for his miniature, of himself or a friend. A man stoking the fire asks, 'Master, is it hot enough now?' Another, holding a club, depicted three times the size of the sacrificed figures, announces: 'This incense shall revive degraded Manhood.'

George described these macaroni characters simply as 'small and effeminate'. Miles Ogborn notes of this incident: 'The Macaronis . . . created problems by turning men's bodies into the wrong sorts of spectacles.'[69] He links the Vauxhall Affray with the crisis of credit that gripped Britain in the 1770s, as 'credit depended upon reputation which, in turn, depended upon self-presentation within the market place'.[70]

The *Whitehall Evening Post* published a poem entitled 'The Macaroniad', which in calling Fitzgerald 'Fitzgiggo' referred to a famous sodomitical satire by David Garrick, which is discussed in the following chapter. The relevant section of the poem follows:

> Fitzgiggo foremost let's describe,
> Memento mori of the tribe,
> A thing so meagre and so thin,
> So full of emptiness – and sin,
> There's nothing comes before – behind
> But stinks on wings of his own wind;
> And yet the things so hung with rings,
> With buckles, baubles, tambour-strings,
> And so baptiz'd with milk of roses,
> Which, with his smells, so strike our noses,
> That ev'ry gentle air that blows,
> Brings something new unto the nose;
> As if young Zeph'rus was turn'd pilot,
> To wast the sweets of some poor vi'let,
> By some unkind mis-hap disgrac'd,
> And on a putrid dunghill plac'd;
> So let Dan Zephyr do his best,
> The dunghill makes his sweets a pest.
> Thus did Fitzgiggo gay advance,
> Like dismal Death dress'd out to dance . . .
> . . . But Macaronies are a sex
> Which do philosophers perplex;
> Tho' all the priests of VENUS' rites
> Agree they are Hermaphrodites.[71]

The rhyme uses a mock-heroic turn of phrase, 'Thus did Fitzgiggo gay advance', whose origins may be found in Homer.

Another periodical included the fictional conversation between the Parson and Fitzgerald:

> Bate to F-G: 'You judge of the fair sex as you do of your own doubtful gender, which aims only to be looked at and admired' . . .

Mr Fitz-Gerall: 'I love the ladies, for the ladies love me.'

Mr Bate: 'Yes, as their panteen, their play-thing, their harmless bauble, to treat as you do them, merely to look at.'[72]

A panteen is a puppet. This extract indicates that the episode was read as an affront to women, with the macaroni lacking interest in the pursuit of women as sexual objects. Women are observed like works of art; the macaroni have made themselves into objects of the gaze. Later commentators in the Edwardian period ignored this nuance and described instead an episode that made little sense, in which the perpetrators 'made a deliberate attempt to stare the beautiful actress out of countenance'.[73] The act of looking, staring and observing, and what that meant to eighteenth-century minds, will be explored in the following chapter concerning the theatre.

Eighteenth-century culture read the sodomite as offensive and threatening primarily to women, not to men. The macaroni, too, was often positioned in this way. He was depicted both confronting and being confronted by women such as the fishwife, who in the caricature *The Enraged Macaroni* thrusts a fish in his face and cuts off his queue: 'The Billingsgate with rude and cutting Jokes / The Macaroni to fierce Rage provokes; / Who threatens Blood and Wounds with glaring Eyes; / But she with vip'rous Tongue his Rage defies' (fig. 5.16). Contemporary accounts of the ordeals of convicted sodomites, when placed in the stocks, indicate that they most feared the torrent of verbal and physical abuse that was hurled at them by working women, who were affronted by behaviour that turned its back on conventional sexual outlets. Prostitutes, in particular, were depicted as outraged at the potential loss of business that an increase in male-to-male sexual contact might produce.[74]

Many satirical poems and stories of the period claimed that the macaroni had nothing active in his pants, that he was of no use to women: 'Nor forget that his breechs be roomy between 'em: / 'Twill shew that a great deal is wanting with-in 'em.'[75] Passivity is his sexual position; he receives rather than gives – the punning conjunction *'donne dans'* is better explained in the case of Onslow, discussed previously.

There seem to be no recorded cases of historical individuals who were both convicted sodomites and known to be macaroni dressers. This is not surprising, as identified sodomites faced execution. However, it would hardly be surprising if some macaroni used their attire to signal to other men their willingness for homosexual encounter. Indeed, there is little doubt that such clothing was deployed at times by individuals who wished to send out signals to like-minded men.

5.16 Philip Dawe (printmaker),
***The Enraged Macaroni,* 13 July
1773**. Mezzotint, sheet 35 × 25 cm.
Courtesy of The Lewis Walpole
Library, Yale University

The ENRAGED MACARONI.

The Billingsgate with rude and cutting Jokes
The Macaroni to fierce Rage provokes,

Who threatens Blood and Wounds with glaring Eyes
But she with viperous Tongue his Rage defies

Performing gender

Judith Butler's *Gender Trouble* of 1990 has been a work of enormous
influence on all studies of dress and gender. Butler argues that gender is
performance, structured through repetition, and that we act out the signs of
gender that are socially sanctioned and inculcated from birth. Eighteenth-
century dress and the macaroni are clearly related to the repetition of
behaviours, and it is therefore not surprising that they have been so richly
reassessed by historians such as Terry Castle and George Haggerty. Philip
Dormer Stanhope, 4th Earl of Chesterfield, in his *Letters . . . to His Son* (on
the Grand Tour in Paris) revealed that clothing was inadequate without
training in how it was to be worn (or performed):

It seems ridiculous to tell you, but it is most certainly true, that your dancing master is at this time the man in all Europe of the greatest importance to you. You must dance well, in order to sit, stand, and walk well; and you must do all these well, in order to please.[76]

The eighteenth-century focus upon the self as a work of art fed into a set of camp behaviours that are associated with a certain type of modern homosexual. Susan Sontag, in *Notes on Camp* (1966), argued that the genesis of camp was in *ancien-régime* manners. And many of the writers in Moe Meyer's sparkling anthology *The Politics and Poetics of Camp* (1994) reworked the lineage that Sontag established, from the eighteenth-century aristocrat to Oscar Wilde to the twentieth-century urban homosexual. Wayne Koestenbaum has put it thus:

By the twentieth century, homosexuality already meant more than just sex acts or desires shared by bodies of the same gender. It implied a milieu and a personality – flamboyant, narcissistic, self-divided, grandiose, excessive, devoted to decor.[77]

Oscar Wilde was once described as Georgian in inflection, rather than as an aesthete: 'Remember at Cambridge to be clever and witty is Victorian and to be aesthetic is to be even more archaic – for Oscar Wilde plagiarized the late Georgians.'[78] His system of 'posing', based on an interest in the Delsarte acting system, and his sartorial props – cane, rings, scent – referred to the attire of the courtier or macaroni. Meyer argued that camp is a body of performative practices used to enact an identity; that camp is not irony, but 'intercontextual manipulation of multiple conventions', queer parody: 'queer performance is not expressive of the social identity but is, rather, the reverse – the identity is self-reflexively constituted by the performances themselves'.[79] The macaroni persona played with the conventions of court dress in different ways; some macaroni may have utilised aspects of high fashion in order to effect new social identities, but others may have asserted what we would now label a queer identity. It seems all the more significant that the macaroni appeared at a time when modern gender identifiers were being consolidated in mainstream society, to become, as Nancy Armstrong contends, the mainstays of late eighteenth- and nineteenth-century middle-class structures.[80] Dominic Janes's recent study of a queer 'archaeology' has confirmed what this author suspected. In working backwards from Oscar Wilde, whom Janes convincingly argues made use of the visual repertoire of the Georgian fop, macaroni and dandy, and forwards to Edwardian stereotypes expressed in sources as diverse as caricatures and the theatre, Janes has revealed the double-sided nature of late-Victorian homophobic humour as simultaneously a destructive space and a creative force. Clothing, body shape, deportment and personal performance come together to create a new queer self-expression, one that still resonates today.[81]

The macaroni images are therefore highly significant in that they mark an emphasis upon men as vain fashion consumers that matches, if not exceeds, attacks on female vanity. Such an attack is found at other times, such as in the reign of James I, when it was also grafted to a concern about a potentially sodomitical court. The macaroni formed a bridge connecting ideas of effeminacy, luxury and display with corruption and homosexuality, an ancient idea that had been revived in seventeenth-century England by those who wished to attack the aristocracy and the court. It fed forwards into late nineteenth-century conceptions of the homosexual as a third sex, a woman trapped in a man's body, with the attributes of femininity, including a type of hysterical instability. The growth of luxury is an important link here between the sexual and sartorial politics. The first-century writer Philo of Alexandria described Sodom as the link:

> The inhabitants owed this extreme licence to the never-failing lavishness of their sources of wealth . . . Incapable of bearing such satiety, plunging like cattle, they threw off from their necks the law of nature and applied themselves to deep drinking of strong liquor and dainty feeding and forbidden forms of intercourse.[82]

The theologian Albertus Magnus (d.1280) argued that sodomy was 'more common in persons of high station than in humble persons'.[83]

If men were becoming too feminine within the commercial culture of eighteenth-century Britain, then women might be becoming more masculine. Images of fashionable women in riding dress, such as the engraving after Hugh Douglas Hamilton's mannish-looking *Lady Spencer*, suggest a type of androgyny taking place in fashionable appearances, in which men and women began to resemble each other – hair, jacket, waistcoat and stock (fig. 5.17). Here was the forerunner of the *amazone*, whom the nineteenth century found so erotic and appealing.

In conclusion here, the macaroni was a departure from the ruggedly bisexual Restoration rake (also a figure of fashion), noted for his random couplings. The caricatures of the macaroni extended the territory of the rake to create a new type of potentially sexually deviant man. Homosexuality was understood less as an affront to men than an attack upon women, for it threatened to make them redundant. Some macaroni may have constituted themselves as a new type of sodomitical character, and they considerably extend what is known about the representation of such stereotypes in eighteenth-century England. Although he was occasionally described as a whoring debaucher, the macaroni was more often represented as effete and homosocial. His pursuits and interests – fashion, appearance, diversions,

wit – were cast more often as feminine, and had the effect of condemning the slavishly fashionable to the side of the sexually suspect for some time, in the Anglo-Saxon world at least. Despite the ground prepared by figures such as David Bowie from the 1970s, it is perhaps only in the last ten years – for a generation who can 'see it all' on social media, from former sports champions to queer muscle-queen performance artists – that the male fear of hyperbolic dressing seems to have been lessening.

CHAPTER 6

'Things of a peculiar species': The Macaroni and English Theatre

*W*hilst fickle Fashion own'd her ruling hand,
  And fix'd the mode, or alter'd, at her dread command.
'Twas she who bid our trembling bard engage
To lash the folly of this fribbling age.

[Robert Hitchcock], The Macaroni, 1773[1]

Theatre was an extremely popular entertainment in eighteenth-century England and an important space for the cultural and social imagination. The Licensing Act of 1737 permitted London plays to be held only at Drury Lane and Covent Garden, with the exception of summer plays at the Haymarket after 1767.[2] Theatre-going was Queen Charlotte's favourite diversion. Charles James Fox's maternal relations, the Lennox women, went to several plays a week, Caroline having a box at both Drury Lane and Covent Garden – playhouses that in the 1780s were connected with the opposition Whig Foxites and William Pitt, and the government, respectively.[3] George III attended Covent Garden about seven times a year, 'but was rarely if ever present at Drury Lane'.[4] The theatre was a barometer of everyday life; it was not simply a reflective mirror, but a place in which opinions and identities were formed, received and tested.

This chapter concerning the relationship between the macaroni and the theatre attempts to rise to the challenge – once presented by Anne Bermingham for eighteenth-century studies – that: 'our models for the consumption of culture may include but must finally move beyond the ideas of emulation to embrace structures of appropriation, circulation and bricolage, and the complex workings of aesthetics, fantasy, discipline, and sexuality'.[5] It also acknowledges the role of performance within an 'inter-arts approach' to the eighteenth century – a necessity, as H. James Jensen argues, because '[t]he arts were seen as parallel in effect, purpose, and means, and the place where all the arts coalesce most clearly is in the theatre.'[6]

Early eighteenth-century stage figures of fops, later 'fribbles' (as they were often called in the 1750s) and macaroni (in the 1770s), were commonly seen on the stage. The fop had been present on the English stage since the Restoration – he was a requisite role in most comedy. In the satirical *Dictionary of Love* of 1777, the fop and macaroni were conflated in a figure described thus: 'He is extremely satisfied with his person; fancies every woman that sees him cannot help dying for him ... He passes most of his time in ogling himself in a glass; primming his figure, and caressing his curls and toupee.'[7]

The stage fop is a repository of attitudes towards male dress of the time. A famous late seventeenth-century example was Colley Cibber's performance of Sir Novelty Fashion in *Love's Last Shift* (1696). John Vanbrugh's ironic sequel to this was *The Relapse* (1696), which includes the male characters of Lord Foppington and the lecherous Coupler, who accosts a young man named Fashion. Stephen Orgel has noted that Coupler is 'the first character I know of who would be recognizable as gay in the modern sense'.[8] Sir George Etherege's *The Man of Mode, or Sir Fopling Flutter* (1676) continued to be popular throughout the eighteenth century. Images of fops appeared in many visual formats, ranging from popular squibs to a printed *toile* design showing the foppish Lord Chalkstone from David Garrick's play *Lethe* (1740).[9] Lord Chalkstone (his name is the colloquial term for kidney stone) was the character of a wealthy, affected and physically debilitated nobleman played by Garrick. In 1756 Garrick wrote a new part in *Lethe*; he also played the Frenchman in this play.

The macaroni was therefore recognisable when he emerged on the stage in the 1770s. Although the fop was allowed to be a sexually ambiguous figure, the macaroni was more often cast as potentially sodomitical. This was overt in Robert Hitchcock's play *The Macaroni* of 1773; coinciding with the expansion of the little industry in macaroni caricatures, the play went through two reprints after its debut in York, one in London and one in Dublin. That it emanated from outside London indicates the wider dissemination of this new type of stage fop. Such plays popularised the novel term 'macaroni' as effectively as the caricatures in the print-shop windows: these macaroni literally came to life, adding speech and movement.

Plays frequently alluded to a wide range of references from visual culture. In particular, the theatre referred in a self-conscious and reflexive way to printed caricatures. As Heather McPherson puts it, 'the potency of satirical prints derives from their multivalence, intertextuality, and ventriloquism'.[10] Daniel O'Quinn, in his history of British political sovereignty and Empire during the 1770s and 1780s, makes this point of the theatre: 'Because of the temporality of performance, the mélange of stock plays and new productions that made up a typical season not only reactivated past representations but also put forth new representational paradigms to explore present social problematics.'[11] Oliver Goldsmith's *She Stoops to Conquer* (1773) pointed to the contemporary craze for macaroni prints. In it, Marlow notes: 'O, confound my stupid head, I shall be laugh'd at over the whole town. I shall be stuck up in caricatura in all the print-shops. The Dullissimo Maccaroni ...'[12] Goldsmith also wrote a 'quarrelling epilogue' for the actresses Mrs Bulkley and Miss Catley, which was printed but not performed, and included the following passage:

> Let all the old pay homage to your merit;
> Give me the young, the gay, the men of spirit.
> Ye travell'd tribe, ye macaroni train,
> Of French friseurs, and nosegays, justly vain,

Who take a trip to Paris once a year.
To dress, and look like awkward Frenchmen here . . . [13]

The Clandestine Marriage of 1766, a collaboration between George
Colman and David Garrick, deferred to Hogarth, as the play was based on
plate 1 of *Marriage à la Mode*. Colman had written to Garrick: 'I had long
wished to see those characters on the stage', and Garrick himself played
the elderly fop Lord Ogleby.[14] The prologue announced: 'Tonight, your
matchless Hogarth gives the thought, / Which from his canvas to the stage
is brought.'[15] In 1762 Garrick wrote a short interlude, about four pages long,
entitled 'The Farmer's Return from London'. A farmer describes sights
of the metropolis such as prostitutes and fops.[16] This format was also very
recognisable within the satirical imagery of the 1770s, with the popular
theme of 'up from the country' (see fig. 3.32).

About 20 years ago Brian Maidment wrote that the relationship between
the popular theatre and the print trade is a complicated one that is still
poorly understood. He posed the provocative questions: 'Did the readers re-
enact the plays from these texts? Or imagine the theatre experience?'[17] The
text of a play is a useful metaphor for surviving examples of clothing, which
need to be put into performance for their full meaning to become apparent.
They are particularly useful for macaroni dress, with its strong performative
element. Gentlemen who identified as macaroni, such as Charles James
Fox, attended performances where their counterparts appeared on stage:
the macaroni was thus played out as a stage representation, as well as being
represented in the boxes and on the streets. This yields insights into the
macaroni character, and probable reflections of the behaviour and dress
of the macaroni audience, who may in turn have imitated the character,
in a spiralling round of exaggerated performance. Jensen notes:

> Because of the public nature of theatrical art, whether musical or
> otherwise, the historical dimensions of fields of reference help define
> the theatrical experience that an audience would be expected to realise.
> It also means an intentionality built into the dramatic work of art based
> on the assumed knowledge or assumptions of both artist and audience.[18]

Thus macaroni characters and macaroni audience members blurred the
distinction between the 'represented' and the 'real'.

Central to the stage representation of the macaroni was no less a
personage than David Garrick. Probably the most recognisable figure
of his age, apart from members of the royal family, Garrick was the most
famous actor and theatre-manager of the period. He was praised for the
new naturalism that he brought to acting style, a point worth remembering
when considering the popularity of his roles as a theatrical fop. Considered by

contemporaries to be very handsome, he was also noted for the flexibility of his face and the enormous variety of facial expressions he could hold. The imagery of the macaroni would inevitably have informed the way in which he performed such roles on stage, performances that in turn would have inflected both the reading and production of prints. Garrick and his wife were extremely interested in sartorial fashions, owned a Thames-side villa with the most up-to-date furnishings, and were retained by the Duke of Devonshire as a 'proxy shopper' to advise on the purchase of his metropolitan court dress.[19] Garrick himself tended to be portrayed in fairly sober but fine dress (fig. 6.1), reminiscent of the 'carmelite'-coloured velvet suit that he had purchased in Italy (fig. 6.2). This is the dress depicted by Batoni in his portrait of Garrick (fig. 6.3). Garrick was wealthy and ended up being next-door neighbour to Horace Walpole, who, as Shearer West argued, looked down upon Garrick's aristocratic airs as 'affectations of nobility' linked to his 'mimic ability, rather than any genuine grace or ease in such society'.[20]

Comic roles were seen as the obverse of the new seriousness and realism that Garrick bestowed on the tragic: a detractor wrote, 'your repertory has let us down; give us the best, your Lears, Hamlets, Richards, not your Lying Valets and Fribbles'.[21] As West has so cogently explained, contemporary aesthetic theories often derided caricature as 'frightful and ridiculous', and this view was expanded by critics who attacked low-life, burlesque and crude images on the stage.[22] Nonetheless, the public liked these roles, just as they liked the images. Garrick had both acted and written various characters representing the foppish type. He had five major roles as a fop in other writers' plays: Clodio in Cibber's *Love Makes a Man*; Witwoud in Congreve's *The Way of the World*; Duretete in Farquhar's *The Inconstant*; Lord Foppington in Cibber's *The Careless Husband*; and Marplot in Centlivre's *The Busy Body*.[23] In the 1750s Garrick popularised the character of the 'fribble', the overly effeminate fop, and then in the 1760s and 1770s that of the macaroni. As the largest part of the theatre audience was of the 'middling sort', Woods interprets the creation of these roles as Garrick's attempt to 'soften some of the resentment which attended his growing wealth and social standing', but with his interest in Hogarthian types, he must also have relished the performances in and of themselves.[24]

As well as playing other writers' roles, Garrick created his own. He wrote for himself the character of Fribble in *Miss in Her Teens* (1747), his seventeenth most frequently performed role out of 96.[25] Garrick advertised that the play was based on Dancourt's *La Parisienne*; his version was popular for the next 30 years.[26] In this play Miss Biddy is courted by several men, including Captain Flash and Fribble; the latter is a rejected suitor, more effeminate than the lady he courts. Miss Biddy describes the fribble thus:

DAVID GARRICK Esqr.

Above left
6.2 **Three-piece suit, Italian, associated with David Garrick,** **1758–61**. Brown velvet. Museum of London

Above right
6.3 **Pompeo Batoni,** *David* *Garrick*, **1764**. Oil on canvas, 76 × 63 cm. Ashmolean Museum, University of Oxford, WA1845.61

[A fribble] speaks like a lady, . . . and never swears, . . . wears nice white gloves, and tells me what ribbons become my complexion, where to stick my patches, who is the best milliner, where they sell the best tea, and which is the best wash for my face, and the best paste for the hands; he is always playing with my fan, and shewing his teeth . . . and cries The Devil take me, Miss Biddy, but you'll be my perdition – ha, ha, ha.[27]

This rather camp conversation is reminiscent of the speech patterns ascribed to mollies, and of molly-house scenes. Fribble then goes on to provide a further vivid account of his real interests:

Frib . . . there is a Club of us, all young Batchelors, the sweetest Society in the World; and we meet three times a Week at each other's Lodgings, where we drink Tea, hear the Chat of the Day, invent Fashions for the Ladies, make Models of 'em, and cut out Patterns in Paper. We were the first Inventors of Knotting, and this Fringe is the original Produce and joint Labour of our little Community.

Biddy. And who are your pretty Set, pray?

Frib. There's Phil Whiffle, Jacky Wagtail, my Lord Trip, Billy Dimple, Sir Dilberry Diddle, and your humble --[28]

These names were well known and circulated, in other contexts: Whiffle has been discussed with reference to Smollett regarding sexuality (pp.171–2), and Billy Dimple was the title appended to a caricature of Richard Cosway painting a portrait (figs 3.22, 3.24).

In *Miss in Her Teens*, Fribble goes on to describe a dreadful fracas in which:

> three drunken naughty Women of the Town burst into our Club-room, curst us all, threw down the China, broke six Looking-glasses, scalded us with the Slop-Bason, and scrat poor Phil Whiffle's Cheek in such a manner, that he has kept his Bed these three Weeks.[29]

The women thus break the individual looking glasses of each fribble – a symbol of both femininity and narcissism – and disfigure Whiffle, an attack on femininity as represented in the male. The slop-basin contains the 'dregs' or waste of the tea: they are literally burned, with a reference to their maligned sexuality. Biddy replies: 'Indeed, Mr Fribble, I think all our Sex have great reason to be angry; for if you are so happy now you are Batchelors, the Ladies may wish and sigh to very little purpose.'[30] Fribble's love-song to Miss Biddy Bellair concludes: 'Then take with me, Love's better Part, / His downy Wing, but not his Dart.'[31] The implication that the fribble's penis is wasted on him is shared with the macaroni caricatures discussed earlier. Garrick also dictated the speech pattern of Fribble, with pronunciations such as 'crateer' (creature), 'meister' (master), 'serous taalk' (serious talk), 'hooman nater' (human nature), the type of intonation possibly taken up by the macaroni, or perhaps echoing speech patterns with which he was already familiar.[32]

The theatre-going experience produced multiple meanings that were openly acknowledged within the organisation of the comedies, in that plays were explicitly structured to appeal to the hierarchical demarcations within the theatre – box, pit and lower and upper galleries. Those with less money to purchase a ticket occupied the latter, and also mixed in the pit with various social groups from the middling sort. Some of the caricature prints we have discussed might be read in a similar manner, with different groups procuring different meanings from each print. Various people came and went as the different genres of plays were performed in the course of the evening: the attempted suppression of this practice was at the base of the 'half-price riots' of 1763. As Marc Baer notes, riots might be as old as theatre itself. The 'half-price riots' had been preceded by a riot at Drury Lane in 1737 when footmen were refused the customary free entry, and Garrick's use of French performers in 1755 led to the windows of his residence being smashed.[33]

Within the theatrical structure, each section felt they were receiving a message from the actor-manager. The function of the prologues inspires a reading of macaroni imagery in which mocking functioned on several levels:

Prologues railed gently at current taste, and bantered in a modified Aristophanic fashion audience, author, and performers, by taking the audience into confidence, assuming its collective intelligence to be brighter than that of the writing or performing crews, and setting it up to belittle the whole process.[34]

Garrick's epilogue to Arthur Murphy's *All in the Wrong* (1761) addressed each part of the theatre separately:

> What shall we do your different tastes to hit?
> You relish satire [to the pit] you ragouts of wit [to the Boxes].
> Your taste is humour and high-seasoned joke [first gallery]
> You call for hornpipes, and for hearts of oak [upper gallery].[35]

George Colman's 'Prologue' to Garrick's *Bon Ton; or, High Life above Stairs* (1775) also addressed different parts of the audience and the ways in which they experienced fashionability. The mocking of the speech patterns and pretensions of the Spitalfields characters Madam Fussock and Miss Observe in Higher Life suggested the aspirations, pursuits and fantasies of the urban dweller in the 1770s, making a striking and direct reference to the caricature prints of Darly:

> FASHION in ev'ry thing bears sov'reign sway,
> And words and periwigs have both their day:
> Each have their purlieus too, are modish each
> In stated districts, wigs as well as speech.
> The Tyburn scratch, thick club, and Temple tye,
> The parson's feather-top, frizz'd broad and high!
> The coachman's cauliflower, built tiers on tiers!
> Differ not more from bags and brigadiers,
> Than great St George's, or St James's stiles,
> From the broad dialect of Broad St Giles.
> What is BON TON? – Oh, damme, cries a buck –
> Half drunk – ask me, my dear, and you're in luck!
> Bon Ton's to swear, break windows, beat the watch,
> Pick up a wench, drink healths, and roar a catch.
> Keep it up, keep it up! damme, take your swing!
> Bon Ton is Life, my boy; Bon Ton's the thing!
> Ah! I loves life, and all the joys it yields –
> Says Madam Fussock, warm from Spital-fields.
> Bone Tone's the space 'twixt Saturday and Monday,
> And riding in a one-horse chair o'Sunday!
> 'Tis drinking tea on summer afternoons
> At Bagnigge Wells, with China and gilt spoons!

'Tis laying by our stuffs, red cloaks, and pattens,
To dance Cow-tillions, all in silks and sattins!
Vulgar! cries Miss Observe in higher life
The feather'd spinster, and thrice-feather'd wife!
The CLUB's Bon Ton. Bon Ton's a constant trade
Of rout, Festino, Ball and Masquerade!
'Tis plays and puppet-shews; 'tis something new!
'Tis losing thousands ev'ry night at lu!
Nature it thwarts, and contradicts all reason;
'Tis stiff French stays, and fruit when out of season!
A rose, when half a guinea is the price,
A set of bays, scarce bigger than six mice;
To visit friends, you never wish to see;
Marriage 'twixt those, who never can agree;
Old dowagers, drest, painted, patch'd, and curl'd;
This is Bon Ton, and this we call the world! . . .
To-night our Bayes, with bold, but careless tints,
Hits off a sketch or two, like Darly's prints.
Should connoisseurs allow his rough draughts strike 'em,
'Twill be Bon Ton to see 'em and to like 'em.[36]

The prologuer shows that he can 'be' anyone by copying their method of
speaking. The expression 'Bon Ton' changes meaning as it is taken up and
performed by each 'character'; the French phrase is imported and then in
turn mistranslated by individuals, like macaroni dress – indeed, potentially
like all fashionable dress. Each protagonist can only be defined and given
meaning by the process they engender: a play by a performance, a caricature
by its consumption, a macaroni in the self-conscious art of living.

Garrick used his acting skills in *Bon Ton* to imitate a wide range of
voices: 'It is said he mimics eleven men of fashion,' wrote Mrs Delany.[37]
Plays, caricatures and macaroni were thus intrinsically multi-vocal and
intertextual, to the point where these became their defining characteristics.
The print industry derived many of its titles and incidents from theatre:
Lady Betty Modish was a character in *The Careless Husband*, famously
played by Peg Woffington, for example. Sophie Von La Roche, a young
German noblewoman visiting London in 1786, noted in her diary that the
epilogue of a play she witnessed had been:

> reckoned for the people, [as it] was in the popular vein. For a French
> dancing-master and an Italian singer were burlesqued. A good,
> conservative old Englishman was plagued by his wife into giving his
> daughter a fashionable education, which resulted in an exaggerated
> caricature of these two, causing much amusement in the gallery.[38]

This is precisely the subject matter of numerous caricature prints regarding the relationship of urban fashionability and rustic common sense. Audiences thus had cues for reading the prints, before they analysed them in more detail. The graphic design of a printed play might itself evoke fashion: the frontispiece of *The Pantheonites* (a copy of which was owned by Horace Walpole) used fonts to create the literal form of a fashionable men's shoe buckle or steel jewellery, but in ink and typography (fig. 6.4). A rare Swedish painted copy of an English caricature print by Darly (see fig. 1.8) makes the relationship between print and theatre explicit, in that the painter has modified the scene by depicting a proscenium stage, topped off with a Swedish-style painted floor cloth (fig. 6.5).

Images sometimes directly followed a popular play. The character of the effeminate Fribble was illustrated in two engraved versions of the duel scene in *Miss in Her Teens* by the end of the first month of its performance (fig. 6.6). Fribble, at the left, played by Garrick, was depicted as small in stature; the viewer would have enjoyed the contrast with Captain Flash. Garrick was a short man, at just over five feet, playing a weak and ineffectual character. Frail and cowering, Fribble is modishly dressed, with a trimmed waistcoat. He holds his sword wanly. He sports a kerchief over his shoulders, worn in a loose, *déshabillé* manner, possibly part of Garrick's stage repertoire. In a more detailed version of the scene, his sleeves are trimmed with ermine and his waistcoat is fashionably fringed (fig. 6.7). His foe, Captain Flash, wears a large trimmed hat decorated with a big rosette, a pearl and feathers, a reference to the Restoration rake. His double-breasted coat with its shoulder frogging is military or riding wear, underlining his virility. The dress depicted in the fribble print reflects many of the characteristics associated later with the macaroni. The scene depicted in the second, Charles Mosley version shows the theatre as reformed by Garrick, and the manner in which the actors were protected from the audience by vicious-looking metal spikes. Although such representations do not necessarily re-create the real appearance of a theatre, they establish a set of conventions about looking at audience and actors alike.

Garrick wrote several other plays that toyed with the word 'macaroni'. *The Male-Coquette: or, Seventeen Hundred Fifty-Seven* (1757), a play that refers back to Restoration comedies such as George Etherege's *Man of Mode*, included the Marquis of Macaroons, also called 'il Marchese di Macaroni' or 'Lord Macaroni', who is here a cross-dressing Italian. Contrasted with the principal character of Daffodil

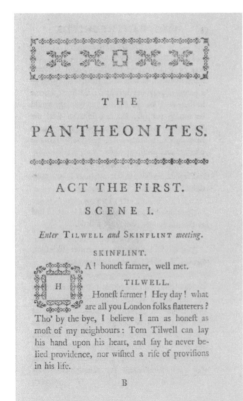

is the 'roast-beef' figure of Tukely, of whom Sophia notes: 'If the gentleman would put his speech into a farce, and properly lard it with roast beef and liberty, I would engage the galleries would roar and halloo at it for half an hour together.'[39]

A short piece entitled *A Peep Behind the Curtain; or, The New Rehearsal* (1767) also included the character of Sir Macaroni Virtu.[40] The term was

The celebrated fighting Scene in Miß in her Teens.

THE MODERN DUEL.
Taken from Miss in her TEENS, as it's now Acted, at Covent-Garden.

thus highly current on the stage. *Bon Ton* played, once again, on the contrast
between the mores of city and country. The first act has the characters about
to attend a masquerade, with affected manners and dress copied from the
continent. The rich but rustic Sir John Trotley complains:

> not a bob or tie-wig to be seen! All the degrees from the parade in St
> James's Park, to the stool and brush at the corner of every street, have
> their hair tied up – the mason laying bricks, the baker with his basket,
> the post-boy crying newspapers, and the doctor prescribing physic,
> have all their hair tied up ... [41]

These were the various characters beloved of Darly's print repertoire.
Later, Sir John notes of Davy: 'This fellow would turn rake and maccaroni
if he was to stay here a week longer – bless me, what dangers are in this
town at every step!'[42] The play includes the characters of the city relative

Lord Minikin and his French servants, Jessamy and Mignon: 'Our beef and pudding enriches their blood so much, that the slaves, in a month, forget their misery and soup maigre.'[43]

Garrick made particularly skilful use of costumes as brilliant devices in his characterisation and acting. His character Sir John Brute in Vanbrugh's *The Provoked Wife* wears a wig suitable for his years, on which is:

> perched a small, beribboned modish hat so jauntily that it covers
> no more of his forehead than was already hidden by his wig. In his hand
> he holds one of those hooked oaken sticks, with which every young
> poltroon makes himself look like a devil of a fellow in the Park in the
> morning . . . [44]

In October 1775, in his cross-dressed role in *The Provoked Wife*, Garrick brought down the house with his feather headdress: 'Mr G.-- never play'd better, & when he was in Woman's Cloaths he had a head drest with Feathers, Fruit etc. as extravagant as possible to Burlesque the present Mode of Dressing – it had a Monstrous Effect.'[45] A newspaper reported that the headdress included feathers, ribbons, oranges and lemons, and flowers: 'The ladies in the boxes drew back their heads, as if ashamed of the picture.'[46] Garrick's headdress was reminiscent of the numerous images of 'preposterous' headdresses created as satirical prints in the late 1770s (see fig. 6.8). Such hairstyles also appeared in contemporary fashion periodicals, as well as in engraved portraits of actresses, prostitutes and other 'gay ladies', indicating the fine line that existed between satire and reportage. In some cases French fashion images were directly pirated for the production of English mezzotints.[47]

The Gentleman's Magazine reported in July 1776 that their majesties had 'laughed immoderately' at a similar performance by the cross-dressed mime artist and satirist Samuel Foote: 'The elegant, becoming manner in which her Majesty's head was dressed was, however, the severest satire on the present filthy fashion.'[48] 'High hair' was clearly very topical, as Horace Walpole wrote to Sir William Hamilton in February 1776: 'I advise Lady Hamilton to beg, buy, or steal all the plumes from all the Theatres on her road: She will want them for a single fashionable headdress, nay, and gourds & melons into the bargain. You will think like William the Conqueror that you meet marching forests.'[49] One of the favourite actress-courtesans of the day, Sophia Baddeley, who worked for a period for Garrick, was depicted in a mezzotint portrait engraved after Zoffany with a high confection of wigging and a small, beribboned cap and dependent pearls (fig. 6.9). As Zoffany himself was remarked to be 'macaroni' when he arrived in London from Switzerland in 1760, it is not surprising that he was such an adept interpreter of this new fashion trend: he 'commenced *maccaroni*, bought a

THE PREPOSTEROUS HEAD DRESS,
or the FEATHERD LADY.

THE OPTIC CURLS.
OR THE OBLIGEING HEAD DRESS

Above left
6.8 M. Darly, *The Preposterous Head Dress, or the Featherd Lady*, 20 **March 1776**. Etching, plate 35 × 24.8 cm, sheet 38 × 27 cm. Courtesy of The Lewis Walpole Library, Yale University

Above right
6.9 R. Laurie after Johann Zoffany, *Mrs Baddeley*, *c.*1770. Mezzotint, plate 37 × 26.8 cm. Courtesy of The Lewis Walpole Library, Yale University

Left
6.10 M. Darly, *The Optic Curls or the obligeing head dress*, 1 April 1777. Etching, 35 × 24.8 cm. British Museum, London

suit à la mode, a gold watch and a gold-headed cane', shortly before falling on hard times.[50] The high hair of fashionable women was sometimes used as a device to underline a point about visibility. In one satirical print, foppishly dressed audience members were satirised peering through the curls of a lady that were being used as optical devices (fig. 6.10). According to Matthew Craske, the eyeglass as a motif exposes 'the intellectual or moral myopia of the lecherous or amorous individual whose attentions are fixed only on shallow sensual objectives'.[51]

Garrick owned a very large collection of prints. In an interesting indication of how such prints might have appeared within a contemporary interior, some of the engravings and mezzotints of Garrick's collection were 'glazed, framed and hung throughout . . . [his] two mansions'.[52] Matthew Darly dedicated one of his 1772 suites of *Macaronies, Characters, Caricatures* to the actor. Stone and Kahrl state that this dedication was 'In recognition of Garrick's patronage of engravers and print sellers', but it was also a witty and topical comment on the importance of Garrick in popularising the macaroni as a stage character and in referring directly to a wide range of visual representations in the text of the plays he himself wrote.[53] Garrick had also requested in a letter of 17 November 1772 that James Boswell purchase for him from a bookseller's catalogue '*Histoire Maccaronique*, 2 Vols', a text that remains unidentified; it might have been macaronic poetry.[54]

Just as fashionability and the fashionable women in the audience were cleverly drawn in and mocked by Garrick, so the macaroni gentlemen present in the theatre were probably acknowledged by actors at various points during the performance. The contemporary theatre was not darkened, but was lit by footlights, sconces and chandeliers, and the audience could be observed throughout the performance. The story of an Irish macaroni figure and his fate in the theatre was recounted in 1826:

> One of the finest gentlemen in Dublin about this time [1760s], indeed the most remarkable for his dress and manner, was a young merchant in Cow Lane who troubled himself no more about business than my Bouquet, the hop merchant in St Mary Axe. This grand gentleman was one night at Crow Street (the play, Murphy's *Orphan of China*). He sat in the left-hand stage box and, though he had the front seat all to himself, this did not content him. Turning his back upon the stage . . . he placed himself upon the edge of the box, his legs stretched out at full length, crossing each other, his arms also folded and his shoulder resting against the side of the box. Under him was the door opening to the pit and the flooring was rather deep. Thus he remained, enjoying his prime wish of an ample display of his person and dress to the whole house. His clothes were silk and richly embroidered; his hair, tastefully dressed with ringlets

that played round his ears; his sword, with a large and magnificent silver sword-knot, stretched itself all along by the side of his legs to complete the view. The eyes of the audience were upon him full front, the eyes of the performers upon the back of his head and shoulder. In the very height of this proud and careless display of his six-foot-long person, whilst lolling with a smile of complacent nonchalance, he at an instant overbalanced himself and tumbled into the pit. A clamour of mirth burst through the whole house and, as no bones were broke, nobody was sorry for his downfall. This, though not the first, was most likely his last attempt to captivate the notice of the audience and turn it from the stage, the true point of attraction, to his own fine self-admired self.[55]

The macaroni's theatrical performance could hardly be better illustrated.

Similarly, Sophie Von La Roche described a group of ultra-fashionable women and fops being literally driven from the theatre by the combined attentions of actors and audience. A group of four ladies:

entered a box during the third play, with such wonderfully fantastic caps and hats perched on their heads, that they were received by the entire audience with loud derision. Their neckerchiefs were puffed up so high that their noses were scarce visible, and their nosegays were like huge shrubs, large enough to conceal a person. In less than a quarter of an hour, when the scene had changed to a market-square in any case, four women walked on to the stage dressed equally foolishly, and hailed the four ladies in the box as their friends. All clapped loud applause. The two gentlemen accompanying the fashionable fools were least able to endure the scorn, for they hastily made away. One of the women held her fan before her face, and was thereupon called by name – and when the expression of the remarks became too strong, they too departed before the end of the sketch, but they were followed out by a number of people from the pit and gallery, and held up to ridicule.[56]

Garrick as Fribble

Garrick's role as Fribble generated a set of written texts and retorts that indicate the degree of circularity in eighteenth-century culture and the manner in which pointed references to older texts were deployed. The first was to the anonymous pamphlet *The Pretty Gentleman* (London, 1747), a doubly satirical attack upon Garrick's roles as a playwright and as an actor playing a fop, discussed in detail below.

Garrick published anonymously in 1761 a poem entitled *The Fribbleriad*, written in order to offend the detractors who had disrupted performances at Drury Lane. This was a devastatingly funny poem, which maligned his theatrical enemies as feminised and Francophile. That Garrick would choose to attack as effeminate fribbles the troublemakers who questioned his theatre management indicates the cultural resonance of this term. In a brilliant twist he addressed the real troublemakers and the fictional authors of the previous document, *The Pretty Gentleman*, at the same time. The viewing and reading public would have revelled in the circularity of this double performance, as the actor-author defended his tenure and directed well-placed barbs back at the audience who viewed his plays and read his pamphlet. His satire, illustrated with an elegantly executed portrait of the fribble Fizgig, was a fine repository of the attributes that were laid at the well-shod feet of the macaroni several years later.

The Pretty Gentleman

In 1747 the anonymous 'Philautus' ('Friend of Himself' or 'Self Love' from various neo-Latin dramas) published *The Pretty Gentleman; or, Softness of Manners Vindicated From the false Ridicule exhibited under the Character of William Fribble, Esq.* This brilliantly satirical work is written from the speaking position of a 'pretty gentleman' who has been affronted by Garrick's character Fribble from *Miss in Her Teens*. He contends that Garrick's Fribble was written in a pique of envy: 'it must have been a secret Admiration of their Elegant and Refined Manners, that called forth your Spleen, to turn into Ridicule those soft Accomplishments you despaired to equal'.[57]

In this satire the pretty gentleman is reading Garrick's characterisation as being in competition with his own (the pretty gentleman's) display. The author then discusses a lineage of foppery. What a 'pretty gentleman' represents is made very clear when the author notes: 'Amidst all my Researches into the History of this Country, I do not find one PRETTY GENTLEMAN, till the glorious reign of King James I.'[58] He complains that Garrick has falsely attempted to deride 'that mollifying Elegance which manifests itself with such a bewitching Grace, in the refined Youths of this cultivated Age'.[59] *The Pretty Gentleman* then describes the activities of the modern male, a wonderful satire that Garrick referred to when he composed *The Fribbleriad* 15 years later:

> The enfeebled Tone of their Organs and Spirits does therefore naturally dispose them to the softer and more refined Studies: Furniture, Equipage, Dress, the Tiring Room, and the Toy-shop. – What a Fund is here for Study! And what a Variety of easy Delights! Or, if the Mind is bent upon Manual Exercise, the Knotting-Bag is ready at hand; and their Skilful Fingers play their Part.[60]

As well as the feminine pursuit of knotting, the pretty gentlemen pass their time in 'the pretty Fancies of Dress, in Criticisms upon Fashions, in the artful Disposition of China Jars, and other Foreign Trinkets; in sowing, in knitting Garters, in knotting of Fringe, and every gentle Exercise of Feminine Oeconomy'.[61] With names like Sippius, Fannius, Sir Thomasin Lepidulus, Narcissus Shadow ('Dere Nessy'), Lord Molliculo, Delicatulus, Lord Molly, Cottilus and Sir Roley Tenellus, their very emotions are delicate. A laugh is vulgar, but a 'tempered Laugh, which plays with such a Grace on the Countenance of a Pretty Gentleman', is acceptable. Fannius is prone to 'Hysterics' at the sight of lamb and 'spinage', and faints dead away. They never eat roast beef, or the flesh of a full-grown animal, preferring cheese-cakes and flommery. Food, once again, has loaded cultural meaning. The 'pretty gentlemen' were assigned to the register of the female gender: 'Hark, with what feminine Softness his Accents steal their Way through his half-opened Lips! . . . it looks as if Nature had been in doubt, to which Sex she should assign Him.'[62] The author calls for the theatres that so unjustly mock the fribble to be closed, for otherwise England may become a nation of 'Brutes, i.e., Masculine, Robust Creatures, with unsoftened Manners'.[63] Here we have an inversion worthy of the macaroni. The theatre was often maligned as frivolous, but here in its masculine guise it is projected as offending the frivolous and harming the sensibilities of the nation. Garrick's play *Miss in Her Teens* was discussed by a later author in 1801 as relating to the phenomenon of 'the pretty gentlemen, who chose to unsex themselves, and make a display of delicacy that exceeded female softness'.[64] Early nineteenth-century biographers thus swiftly recognised the connection between the 'pretty gentleman' incident and a category of effeminate men.

Fops, fribbles and Fizgig: David Garrick's 'The Fribbleriad' and the 'X.Y.Z.' attack

In 1761 Garrick used the repertoire of the effeminate male deployed in *The Pretty Gentleman* to attack an enemy. In using such a parodic form and trivial associations, he was suggesting that his enemy was as ludicrous as his lampoon. Garrick's biographers have not generally noted that the weapon he used to mock and chastise them was effeminacy. Nor have biographers much recognised the importance of Garrick's career in connecting the fop, the fribble and the macaroni, thus drawing together theatrical conventions from the early to the late eighteenth century.

In the 1760s Garrick was reforming the theatre. In an attempt to improve the reputation of actors and acting, he banned the drunken loungers who had been allowed to sit on the stage and disrupt the plays, falling at the heroine's feet or interjecting at moments of pathos. He had mocked their arrogance in his play *Lethe*. As the 'Fine Gent' noted to Aesop: 'I dress in the Evening, and go generally behind the Scenes of both Play-houses; not, you may imagine to be diverted with the Play, but to intrigue, and shew my-self

--- I stand upon the Stage, talk loud, and stare about – which confounds the Actors, and disturbs the Audience.'[65] The privileged were banned by Garrick from the wings, the green room and the dressing rooms. Lighting was improved, in the interests of good acting. The theatre audience was subjected to the process of discipline that would much later result in a relatively passive audience.

As well as forming enemies of slighted writers and actors, Garrick's management of the theatre drew many critics. Most controversially, Garrick was trying to abolish half-price entry after the third act at Drury Lane, where the pantomime or short farcical pieces were placed. Thaddeus 'Thady' Fitzpatrick, leader of an anti-Garrick group of young men who called themselves 'the Town', led the attack.[66] For about a year in *The Craftsman* and other weekly periodicals, Fitzpatrick, possibly William Shirley and others under the initials 'X.Y.Z.' wrote letters attacking Garrick's acting, or lack thereof, and his vanity on stage. In late 1760 these attacks were gathered and printed together with Fitzpatrick's *An Inquiry into the Real Merits of a Certain Popular Performer.*[67] Garrick was called the Nero of his profession, and his avarice as a manager attacked: 'you acquire a large stock of fame upon the credit of theatrical science which you never possessed'. He replied in a letter dated 3 August 1759: 'I despise the attacks & Misrepresentations of Blockwig, but shall be Ever Truly Sorry when I am misunderstood by a Man of Genius.'[68]

Stone and Kahrl argue that *The Fribbleriad* was Garrick's response to this criticism. The playwright's Horatian verse brands the X.Y.Z. writers as gender and sexual neuters, fashion victims, impressed by all they read and write. Fizgig – clearly intended for Fitzpatrick, and certainly interpreted as such at the time – becomes 'Cock Fribble'. J.D. Hainsworth has noted, 'the poem suggests that Fitzpatrick's attack on Garrick was in revenge for the ridicule of fribbles in *Miss in her Teens.* But this suggestion is itself part of the satire.'[69] The text is modelled on Satan's Assembly in Hell in Book II of *Paradise Lost.* A convention of Fribbles debates how best to annoy Garrick by ungracious theatre behaviour. A Regency memoir noted:

> A poem was published, called *The Fribbleriad*, which was universally and justly attributed to Mr Garrick. With much humour, great vivacity, pleasantry and wit, he played with the tremendous plot of Fizgig, the hero of the poem, and the members of his contemptible club. He characterizes them as things of a peculiar species, who met together in assembly at Hampstead, to plot the downfall of Garrick, their great enemy, who had most abominably exposed them in his farce of *Miss in her Teens.*[70]

The satire is an important repository of the gendered characteristics associated in England with the figure of the fop. The realm of crafting the ornamental and managing the domestic had been gendered feminine; the fribbles were mocked for bringing their own chairs with them, satin ones that they had worked themselves:

> Which nicely quilted, curtan'd pleat'd,
> Did all their various skill display:
> Each work'd his own to grace the day – [71]

Furthermore, the satire posits a direct link between an extravagant sartorial manner and sodomy. This connection was ignored by nineteenth-century writers. Stephens published an excerpt from the poem in his catalogue of the British Museum's print collection, but omitted the following passage, which was more specific than the inclusion of the reference to the 'Master-Misses':

> So dainty, so dev'lish, is all that you scribble,
> Not a soul but can see 'tis the spite of a *Fribble*;
> And all will expect you, when forth you shall come,
> With a *round smirking face*, and a *jut with your bum*. [72]

As it is particularly apposite to the formation of the macaroni stereotype, I shall quote several sections at length:

> *A Man* it seems – 'tis hard to say –
> a *Woman* then? – a moment pray –
> Unknown as yet by sex or feature,
> Suppose we try to guess the creature;
> Whether a *wit*, or a *pretender*?
> Of *masculine* or *female* gender?
>
> Some things it does may pass for either,
> And some it does belong to neither:
> It is so fibbing, slandering, spiteful,
> In phrase so dainty, so delightful;
> So fond of all it reads and writes,
> So waggish when the maggot bites:
> Such spleen, such wickedness, and whim,
> *It* must be *Woman*, and a *Brim*.
> But then the learning and the Latin!
> The ends of *Horace* come so pat in,
> In short 'tis easily discerning,
> By here and there a patch of learning,
> The creature's *Male* – say all we can,
> It must be something *like* a man – . . .

What! of that wriggling, fribbling race,
The curse of nature, and disgrace?
That mixture base, which fiends sent forth
To taint and vilify all worth – . . .
So smiling, smirking, soft in feature,
You'd swear it was the gentlest creature –
But touch its pride, the *Lady-fellow*,
From sickly pale, turns deadly yellow –
Male, female, vanish-fiends appear –
And all is malice, rage and fear – . . . [73]

Sir Diddle, Sir Cock-a-Doodle, Baronet, Captain Pattypan – 'with kimbow'd arm, and tossing head' – Mister Marjoram and other fribbles convene a 'Panfribblerium' and elect a new chair, Fizgig, who is described thus:

with visage sleek, and swelling chest,
With stretch'd out fingers, and a thumb
Stuck to his hips, and jutting bum.

Phil. Whiffle notes in response to having seen Garrick mock the fribbles on stage:

For he, that play'r so mock'd our motions,
Our dress, amusements, fancies, notions,
So lisp'd our words and minc'd our steps,
He made us pass for *demi-reps*.
Tho' wisely then we laugh'd it off,
We'll now return his wicked scoff.

If the sodomitical allusion was not clear enough, then the fribbles note, in a rather hilarious section:

But how attack him? far, or near?
In front, my friends, or in the rear? . . .
The kiss goes round the parting friends –
The chair is left – th'assembly ends.

They all go home: 'Save one, who, harrass'd with the chair, / remain'd at *Hampstead* for the air'.[74] This phrase links the fribbles to the sodomitical space of the cruising ground.

The satire was accompanied by an engraving, finely executed in the French manner of the first third of the eighteenth century, the character of which Stephens describes as having an 'affected attitude of mixed surprise and pleasure' (fig. 6.11).[75] It depicts a mannered man in court dress, with 'jutting bum' and a simpering smile that suggested French *esprit*. He is made doubly ridiculous in that the clothing is slightly old-fashioned, the large cuffs recalling styles of the 1750s. A song entitled 'Fizgig's Triumph' was subsequently published in London in 1763 with the exact outline reprinted, but with slightly different shading.[76]

The theatre is an extremely important site for reimagining lost moods, visual acuity, feelings and innuendo concerning queer men and fashion. Although no theatrical performance can be re-created, other cultural formats provide clues. Porcelain figures, modelled to be viewed in the round, give a glimpse of an actor turning on the stage or of a fop moving across an assembly. The pose, clothing and facial expression of the engraved

FIZGIG.

figure of Fizgig relate closely to a porcelain figurine of Octavio, produced
by Nymphenburg as part of their *commedia dell'arte* series. Octavio is one
of the florid names given to the male lover (also including Flavio, Cinthio
and Lelio), who epitomises gallantry and elegance in the play. Octavio was
viewed as a lightweight and foppish man, characterised by his elegant,
affected pose, particularly as visualised by Bustelli's famous figures,
variously coloured in rich hues, modelled in *c.*1760 (fig. 6.12).[77] The design
of such figures was related to the poses found in older printed books that
included gesture, such as Cesare Ripa's *Iconologia*, whose second illustrated
edition appeared in 1603 and was much reprinted. Octavio is one of the
commedia characters that does not wear a costume, but rather fashionable
dress, which makes a paradox on the stage, as we have also seen with
masquerade participants. Another such example is the *Dancing Cavalier*,
by Meissen, probably modelled by Johann Joachim Kaendler and produced
between 1740 and 1745 (fig. 6.13). The richly brocaded waistcoat with
matching cuffs flares out, in strong contrast to the block of white porcelain
used to model the coat.

Fine-quality objects such as this were likely to have been made for the
banquet table or aristocratic *cabinet* by the 1760s, although *The Lover* (1714)
'treats on the absurdity of filling the best rooms of fashionable females with
china', and notes that the vendors of the more plebeian ceramics usually

'bartered them for rejected cloathing, a custom now faintly discernible amongst certain Jews, who exchange glass, earthen-ware, and a little china, for old cloaths, with servants'.[78] Thus typologies and representations of foppish and queer male 'fashionables' had complex threads of interconnection across cultures, media and formats. We see in these three-dimensional figures how the theatre was significant in creating ideals and images of fashion.

Garrick and other sophisticated viewers would have been aware of many of these associations, not all of them positive. Stephens notes a similar portrait to Garrick's *Fribbleriad*, published by Charles Churchill in *The Rosciad* of 1761:

> A motley figure, of the fribble tribe,
> Which heart can scarce conceive, or pen describe,
> Came simp'ring on; to ascertain whose sex
> Twelve, sage, impanell'd matrons would perplex;
> Nor male, nor female; neither, and yet both;
> Of neuter gender, though of Irish growth;
> A six-foot suckling, mincing in Its gait,
> Affected, peevish, prim and delicate;
> Fearful It seem'd, though of athletic make,
> Lest brutal breezes should too roughly shake
> Its tender form, and savage motion spread,
> O'er its pale cheeks, the horrid manly red . . . [79]

Garrick's attack may well have enraged Fitzpatrick, who was clearly identified in the pamphlet. The latter kept up the attack in *The Muses' Address to David Garrick* (1761) and *The Battle of the Players* (1762). More effectively, Fitzpatrick engineered a riot in Drury Lane Theatre, on 25 January 1763, during a performance of Shakespeare's *The Two Gentlemen of Verona*. Garrick was charging full price for a play with no pantomime. He had printed on the playbill that 'nothing under full price will be taken'; Fitzpatrick responded with posters signed 'An Enemye of Imposition', in which he protested against this.[80] At the sixth performance the audience called out for Garrick to speak to them, then rioted, breaking the chandeliers, pit barriers and boxes, setting the scenery nearly on fire. A riot occurred the following night as well. The fracas was a violent audience reaction to Garrick's suppression of their role in 'theatre'. His reforms were a struggle over the forces of theatricality, actor versus audience. Newspaper reports were generally critical of the 'half-price riots' or 'Fitzgig's Triumph', and of Fitzpatrick, calling him 'Fitzgig', or 'Fizgig' for comic effect. Fitzpatrick was not deterred, leading a similar riot at Covent Garden during a performance of Dr Arne's *Artaxerxes* on 24 February 1763. This indicates

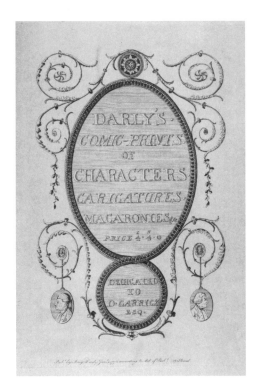

6.14 Mary Darly, *Darly's Comic-Prints of Characters, Caricatures, Macaronies, &c. Dedicted to D. Garrick Esq.*, 1776. Title page. Courtesy of The Lewis Walpole Library, Yale University

the topicality of the macaroni to sensational events such as the near-destruction of two theatres. When Matthew Darly dedicated his 1772 suite of macaroni engravings to Garrick, this was a move that would have referred to both the famous fribble incident and to his performance of such roles; Mary Darly repeated the gesture in 1776 (fig. 6.14).

Robert Hitchcock's 'The Macaroni' (1773)

When Garrick included Lord Macaroni in his play *The Male-Coquette* (1757) he introduced the macaroni in that guise to the English stage. The audience would have recognised characteristics associated with the fribble: effeminate and self-indulgent posturing and a slavish devotion to fashion. These characteristics carried over into a play devoted to the macaroni and published at the time when the macaroni were in full force in the print-shops. The premise of this comedy – Robert Hitchcock's *The Macaroni*, performed in York in 1773 – is that the macaroni belongs to an ambiguous or 'amphibious' sex, one that has no name but is clearly different from normative modes.

Act 1 opens in the dressing room of the macaroni Epicene's house. Whilst dressing with his French valet Fourbe (a name that means 'deceitful'), Epicene notes, 'What a great pity 'tis, Fourbe, we can't entirely introduce the Italian manners and customs here?'[81] Epicene is betrothed to Lord Promise's sister Fanny; he must marry her or forfeit £30,000. Epicene is more interested in the essential business of decorating his person, and there is considerable dialogue about sexual relations: 'How do you intend to manage in that affair?'[82] Promise enquires whether Epicene's morning dress is a masquerade garment, and hopes that it is not a wedding suit: 'Upon my soul you will make such large advances to the feminine gender, that in a little time 'twill be difficult to tell to which sex you belong.'[83] Of Epicene's potential to perform conjugal duties, Fanny exclaims:

> Quite the contrary to a woman of spirit – Oh, I have not patience every day to see such crowds of mincing, whiffling, powder'd Master Jemmys fill our public places, who only want to assume the petticoat, to render them compleat Misses.

'Jemmy' is a corruption of James, the name of a famous sodomite, King James I, and thus also a Stuart and papist reference, with the ghost of George Villiers, the Duke of Buckingham, looking on from the wings.[84]

Within a convoluted farcical plot that involves various people cross-dressing and the disguise of different social 'orders' undertaken by both men and women, Promise and Epicene are eventually chastised by the female characters for symbolising two flawed types of English manhood. In the following exchange Epicene is forced to repeat after Lord Promise:

> I confess, that a Macaroni is the most insignificant – insipid – useless – contemptible being – in the whole creation – Very well, you are docile, I find – Lastly, you must entirely quit the appearance of such a despicable species, and endeavour to assume the Man.[85]

Epicene cries: 'That's hard, nay, I am afraid impossible – You may as well bid me to shake off my existence', to which Lord Promise exclaims:

> For shame! – Think who you sprung from[,] a race of hardy, virtuous, conquering Britons, and blush at your own degenerate exotic effeminacy – But I have done, and be assur'd, my sole motive was to set you up a glass, wherein you might behold a faithful image.[86]

The epilogue, spoken in the character of a macaroni, reiterates the range of macaroni conjured up in caricature engravings and suggests the theatre as a corrective space:

> It matters not, good folks, say what you will,
> Approve, or disapprove our author's skill,
> 'Tis sure there must be Macaronies still.
> For phantom-fashion leads us by the nose,
> And makes us die for every whim she shews.
> A coat, a club, a feather, will engage
> A genius of the *Bon Ton* for an age;
> Like *Newton's* system, bear th' inventor's name,
> And rank him higher in the lists of fame.
> In *English garb*, we know, plain common-sense
> To modish understanding gives offence;
> And modest merit, if perchance one meets,
> How awkward creeps the stranger thro' the streets!
> Whilst fan-tail'd folly, with *Parisian* air,
> Commands that homage sense alone shou'd share.
> The world's so *macaronied* grown of late,
> That common mortals now are out of date;
> No single class of men this merit claim,
> Or high, or low, in faith 'tis all the same;
> For see the Doctor, who, with sapient wig,
> Gold cane, grave phiz, ere while look'd more than big,
> With *France's* foretop decorates his face,
> Prescribes and dresses with *macaronied* grace;

Then swears he hates all formal stuff,
For gravity in practice is a puff.
The Soldier, once that hardy son of arms,
Whose soul was rouz'd, was fir'd with war's alarms,
Forgets the eminence on which he stood,
Whene'er his country call'd, how boil'd his blood!
Resigns the glory his forefathers won,
And lives *Britannia's* alienated son.
Still lower let us fall for once, and pop
Our heads into a modern *Barber's* shop;
What the result? or what behold we there?
A set of *Macaronies* weaving hair.
Such gen'ral folly your attention claims,
And satire here at reformation aims;
O me this night exerts its utmost skill,
Corrects, reforms, and moulds me to its will.[87]

Even hair, that natural protuberance, is 'woven' by artifice. Theatre tries to shake its 'real life' counterpart, the macaroni, to ensure its own existence. It cannot help but perpetuate the image, however, because the macaroni is nothing less than the theatre, a celebration of a performance. The play was noteworthy, as Horace Walpole pasted the 'Epilogue to the new comedy of the Macaroni. Spoken by Mr Cresswicke' in one of his 'books of materials' and marked it 'September 1773'.[88]

The macaroni also appeared in the stage-act and publication by the famous George Stevens, *A Lecture on Heads* (*c.*1765). Stevens was a failed actor who first performed his show at the Haymarket in 1764. It toured the provinces and the American colonies, and was published in several versions until the 1780s.[89] The *Lecture* was a performance with wood and pasteboard heads illustrating various racial and social types, 'to denote that there are not only Block heads, but Paper Sculls'.[90] These represented characters such as a Frenchman, an Old Maid, a Billingsgate Moll, a Ranelagh Hood and a Lady of the Town. A print was issued in two versions with different keys (see fig. 6.15). The imagery of busts with various emblematic hairstyles is related to older French printed images that connect women, wigging and the arbitrary nature of fashion.[91] The notion that wigging, physiognomy and personal qualities were connected can also be seen in caricatures such as 'Quidnunc, or the Upholsterer Shaving' (fig. 6.16).[92] The wig-stands illustrated here function also as caricatures, ranging from judges to ladies. Images of wigs and wig-stands, from trade-cards (fig. 6.17) to caricatures, underline the paradox that wigs either conferred dignity or covered empty heads. The image of the mannequin wig-stand underlining the folly of fashion continued into the

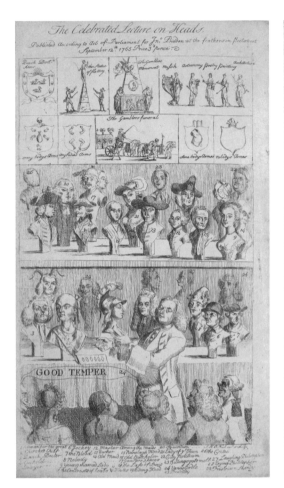

Above left
6.15 *The Celebrated Lecture on Heads*, 12 November 1765. Frontispiece. British Museum, London

Above right
6.16 'Quidnunc, or the Upholsterer Shaving', *Every Man's Magazine*, 1 January 1772. British Museum, London

Right
6.17 'Wm Everingham sculp.', D: Cook Peruke-maker, Hair Cutter & Dresser, at the Star & Peruke in Carey Street near Lincoln's Inn Fields, London, *c.*1770. Trade-card. Courtesy of The Lewis Walpole Library, Yale University

post-revolutionary period, as can be seen in the French caricature *Toupet,
Perruquier*, in which an Englishman in his own hair and comfortable
clothing asks an effete, wizened wig-maker, 'I say, quel chemeng [chemin]
à la Pally Royal?' ('which way to the Palais-Royal?') (fig. 6.18).

In Stevens's *Lecture*, entertainment merges with the more detailed
classificatory urge of the age. The burgeoning study of physiognomy, derived
from the texts of Charles Le Brun and Gerard de Lairesse, would have
intrigued a student of manners such as Garrick, who also owned an edition
of Alexander Cozen's *Principles of Beauty Relative to the Human Head* (1778).[93]
The uncanny nature of detached human heads as fetishistic artefacts passed

I say, quel chemeng
à la Pally Royal?

Voyez, Monsieur, prenez
la troisième rue à main
droite, et vous tomberez
du Palais Royal.

into the pseudo-science of phrenology, and two centuries later into the Surrealist art practice and other speculations of the period 1920–40.[94]

Stevens's *Lecture* also generated various responses related to macaroni men. Head number 10 in the separate print issued in 1765 (fig. 6.15) illustrated macaroni headwear, the tiny hat named after the French envoy in London, the duc de Nivernois (to whom the extraordinary cross-dressing Chevalier d'Éon was secretary). As French Ambassador in London, Nivernois was responsible for negotiating the Treaty of Paris; thus to call a hat a *nivernois* was quite charged, as many Englishmen felt that peace should not have been negotiated at any price; the hat can be read as a deferral to a foe, to passivity. 'This is a HAT in the true spirit of the MODE. This is a Niverne, or a Nivernoise; or a Nivernoi se; or a Never-enough.'[95] Head number 9 was 'Sr Langrish Lisping', a gentleman 'upon town'. Of this type, Stevens noted:

> They smile and simper; they ogle and admire every lady, and every lady alike. Nay, they copy the manners of the ladies so closely, that grammarians are at a loss whether to rank them with the masculine or feminine, and therefore put them down as the Doubtful Gender; . . .[96]

This connection helps us understand a little better the Vauxhall Affray, the fracas discussed previously (see Chapter 5). It suggests that the macaroni, rather than objectifying women, had taken on women's aims and objectified themselves. As Kristina Straub has said of these men, the politics of spectatorship was being contested in this period: 'are they the active agents, the possessors of the power to look, or "pretty beings", spectacles in and of themselves?'[97] The large number of macaroni caricatures also had this effect, of objectifying a set of men who transgressed the demands of their gender. The macaroni were presented as devoid of content, emptied of their masculinity: 'the extreme delicate creatures these represent, seldom make any other use of their heads, than to have their hair or wigs dressed upon them'.[98]

This type of performance with mannequin heads continued to be popular until at least 1780; a text similar to Stevens's *Lecture*, Edward Beetham's *Moral Lectures on Heads* included a head of the effeminate Captain Whiffle, and the head of 'Mr NON-INTELLECT, a macaroni':

> It resembles a skull with two bull's eyes inserted in the sockets . . .
> I cannot put him in the neuter gender, because his wife bore him five fine children. His meagre looks were probably the effects of religious abstinence, for he was a Roman Catholic . . . Macaronies walk just as if they were treading upon eggs, and to appear vastly consequential, they carry a cane like a bailiff's staff. In order to avoid the ridiculous appellation of *nobody*, they are determined to be *all-body*, and therefore they have no

skirts to their coat . . . He would make a good ladies lap-dog, would cut a
pretty ridiculous figure on a chimney-piece between two urns . . . they are
all exceedingly calculated for those ladies, who are particularly fond of
monkeys . . . I shall always be ready with my correcting whip, to drive such
noxious vermin away, from the society of mankind . . .[99]

Stevens's stage act probably referred to these colourful notions that linked
a foreign religion, new objects and means of consumption, and changing
notions of appropriate manhood.

Samuel Foote's play *The Nabob* (1778) related to the macaroni as well as the
major developments regarding the transformation of the East India Company
from a trading company to an entity with extraordinary governmental
authority. A nabob was a wealthy, vulgar man returned from the Company
who indulged in conspicuous expenditure and dressing. He took his place
alongside those who had made fortunes from sugar plantations in the
West Indies, often from Bristol and Liverpool. In both the eighteenth and
nineteenth centuries, clothing worn by Europeans in India continued to be
generally more expensive and elaborate than that worn in Europe. Men often
wore all-white suits there, of light silk or nankeen, a type of cotton, sometimes
with Indian slippers. In Foote's theatrical version, the nabob Sir Matthew
Mite conducts a comical scene with a flower-seller, whom he criticises for
crafting a vulgar ornament: 'You might as well have tied me to a bundle of
sun-flowers!' Rather than using the natural stock of the humble seller, he
turns to 'the artificial flowers I brought from Milan'.[100] Walpole had referred
to the cult of macaroni nosegays in his correspondence, and they emphasise
the notion of foreign manners infecting solid English stock, even indigenous
flowers. We have already seen how William Hickey described that men
brought elaborate French clothes and a *nivernois* hat to take with them to
Bengal. Hickey spent time in India and described a friend thus in 1769:

instead of the plain brown cloth suit we had last seen him in, with
unpowdered hair and a single curl, we now beheld a furiously powdered
and pomatumed head with six curls on each side, a little skimming dish
of a hat . . . His coat was of a thick silk, the colour sky blue and lined with
crimson satin . . . The cut too was entirely different from anything we had
seen, having a remarkable long waist to the coat with scarce any skirts.[101]

The Cunningtons, in their *Handbook of English Costume in the Eighteenth
Century* (1964), claimed that the macaroni were a protest against this vulgar
display of Indian-derived wealth, that they were 'a kind of "resistance
movement" to the crude tastes of the period, not unlike the "Aesthetic
Movement" of a century later'.[102] This is an interesting assessment of the
macaroni men, but it fails to recognise that they were far from averse to

the splendid clothing embroidered with spangles and tinsel worn by the likes of Clive of India upon returning to England. It also contradicts the Francophile and cosmopolitan interests of the macaroni, but it does suggest that they might have made themselves dilettantes of dressing. *The Nabob* was, according to Daniel O'Quinn, an example of 'the theatricalization of imperial affairs in late eighteenth-century London' and in part a topical response to the credit crisis of 1772.[103]

Acting a part

To an eighteenth-century audience, it must have been an obvious irony that acting was very similar to the pursuit of a courtly persona. As Marc Baer notes, more anthropological concepts of theatricality can obscure its original meaning to an eighteenth-century subject, which was 'an instinctually theatrical manner of conduct' or 'consciously being theatrical', without negative connotation: 'Theatricality, then, is appropriation from the stage and ... from audience behaviour as well.'[104] As E.P. Thompson noted of his view of patricians, the appearance of the aristocracy had 'the studied self-consciousness of public theatre ... a studied and elaborate hegemonic style, a theatrical role in which the great were schooled in infancy and which they maintained until death'.[105] Thompson understood dress in a fairly straightforward way as a vehicle of management: 'The ostentatious display, the powdered wigs and the dress of the great must be seen also – as they were intended to be seen – from below, in the auditorium of the theatre of class hegemony and control.'[106]

He went on to note that to speak of dress as 'theatre' is not to diminish its power and importance: 'A great part of politics and law is always theatre ... What one remarks of the eighteenth century is the elaboration of this style and the self-consciousness with which it was deployed.'[107] This is Thompson's notion of 'counter-theatre', a structural model that, as Marc Baer notes, provides an influential model for understanding 'theatre and disorder' as central to eighteenth-century life.[108] Aristocratic methods of carriage and demeanour, of which Roman theatrical gesture is the basis, could be copied by all classes; pocket books such as *The Polite Academy, or School of Behaviour for Young Gentlemen and Ladies* ... put the ideas within the reach of the middling sort, providing instruction for 'a polite Carriage' and appropriate images. These texts explained the carriage in walking, how to stand, how to make a bow, how to offer or receive, how to dance a minuet. The manipulation of the hands and the waistcoat was central to the appearance of a gentleman:

> 11. Put one Hand easy and free into the bosom of your Waistcoat, and the other under the Flap of it.

12. Your Right Hand is best in your Waistcoat, and your left under the Flap.
13. Don't button more than the three lowest Buttons of your Waistcoat, that your Hand may not be raised too high.
14. Do not thrust your Hand into your breeches, as vulgar Boys do, but let it fall with Ease under the Flap of the Waistcoat.[109]

Carriage and demeanour were well rehearsed for both men and women of high social standing in eighteenth-century life. 'The orator . . . must go through a sequence of pantomimes; without them, his words lack force,' notes Richard Sennett.[110]

The macaroni exceeded the polite bounds of decorum to create a mode of mannered behaviour that sometimes edged towards or toppled into burlesque parody; figures such as Richard Cosway literally fell over at times because of their dress or 'habit'. Fops, fribbles and macaroni were important theatrical figures because they most clearly represented the theatricality of parts of the audience, who saw in these stage figures something of the total 'performance' of life, sometimes even their own.

CHAPTER 7

Conclusion: 'Fashion Victims';[1] *or, Macaroni Relinquishing Finery*

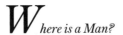

Where is a Man?

Walter Vaughan, *An Essay Philosophical
and Medical Concerning Modern Clothing*, 1792[2]

Frédéric-Samuel Audéoud-Fazy was born in 1767, at the height of the
English macaroni craze, and lived to the age of 64. He looked dramatically
different from a macaroni when he was painted in *c.*1796–1800 by the Genevan
artist Jacques-Laurent Agasse (fig. 7.1). The charming sitter wears long
grey pantaloons with ribbon ties near the foot, and a tall black English-style
hat of great elegance. He wears shoe-ties, not buckles. The sartorial effect
consists of subtle grey and black tones. Although the sitter was born during
the macaroni period, he is clearly of the next generation. His ambience is
English, inflected by French style. 'Swiss style' here becomes more English
than French, and this is but one example of the fashion change in which
Anglophile modes for men gained firm European ascendancy after 1790.

Macaroni men continued to be part of visual culture at this time – but
as something of an amusement. A Viennese coffee cup decorated in 1826
depicted 'L'amour de la Ville', an image of an English macaroni or French
fop of the 1770s (fig. 7.2). The matching saucer has an image of a woman's
hairstyle, 'Coiffure en Colisée', which was in turn copied directly from the
French periodical, *Gallerie des Modes* of 1778. Macaroni men as the 'love of
the town', and high hair for men and women, had now become something of
a novelty or a joke for the next generation.

The transition from male courtly dress to the bourgeois cult of
sobriety has traditionally been associated with the French Revolution and
subsequent attacks on *ancien-régime* symbols. The cataloguer of the British
Museum satirical print collection, Frederic George Stephens, interpreted
the function of the macaroni type in precisely these terms:

> The Macaronies were scorned less on account of their affectations,
> unmanly refinements, and luxury than because they were the very
> froth of the ever-shifting crown of those social waves under which the
> deeply-stirred, ocean-like nation heaved, until it fell upon them. These
> satires on the Macaronies were, indeed, the heralds of a storm which
> culminated in the Conciergerie and the Temple at Paris, and poured
> waves of blood on the pavements of that city.[3]

This is perhaps an over-interpretation of dress portending social change,
but it is interesting nonetheless for the way it makes fashion central to the
wider transformations to which it is both witness and contributor.

Right
7.1 **Jacques-Laurent Agasse,**
Portrait de Frédéric-Samuel
Audéoud-Fazy (1767–1831),
*c.*1796–1800. Oil on card, 23.2 ×
29.6 cm. Musée d'Art et d'Histoire,
Geneva, 1913-0068

Opposite
7.2 **'L'amour de la Ville', cup and**
saucer (detail), Vienna Porcelain
Factory, 1826. Moulded porcelain,
painted in polychromy and gold,
saucer h. 10 cm, d. 15 cm; cup 9.5 × 7.4
× 9.5 cm. Collection Musée Ariana,
Geneva

It is a reasonable argument to suggest, as most historians have done, that the demise of extravagant male dressing occurred because of the shift of cultural capital from the aristocracy to the middle class, accompanied by the assertion of middle-class values of thrift and sobriety. But it is certainly worth noting that this shift was by no means universal – the recalcitrance of the macaroni being the case in point. For one reason or another, these individuals refused to give up their sartorial extravagance, inviting interrogation of that cultural shift, be it framed in terms of class, gender, nationhood, religion or sexuality.

The macaroni may have caused so much cultural consternation precisely because they appeared at a time when dress and demeanour were developing strong gender binaries. The fuss, attention and anxiety attending the appearance of the macaroni were in part related to growing sexual suspicion connected with a love of clothes, which played a major role in a realignment of the sartorial system along gender lines in the late eighteenth and early nineteenth centuries.

In the 1780s a guide to drawing caricatures was issued by Francis Grose, but his work now contained a corrective air, something of a return of the views of Hogarth regarding caricature, who famously disliked the comic grotesque (see fig. 7.3). Grose was a retired military man, antiquarian collector and lexicographer who formed a large collection of caricatures himself, and issued books, including the *Dictionary of the Vulgar Tongue*, which opened the present work. Grose's *Rules for Drawing Caricaturas with*

Lamour de la Ville.

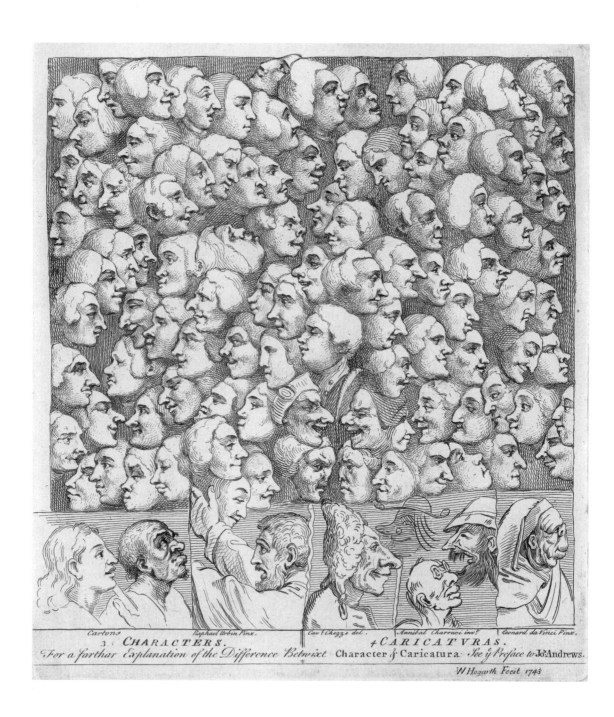

7.3 **William Hogarth,** *Characters*
& Caricaturas, **subscription ticket**
to 'Marriage à la mode' series, 1743.
Etching and engraving, third of three
states, plate 20.6 × 20 cm. National
Gallery of Victoria, Melbourne. Gift
of Professor P.W. Musgrave, 1995

7.4 Francis Grose, *Rules for Drawing Caricaturas with portraits and four plates, and an essay on comic painters* (London: S. Hooper, 1788), plate I. Etching, sheet 12.1 × 19.7 cm. Courtesy of The Lewis Walpole Library, Yale University

portraits and four plates, and an essay on comic painters, of 1788, presented all manner of distortions of the face and commended the caricaturist as a new type of public communications figure (fig. 7.4). To Grose, the caricaturist was a 'dangerous figure, to be feared rather than esteemed', but like William Hazlitt in relation to the theatre a little later, he believed that extreme mockery might have a corrective ambition.[4] Grose's approach was later taken up by Pierce Egan in the Regency period and did much to shape our understanding of eighteenth-century vulgar and low life. The historiography – the self-conscious understanding – of eighteenth-century print culture was something that already existed before the end of the long eighteenth century.

Images of male fashionability now turned to informal English country dress, to which the French added their own jaunty air and accessories. French suits of the 1790s might still be made of silk, but they had a simpler and elongated, neoclassical and tapered look that made the dress of 1770 seem distinctly old-fashioned (fig. 7.5). This blending of a new formulation of masculinity can be readily observed in John Caspar Lavater's *Essays on Physiognomy*, a major illustrated work designed to promote 'the knowledge and the love of mankind'; 800 comparative engravings analysed the silhouette of men's faces from Antiquity to the present day. The soft, aristocratic face, with hair curled at the side, was described as 'absolutely incompatible with Philosophy and Poetry, with the talents of the Politician,

or the heroism of the Soldier'.[5] Another example displayed 'weakness,
presumption, insensibility – but it needs no commentary'.[6] 'Contrasted
attitudes [of] a man and a fribble' pitted the construction of modern
masculinity as forthright and unaffected, in greatcoat and boots with
bolt-upright stance, with the *ancien-régime* fribble, whose clothing sums
up the macaroni type (fig. 7.6). The fribble wears high, powdered hair in an
absurd shape, a patterned silk coat, lace at his cuffs, silk stockings, heels
and breeches, and is short, and slouched by the weight of a large nosegay.
The figure of Fribble was copied closely from *Mr King in the Character of*
Lord Ogleby in The Clandestine Marriage (engraved by Smith and Sayer in
1769), underscoring again the circulation of images between dress, theatre,
popular illustration and pseudo-science. Ogleby retreats a little more from
the forthright modern man in the copy, rather than brandishing his bouquet
wildly towards a character on stage. Lavater asked of the image:

> which of these figures announces a hairbrained coxcomb, a petit-maitre
> – a man whose conversation is equally insipid, tiresome, and teasing –
> a mind incapable of feeling either the great and beautiful, or the simple
> and natural – a being who … will pass his whole life in an eternal
> childhood.[7]

As the macaroni was so frequently pilloried as enfeebled, impotent and unhealthy, the medical ideas have particular relevance for reading the macaroni as a cultural type – a 'typing' more convincing for the strength of subsequent discourses rendering the 'effeminate' man psychologically sick in the nineteenth and twentieth centuries.

The courtier, then, could appreciate neither the delights of the sublime nor natural simplicity; he had lost touch with the currents of his day. Reminiscent of Stevens's *Lecture on Heads*, other plates by Lavater were illustrated with figures dressed in various types of hats, 'which may be called characteristic'.[8] Clothing became synonymous here with a new mindset: the aristocratic pose represented 'affected indifference of self-conceit' and was contrasted with 'meditation'.[9] Bodies as well as clothing exhibit the forms of debilitation: 'insensibility and insolence are painted on the face and in the attitude of the Son ... the under-lip and chin ought also to have advanced more'.[10] Moral corruption was registered on the body covered by even more debased clothes. Men's bodies and even the genital organs, an increasing number of medical treatises argued, were being eroded through the wearing of knee breeches, tightly woven silk, velvet textiles and dressed hair.

Henry Siddons's *Practical Illustrations of Rhetorical Gesture and Action, Adapted to the English Drama* (1807) noted of the new type of male subject:

> If the gestures are the exterior and visible signs of our bodies, by which the interior modifications of the soul are manifested and made known, it follows that we may consider them under a double point of view:
> In the first place as visible changes of themselves; – secondly, as the means indicative of the interior operations of the soul.[11]

A series of male poses familiar from the conventions of painting that had previously indicated an august and noble persona now represented 'Conceit'; the fine clothing that had once conveyed dignity and rank now connoted 'Vulgar Arrogance' (fig. 7.7):

> if you are desirous of a strong and full expression, do not chuse your examples from those who have been educated in the principles of what is termed 'scavoir vivre', or beau monde; an education of this kind, teaches a man the art of dissembling in a double way.[12]

Ironically, theatrical conventions and an acting manual now helped mould a new man who was resisting metropolitan and urbane associations. Some felt that people of the town were 'that hermaphrodite race of feeble creatures, classed in natural history under the name of people of fashion ... they are not of the genuine British growth'.[13] Views concerning the role of theatre-going were not monocultural, however. Stage fops were also viewed as corrective measures. The great critic Hazlitt wrote that 'the stage not only

refines the manners, but it is the best teacher of morals, for it is the truest
and most intelligible picture of life'.[14] Even the English court was changing
– and at the very top. King George III was reported as having worn to court
in 1794 'a brown cloth coat and breeches, with plain steel buttons, and white
silk waist-coat'.[15]

A new type of ideal male body emerged over the course of the eighteenth
century. The aristocratic and rather effeminate body, with a particular
repertoire of courtly gestures learned from the dancing master and an
observation of urban rituals, was to be replaced with the 'natural' body
that resisted such vain and foppish gesture. And this natural body tended
to be dressed in woollens – which in England carried patriotic meanings
regarding local production and consumption – rather than silks.

Vulgar Arrogance

Printed for Richard Phillip's New Bridge St 1807

In 1775 Fanny Burney noted that the word 'macaroni' was no longer the 'ton': the very name had lost its fashionable cachet.[16] Christopher Anstey penned *Liberality; or, The Decayed Macaroni. A Sentimental Piece* in around 1788, which was illustrated with an image of dishevelment, even madness (fig. 7.8). The macaroni was left for some time to populate the novels of Jane Austen and Charles Dickens as an ailing and ridiculous fop, generally resident in Bath, at odds with youthful masculinity. *Persuasion* (1818) included the character of Sir Walter Elliot, the vain and obsequious father of Anne, who revels in the society of Bath, disavowed by Anne in favour of the seaside: 'Vanity was the beginning and the end of Sir Walter Elliot's character; vanity of person and of situation.'[17] *The Pickwick Papers* (1836–7), set in around 1827, included a 50-year-old macaroni, master of ceremonies at the Assembly Rooms, with affected manners and speech: 'it was difficult at a small distance to tell the real from the false'.[18]

By the Edwardian period, the macaroni was reduced to a figure of 'olden times', from a world 'where grace and charm were omnipotent, where worth without wit, or wisdom without brilliance were of small account'.[19] He passed into the 'silver fork' short stories, as a 'lahdy-da' or macaroni in 1935,[20] and as late as 1938 was mentioned in one such story in *Australian Woman's Weekly*.[21] He was also alluded to, wittily, in the trade-name of Cavalier food products, described as 'Australia's most modern macaroni factory' for its

THE
DECAYED MACARONI,
A SENTIMENTAL PIECE.

I.

I AM a decay'd Macaroni,
  My Lodging's up three Pair of Stairs;
My Cheeks are grown wondroufly bony,
  And grey, very grey, are my Hairs:

My

vermicelli and semolina pastes, based in Collingwood, Melbourne.[22] Macaroni had come full circle, ready to be consumed as everyday food on Australian dining tables.

The word seemed to fall away in the post-war period, although Caroline Kennedy's pony in the 1960s was called Macaroni – probably her mother's knowing reference to the American ballad and a reflection of Jackie's love of the Anglo-French eighteenth century.[23] But the macaroni seems to be returning today, courtesy of social media and the new visual flamboyance of much men's fashion. On Instagram may be found a young Thai hairdresser and socialite, Mark Thawin P. Siaotong, whose social media name is Markaroniii. With 18,700 'followers' (as at October 2017), he posts his self-portrait daily, wearing customised Valentino and ladies' Chanel jackets, and carrying various ladies' mini-Birkin handbags, always with an artful touch of *maquillage*. Markaroniii revels in clashing colours, patterns and components of the latest designer clothes, and seems a worthy inheritor of the name.

The macaroni, by his very nature, problematises the idea that any type of clothing can express a stable, continuous and inherent self-being. Sometimes he exists only in performance, in a joke- or songbook, or on the white ground of ceramic or glass, and he has to be brought to life through an understanding of how his dress related to body, gesture and speech. The macaroni cannot simply be understood, therefore, by analysing clothing, deposited as surviving examples in the world's great museums. In the same way, the text of a play languishing unrealised without a stage is diminished in its meaning. A new picture of macaroni clothing and its wearers brings to life the visual drama that such garments brought to the urban landscape of the city of London. In the dissemination of the term, from the North American colonials to India, the macaroni broke the bounds of the English metropolis to become an icon of male fashionability.

Notes

For the abbreviations used in the notes, see the list at the head of the Bibliography on page 242.

Preface

1   Keith Thomas, 'Introduction', in Jan Bremmer and Herman Roodenburg (eds), *A Cultural History of Gesture* (Ithaca, NY: Cornell University Press, 1991), pp.2, 10.

2   Kelly Olson, *Masculinity and Dress in Roman Antiquity* (London: Routledge, 2017).

3   Marcia Pointon, *Brilliant Effects: A Cultural History of Gem Stones and Jewellery* (London and New Haven: Yale University Press, 2010); Susan Siegfried, 'The Visual Culture of Fashion and the Classical Ideal in Post-revolutionary France', *Art Bulletin*, vol. 97, no. 1 (March 2015), pp.77–99; Susan Siegfried, 'Portraits of Fantasy, Portraits of Fashion', *Nonsite.org* (15 December 2014) <http://nonsite.org/article/portraits-of-fantasy-portraits-of-fashion> [Accessed 2 November 2015].

Chapter 1

1   Pierce Egan, *Grose's Classical Dictionary of the Vulgar Tongue* (London: for the Editor, 1823 [1785]), unpag. under 'M'. As George Paston noted in 1905, 'It will be noted that there is a pleasing variety about the spelling of the word "Maccaroni"'. George Paston [pseudonym of Miss E.M. Symonds], *Social Caricature in the Eighteenth Century* (London: Methuen, 1905), p.18. I observe the following spellings in eighteenth-century sources: 'macaroni', 'macarony', 'maccaroni', 'macaronie', 'macaronis', 'macaronies', even 'macoroni'. For consistency, I adopt the more common 'macaroni', which also functions as a plural throughout my text, unless citing a primary source.

2   It continued to circulate: the macaroni were described and illustrated by a nineteenth-century drawing in the weekly magazine edited by R. Chambers, *The Book of Days*, vol. 2 (7 July 1864), pp.31–3.

3   Cited in Trevor Fawcett, 'Eighteenth-century Shops and the Luxury Trade', *Bath History*, vol. 3 (1990), p.65.

4   The English referred to North Americans as 'macaroni' in printed caricatures in 1774: see Carington Bowles (pub.), *A New Method of Macarony Making, as Practised at Boston in North America*, 12 October 1774, in which two Bostonians tar-and-feather a customs officer.

5   Paul Langford, *A Polite and Commercial People: England 1727–1783* (Oxford: Oxford University Press, 1989), p.577.

6   Sword-knots were sometimes distributed to members of the French aristocratic wedding party. See Kimberly Chrisman-Campbell, *Fashion Victims: Dress at the Court of Louis XVI and Marie-Antoinette* (New Haven and London: Yale University Press, 2015), p.87.

7   Courtesy of Edward Maeder.

8   Daniel Roche, *The Culture of Clothing*, trans. Jean Birrell (Cambridge: Cambridge University Press, 1994 [1989]), p.91.

9   François Boucher, *A History of Costume in the West*, trans. John Ross (new edn, London: Thames and Hudson, 1987 [1966]), p.291.

10   Kaja Silverman, 'Fragments of a Fashionable Discourse', in Tania Modleski (ed.), *Studies in Entertainment: Critical Approaches to Mass Culture* (Bloomington: Indiana University Press, 1986), p.139.

11   Kaja Silverman, *Male Subjectivity at the Margins* (New York and London: Routledge, 1992).

12   Joseph Monteyne, *From Still Life to the Screen: Print Culture, Display, and the Materiality of the Image in Eighteenth-century London* (New Haven and London: Yale University Press, 2013).

13   Wilmarth S. Lewis (ed.), *The Yale Edition of Horace Walpole's Correspondence*, 48 vols (New Haven and London: Yale University Press, 1937–83), vol. 38, p.306.

14   Karin Tetteris, 'Pocket Watch with Châtelaine', in Lena Rangström (ed.), *Lions of Fashion: Male Fashion of the 16th, 17th, 18th Centuries (Modelejon Manligt Mode: 1500-tal, 1600-tal, 1700-tal)* (Stockholm: Livrustkammaren Atlantis, 2002), p.389.

15   Courtesy of Peter Finer, London.

16   David Cast, 'Review of Viccy Coltman, *Classical Sculpture and the Culture of Collecting in Britain since 1760. Classical Presences*', *Bryn Mawr Classical Review* (March 2010) <http://bmcr.brynmawr.edu/2010/2010-03-46.html> [Accessed 5 October 2015].

17   Patrik Steorn, 'Migrating Motifs and Productive Instabilities: Images of Fashion in Eighteenth-century Swedish Print Culture', *Konsthistorisk tidskrift/Journal of Art History*, vol. 82, no. 3 (September 2013), pp.219–34.

18   Patrik Steorn, 'Object in Focus', *Fashioning the Early Modern*, <http://www.fashioningtheearlymodern.ac.uk/object-in-focus/swedish-faience-tray/> [Accessed 5 September 2015].

19   Peter McNeil and Patrik Steorn, 'The Medium of Print and the Rise of Fashion in the West', *Konsthistorisk tidskrift/Journal of Art History*, vol. 82, no. 3 (September 2013), pp.135–56.

20   Gillian Russell, *Women, Sociability and Theatre in Georgian London* (Cambridge: Cambridge University Press, 2007), p.109.

21   Aileen Ribeiro, 'The Macaronis', *History Today*, vol. 28, no. 7 (July 1978), pp.463–8; Valerie Steele, 'The Social and Political Significance of Macaroni Fashion', *Costume*, vol. 19, no. 1 (1985), pp.94–109; Peter McNeil, 'Macaroni Masculinities', *Fashion Theory*, vol. 4, no. 4 (2000), pp.373–404; Peter McNeil, '"That Doubtful Gender": Macaroni Dress and Male Sexualities', *Fashion Theory*, vol. 3, no. 4 (1999), pp.411–47; Amelia Faye Rauser, 'Hair, Authenticity, and the Self-made Macaroni', *Eighteenth-century Studies*, vol. 38, no. 1 (2004), pp.101–17.

22   Aileen Ribeiro, *The Art of Dress: Fashion in England and France 1750–1820* (New Haven and London: Yale University Press, 1995).

23   Diana Donald, *The Age of Caricature: Satirical Prints in the Reign of George III* (New Haven and London: Yale University Press, 1996); Miles Ogborn, 'Locating the Macaroni: Luxury, Sexuality and Vision in Vauxhall Gardens', *Textual Practice*, vol. 11, no. 3 (1997), pp.445–61; Shearer West, 'The Darly Macaroni Prints and the Politics of Private Man', *Eighteenth-century Life*, vol. 25, no. 2 (2001), pp.170–82.

24   Russell, *Women, Sociability and Theatre*.

25   Aileen Ribeiro, 'Re-fashioning Art: Some Visual Approaches to the Study of the History of Dress', *Fashion Theory*, vol. 2, no. 4 (December 1998), pp.315–26.

26   Costumes were by Jenny Beavan.

27   Natalie Rothstein, 'The Excellence of English Brocades', in Regula Schorta and Natalie Rothstein (eds), *Seidengewebe des*

18. Jahrhunderts: Die Industrien in England und in Nordeuropa
(Riggisberg: Abegg-Stiftung, 2000), p.230.

28 Ibid., p.20.

29 Michael Snodin, 'Interiors and Ornament', in John Harris and
Michael Snodin (eds), *Sir William Chambers: Architect to George III*
(New Haven and London: Yale University Press, 1996), p.148.

30 Carolyn Sargentson, *Merchants and Luxury Markets: The
Marchands Merciers of Eighteenth-century Paris* (London: V&A,
1996), p.125.

31 [Louis-Antoine de Caraccioli], *Dictionnaire Critique, Pittoresque et
Sentencieux, propre à faire connoître les usages du siècle, ainsi que ses
bisarreries* (Lyons: Benoît Duplain, 1768), vol. 2, p.1.

32 Meredith Chilton, 'The Spaghetti Eaters', *Metropolitan Museum
Journal*, vol. 37 (2002), pp.223–9.

33 Peter Burke, *Popular Culture in Early Modern Europe* (London:
Temple Smith, 1978), p.185.

34 Chilton, 'The Spaghetti Eaters', p.227.

35 Juliet Fleming, *Graffiti and the Writing Arts of Early Modern
England* (London: Reaktion Books, 2001), p.163.

36 Cited in Karl Beckson, 'Aesthetics and Eros in Wilde' [review of
Patricia Flanagan Behrendt, *Oscar Wilde: Eros and Aesthetics*],
English Literature in Translation, 1880–1920, vol. 36, no. 2 (1993),
p.212.

37 *London Magazine*, vol. 97, no. 41 (April 1772), pp.192–4. BM.

38 Elizabeth Currie, *Fashion and Masculinity in Renaissance Florence*
(London: Bloomsbury, 2016).

39 Moe Meyer (ed.), *The Politics and Poetics of Camp* (London and
New York: Routledge, 1994).

Chapter 2

1 Frederic George Stephens and Edward Hawkins, *Catalogue of
Prints and Drawings in the British Museum. Division I. Political and
Personal Satires*, vol. 4, 1761–*c.*1770 (London: Trustees of the British
Museum, 1883) [hereafter FGS], p.cviii.

2 E.H. Gombrich, 'The Cartoonist's Armoury', lecture given at Duke
University, 1962, in *Meditations on a Hobby Horse* (4th edn, London:
Phaidon, 1985), p.127.

3 The painting shows Patch himself climbing the Venus, as well as a
caricature of Sir Horace Mann. See F.J.B. Watson, 'Thomas Patch
(1725–1782): Notes on his Life, together with a catalogue of his
known works', special printing as published in *Walpole Society*, vol.
27 (1939–40), pp.15–50. LWL Quarto 75.P27.S940 Extra Ill.

4 Brinsley Ford, 'Thomas Patch: A Newly Discovered Painting',
Apollo, vol. 77 (March 1963), p.173.

5 *Darly's Comic Prints*, vol. III (1772). *Darly's Comic Prints*, vol. V. LWL.

6 George Paston [pseudonym of Miss E.M. Symonds], *Social
Caricature in the Eighteenth Century* (London: Methuen, 1905).

7 M. Dorothy George, *London Life in the Eighteenth Century*
(Harmondsworth: Penguin, 1966 [1925]); *England in Johnson's Day*
(London: Methuen, 1928); *Hogarth to Cruikshank: Social Change in
Graphic Satire* (London: Allen Lane/Penguin, 1967).

8 Shearer West, *The Image of the Actor: Verbal and Visual
Representation in the Age of Garrick and Kemble* (New York:
St Martin's Press, 1991).

9 Cited in FGS, p.827.

10 *Town and Country Magazine*, vol. 4 (March 1772), pp.151–2.

11 Philip Carter, 'An "Effeminate" or "Efficient" Nation? Masculinity
and Eighteenth-century Social Documentary', *Textual Practice*,
vol. 11, no. 3 (1997), p.430.

12 Randolph Trumbach, 'The Birth of the Queen: Sodomy and the
Emergence of Gender Equality in Modern Culture, 1660–1750', in
Martin Bauml Duberman, Martha Vicinus and George Chauncey
Jr (eds), *Hidden from History: Reclaiming the Gay and Lesbian Past*
(London: Penguin, 1991 [New American Library, 1989]), p.134.

13 Carter, 'An "Effeminate" or "Efficient" Nation?', p.438.

14 *A Hieroglyphic Epistle from a (Macaroni) to a Modern Fine (Lady)*,
25 May 1772; *The Answer: An Hieroglyphic Epistle from a (Macaroni)
to a Modern Fine (Lady) to a Maccaroni*, invented and published by
Wm Tringham, 20 June 1772, cited in M. Dorothy George, *Catalogue
of Political and Personal Satires Preserved in the Department of
Prints and Drawings in the British Museum*, vol. 5, 1771–83 (London:
Trustees of the British Museum, 1935) [hereafter DG], 5079, 5080.

15 *The Bottle and Friends Garland, containing Four Excellent New
Songs . . . V. The Macaroni* (n.p.: n.d. [*c.*1765]).

16 Anon., *The Macaroni Jester, and Pantheon of Wit . . .* (London:
J. Cooke et al., n.d. [*c.*1773]).

17 Daniel Roche, *The Culture of Clothing*, trans. Jean Birrell
(Cambridge: Cambridge University Press, 1994); Lorna Weatherill,
Consumer Behaviour and Material Culture in Britain, 1660–1760
(London and New York: Routledge, 1996 [1988]). See also Neil
McKendrick, John Brewer and J.H. Plumb, *The Birth of a Consumer
Society: The Commercialization of Eighteenth-century England*
(Bloomington: Indiana University Press, 1982); John Brewer and
Roy Porter (eds), *Consumption and the World of Goods* (London:
Routledge, 1993); Ann Bermingham and John Brewer (eds), *The
Consumption of Culture 1600–1800: Image, Object, Text* (London and
New York: Routledge, 1995).

18 *Universal Magazine of Knowledge and Pleasure* (October 1772),
p.209.

19 *London Chronicle* (4–6 January 1757), 1.22c. LWL card catalogue.

20 Analysis courtesy of Giorgio Riello.

21 G.J. Barker-Benfield, *The Culture of Sensibility: Sex and Society
in Eighteenth-century Britain* (Chicago and London: University
of Chicago Press, 1992), p.176.

22 Anne Buck, *Dress in Eighteenth-century England* (New York:
Holmes & Meier, 1979), p.100.

23 R. Campbell, *The London Tradesman* (1747), cited in Trevor
Fawcett, 'Eighteenth-century Shops and the Luxury Trade', *Bath
History*, vol. 3 (1990), p.57.

24 Christopher Anstey, *Liberality; or, The Decayed Macaroni.
A Sentimental Piece* (London: Dodsley, Robson, Cadell and Dilly,
n.d. [*c.*1788]); *The New Bath Guide: or, Memoirs of the B--R--D
Family. In a Series of Poetical Epistles* (7th edn, London: J. Dodsley,
1770); *The New Bath Guide*, Introduction and notes by Gavin
Turner (Bristol: Broadcast Books, 1994 [1766]); *An Election Ball*,
Introduction and notes by Gavin Turner (Bristol: Broadcast Books,
1994 [1766]).

25 Illustrated in Fawcett, 'Eighteenth-century Shops and the Luxury
Trade', fig. 2.

26 George, *London Life*, p.37.

27 Ibid., p.29.

28   Anon., *The Man of Manners: or, Plebeian Polished . . .* (London: printed for J. Roberts, n.d.), p.11.

29   C. Jenner, *Time was in Town Eclogues* (2nd edn, 1773), cited in George, *England in Johnson's Day*, pp.166–7.

30   Wayne Dynes, *Homolexis: A Historical and Cultural Lexicon of Homosexuality,* Gai Saber Monograph no. 4 (New York: Gay Academic Union, 1985), p.33.

31   R. Chambers (ed.), *The Book of Days*, vol. 2 (7 July 1864), p.32.

32   *Universal Magazine* (October 1772), p.209.

33   'Masquerade Intelligence', *Macaroni, Scavoir Vivre, and Theatrical Magazine* (February 1774), p.205.

34   Hannah Greig, *The Beau Monde: Fashionable Society in Georgian London* (Oxford: Oxford University Press, 2013), pp.43–4.

35   Coloured hair can be clearly seen in the portrait miniatures of men and women by John Smart, some of which were painted in India.

36   Lynn M. Festa, 'Personal Effects: Wigs and Possessive Individualism in the Long Eighteenth Century', *Eighteenth-century Life*, vol. 29, no. 2 (2005), p.59.

37   Michael Kwass, 'Big Hair: A Wig History of Consumption in Eighteenth-century France', *American Historical Review*, vol. 3, no. 3 (2006), pp.631–59.

38   Mikkel Pedersen, 'Status', in Peter McNeil (ed.), *A Cultural History of Dress and Fashion in the Age of the Enlightenment* (London and New York: Bloomsbury, 2017), pp.123–38.

39   Festa, 'Personal Effects', p.52.

40   Diary and account book of a minor aristocrat, resident south of Avignon, France, 1753–78. MS, private collection, France.

41   Sophie Von La Roche, *Sophie in London, 1786: Being the Diary of Sophie V. La Roche*, trans. Clare Williams (London: Jonathan Cape, 1933 [1786]), p.80.

42   Susan M. Radcliffe (ed.), *Sir Joshua's Nephew: Being Letters Written, 1769–1778, by a Young Man to His Sisters* (London: John Murray, 1930), pp.92–3.

43   Ibid., p.96.

44   Ibid., p.119.

45   Alfred Spencer (ed.), *Memoirs of William Hickey*, vol. 1, 1749–75 (London: Hurst and Blackett, 1919), p.56.

46   Wilmarth S. Lewis (ed.), *The Yale Edition of Horace Walpole's Correspondence*, 48 vols (New Haven and London: Yale University Press, 1937–83), vol. 37, p.250.

47   Walpole to Henry Seymour Conway, 9 July 1775, ibid., vol. 39, p.250.

48   B.C. Walpole, *Recollections of the Life of the Late Right Honorable Charles James Fox . . .* (London: James Cundee, 1806), p.23. For songs and satires, see George Otto Trevelyan, *The Early History of Charles James Fox* (London: Longmans, Green and Co., 1880), p.484.

49   Trevelyan, *Early History of Charles James Fox*, p.484.

50   Stanley Ayling, *Fox: The Life of Charles James Fox* (London: John Murray, 1991), p.38.

51   Daniel O'Quinn, *Staging Governance: Theatrical Imperialism in London, 1770–1800* (Baltimore: Johns Hopkins University Press, 2005), pp.68–9.

52   Cited in Trevelyan, *Early History of Charles James Fox*, pp.483–4.

53   Sheila O'Connell, *The Popular Print in England 1550–1850* (exh. cat., British Museum, London, 1999), p.132.

54   *London Magazine*, cited in O'Quinn, *Staging Governance*, p.67.

55   Lewis (ed.), *Walpole's Correspondence*, vol. 38, p.306, notes 4–5.

56   E. Beresford Chancellor, *The XVIIIth Century in London: An Account of Its Social Life and Arts* (London: B.T. Batsford, n.d.[1920]), p.120.

57   Ayling, *Fox*, p.37.

58   Gillian Russell, *Women, Sociability and Theatre in Georgian London* (Cambridge: Cambridge University Press, 2007), p.65.

59   Ibid.

60   Ibid.

61   'Etchings by Henry William Bunbury, Esq. and After His Designs: Horace Walpole's scrapbook collection of 280 etchings, prints and drawings in the Lewis Walpole Library', 2 vols, fol. 49/3563./v.1.2, at p. 2. LWL 765 0 85dr.

62   Walpole to Lord Harcourt, 27 July 1773, in Lewis (ed.), *Walpole's Correspondence*, vol. 35, p.458.

63   Cited in FGS, p.826.

64   A.M.W. Stirling, *Annals of a Yorkshire House from the Papers of a Macaroni and His Kindred* (London: John Lane, 1911), vol. 1, p.323.

65   *Bon Ton* (November 1791), p.357.

66   Walpole to Lord Hertford, 8 June 1764, in Lewis (ed.), *Walpole's Correspondence*, vol. 38, p.401.

67   Walpole to Lord Hertford, 25 November 1764, ibid., p.470.

68   Walpole to the Countess of Upper Ossory, 19 February 1774, ibid., vol. 32, p.191.

69   Walpole to Revd William Mason, 3 April 1775, ibid., vol. 28, p.186.

70   *Matrimonial Magazine* (March 1775), vol. 1, pp.138–9, cited in Lewis (ed.), *Walpole's Correspondence*, vol. 32, p.191, note 8.

71   Radcliffe (ed.), *Sir Joshua's Nephew*, pp.40–41.

72   On the portrait, see Susan Legouix Sloman, '"The immaculate Captain Wade": "Arbiter Elegantiae"', *Gainsborough's House Review* (1993–4).

73   Chesterfield to Henrietta, Countess of Suffolk, 2 November 1734, cited in *New Monthly Magazine and Literary Journal*, vol. 10 (1824), p.543.

74   Susan Sloman, *Gainsborough in Bath* (New Haven and London: Paul Mellon Centre for Studies in British Art and Yale University Press, 2002), p.12.

75   Holkham Hall was commenced in 1730 and took 30 years to build.

76   Hugh Montgomery-Massingberd and Christopher Simon Sykes, *Great Houses of England and Wales* (London: Laurence King, 1994), pp.339–40.

77   Aileen Ribeiro, *The Art of Dress: Fashion in England and France 1750–1820* (New Haven and London: Yale University Press, 1995), pp.203–13.

78   J. Paul Getty Museum <http://www.getty.edu/art/collection/objects/129840/jean-etienne-liotard-portrait-of-john-lord-mountstuart-later-4th-earl-and-1st-marquess-of-bute-swiss-1763/> [Accessed September 2015].

79   Spencer (ed.), *Memoirs of William Hickey*, p.280.

80   Jean Cuisenier (ed.), *Costume, coutume* (exh. cat., Grand Palais, Paris, 1987), p.178 and figs 33–4.

81   'Monday Dec 22, 1788 [Kew] During this day H. My . . . took a dislike to a Picture which hung in his room. It was the School of Florence by Zoffany. He had it immediately off the Nails on the Floor before he was perceived to be busy with it. The picture was removed into the Next room.' *The Diaries of Robert Fulke Greville* (1930), p.130, tipped in opposite p.28 of F.J.B. Watson, 'Thomas Patch (1725–1782)'

Watson himself affixed this page in the extra-illustrated copy of the journal.

82 Greig, *The Beau Monde*.

83 Aileen Ribeiro, *Dress in Eighteenth-century Europe, 1715–1789* (London: B.T. Batsford, 1984), p.142. See also C. Willett Cunnington and Phillis Cunnington, *Handbook of English Costume in the Eighteenth Century* (Boston: Plays Inc., 1972 [1964]).

84 Natalie Rothstein (ed.), *Four Hundred Years of Fashion* (London: V&A, 1984), p.58.

85 An example is held at Spencer House, London.

86 Guy Chaussinand-Nogaret, *The French Nobility in the Eighteenth Century: From Feudalism to Enlightenment,* trans. William Doyle (Cambridge: Cambridge University Press, 1985), p.120.

87 Illustrated in Henry René d'Allemagne, *Les Accessoires du costume et du mobilier, depuis le treizième jusqu'au milieu du dixneuvième siècle* (Paris: Schemit, 1928), vol. 1, pl. CCCIV.

88 Walpole to Revd William Mason, 3 September 1773, in Lewis (ed.), *Walpole's Correspondence*, vol. 28, p.105.

89 9 August 1773, ibid., vol. 32, p.136.

90 FGS 4852.

91 E.P. Thompson, *Customs in Common* (London: Penguin, 1993 [1991]), p.55.

92 Walpole to Horace Mann, 13 July 1773, in Lewis (ed.), *Walpole's Correspondence*, vol. 23, pp.498–9.

93 Ibid., p.499.

94 Walpole to the Countess of Upper Ossory, 29 September 1777, ibid., vol. 32, p.382.

95 Paget Toynbee (ed.), *Satirical Poems Published Anonymously by William Mason with Notes by Horace Walpole, Now First Printed from His Manuscript* (Oxford: Clarendon Press, 1926), pp. 69–70; see also Lewis (ed.), *Walpole's Correspondence*, vol. 10, p.139, note 11.

96 '"Little master" (fop). It is above all capriciousness and futilities, who takes all sorts of faces and who appears in I don't know how many combinations of colours. He is at the gambling, at festivities, at the court, in the town, on the streets, at the Palais-Royal; the sort that one sees everywhere at the same time, and it's his passion to multiply himself' [my translation]. [Louis-Antoine de Caraccioli], *Dictionnaire Critique, Pittoresque et Sentencieux, propre à faire connoître les usages du siècle, ainsi que ses bisarreries* (Lyons: Benoît Duplain, 1768), vol. 2, pp.6–7.

97 Thompson, *Customs in Common*, p.67.

98 James Peller Malcolm, *Anecdotes of the Manners and Customs of London, during the Eighteenth Century*, 2 vols (London: Longman, Hurst, Rees and Orme, 1808–11), pp.219–20.

99 Kimberly Chrisman, *'L'émigration à la mode*: Clothing Worn and Produced by the French Émigré Community in England from the Revolution to the Restoration', MA dissertation (Courtauld Institute of Art, History of Dress, 1997).

100 Walpole to Sir William Hamilton, 22 February 1774, in Lewis (ed.), *Walpole's Correspondence*, vol. 35, p.419.

101 *Fashion in Colors: Viktor & Rolf and KCI* (exh. cat., Kyoto Costume Institute, 2004), p.17.

102 John Brewer, cited in Thompson, *Customs in Common*, p.89.

103 Thompson, *Customs in Common*, pp.45–6.

104 Greig, *The Beau Monde*, p.254.

105 Mark Motley, *Becoming a French Aristocrat: The Education of the Court Nobility, 1580–1715* (Princeton: Princeton University Press, 1990).

106 Siegfried Wenzel, *Macaronic Sermons: Bilingualism and Preaching in Late-medieval England* (Ann Arbor: University of Michigan Press, 1994), pp.2–3.

107 Ibid., p.4.

108 Ibid., pp.3–4.

109 [W. Sandys (ed.)], *Specimens of Macaronic Poetry* (London: Richard Beckley, 1831).

110 Joseph Addison, *The Spectator*, no. 47, cited in Robert Gordon Latham, *A Dictionary of the English Language* (London: n.p., 1870), vol. 2, part 1, p.140.

111 *A Book of Caricatures on 59 Copper Plates, with Ye Principles of Designing, in that Droll and pleasing manner, by M. Darly . . . Printed for R. Wilkinson, Cornhill* [1763]. LWL 779 0 42.

112 Stirling, *Annals*, p.322.

113 LWL card cat., typed and dated 30 March 1949.

114 Terry Castle, *Masquerade and Civilization: The Carnivalesque in Eighteenth-century English Culture and Fiction* (Stanford: Stanford University Press, 1986), p.36.

115 'The Transformation', in *The Merry Andrew; or, Macaroni Jester. A Choice Collection of Funny Jokes, Merry Stories, Droll Adventures, Frolicksome Tales, Witty Quibbles, Youthful Pranks . . .* (London: n.p., 1786), pp.50–51.

116 [C. Plunkett], Lord Dunsany, *If I Were Dictator: The Pronouncements of the Grand Macaroni* (London: Methuen, 1934).

Chapter 3

1 In Wilmarth S. Lewis (ed.), *The Yale Edition of Horace Walpole's Correspondence*, 48 vols (New Haven and London: Yale University Press, 1937–83), vol. 25, p.23.

2 John Money, 'The Masonic Moment: Or, Ritual, Replica, and Credit: John Wilkes, the Macaroni Parson, and the Making of the Middle-class Mind', *Journal of British Studies*, vol. 32 (1993), p.360.

3 Bernard M. Watney, 'Origins of Designs for English Ceramics of the Eighteenth Century', *Burlington Magazine*, vol. 114, no. 837 (December 1972), p.825.

4 Herbert M. Atherton, *Political Prints in the Age of Hogarth: A Study of the Ideographic Representation of Politics* (Oxford: Clarendon Press, 1974), pp.18–19.

5 From an engraved page placed after the title page of Darly's macaroni prints, cited in DG, p.xxxiv.

6 Diana Donald, *The Age of Caricature: Satirical Prints in the Reign of George III* (New Haven and London: Yale University Press, 1996), p.3.

7 Joseph Monteyne, *From Still Life to the Screen: Print Culture, Display, and the Materiality of the Image in Eighteenth-century London* (New Haven and London: Yale University Press, 2013), pp.87–115.

8 FGS, p.786.

9 We find this physiognomy in Edward Newenham's etching *Le Chercheur de 20 pr cent* of *c.*1771 [DG 4926], of which Dorothy George wrote: 'He has a long nose and pendulous under-lip . . . He is probably a Jew'. DG, p.44. Darly's hump-backed and ugly hairdressers are related to an earlier English print tradition, for example *The Morning Tast; or Fanny M—'s Maid, washing her Toes,*

*c.*1733 [Fanny Milton], illustrated in Charles Saumarez Smith, *Eighteenth-century Decoration: Design and the Domestic Interior in England* (London: Weidenfeld and Nicolson, 1993), p.109, plate 93.

10 The Abbé Luigi Lanzi (1732–1809), author of *History of Painting in Italy*, cited in Michael N. Benisovich, 'Ghezzi and the French Artists in Rome', *Apollo* (May 1967), p.347.

11 Ibid., pp.340–47.

12 Bookseller's description, pasted in G.C. Walter [*sic*], *Recueil de quelques dessins de plusieurs habiles maitres, tirés du cabinet de Mr le comte de Brühl, a Dresde* (1752) [49 engraved caricatures]. LWL. See also G.C. Walther [*sic*], 'Ghezzi', *Raccolta di XXIV Caricatura* (Dresden: 1750). LWL.

13 Benisovich, 'Ghezzi and the French Artists', p.340.

14 Cited in ibid., p.342.

15 John Brewer, *The Common People and Politics, 1750–1790s* (Cambridge: Chadwyck-Healey, 1986), p.21.

16 Alicia Kerfoot, 'Declining Buckles and Movable Shoes in Frances Burney's *Cecilia*', *Burney Journal*, vol. 11 (2011), pp.55–6.

17 *Morning Post* (14 January 1777), cited in DG, p.236.

18 On the comte d'Artois, see J. Quicherat, *Histoire du costume en France depuis les temps les plus reculés jusqu'à la fin du XVIIIe siècle* (Paris: Hachette, 1875), p.604. On pornographic and rebus buttons, see Louis Petit de Bachaumont, 'Les Mémoires secrets', in Henry-René d'Allemagne, *Les Accessoires du costume et du mobilier…* (Paris: Chez Schemit, 1928), p.59.

19 *Indispensables accessoires XVIe–XXe siècle* (exh. cat., Musée de la Mode et du Costume, Paris, 1983), p.117.

20 George Otto Trevelyan, *The Early History of Charles James Fox* (London: Longmans, Green and Co., 1880), p.64.

21 Stella Tillyard, *Aristocrats: Caroline, Emily, Louisa, and Sarah Lennox 1740–1832* (New York: Farrar, Straus and Giroux, 1994).

22 Letter, unknown correspondent to Lord Ilchester, 8 September 1763, in Leslie George Mitchell, *Charles James Fox* (Oxford: Oxford University Press, 1992), p.9.

23 Lord Holland to Sir G. Macartney, 30 June 1766, ibid., p.10.

24 B.C. Walpole, *Recollections of the Life of the Late Right Honorable Charles James Fox…* (London: James Cundee, 1806), p.14.

25 Alexander Dyce, *Reminiscences and Table-talk of Samuel Rogers* (London: R. Brimley Johnson, 1903), pp.72–3. On Fox as a macaroni, see also G.H. Powell, *Reminiscences and Table-talk of Samuel Rogers: Banker, Poet and Patron of the Arts 1763–1855…* (London: R. Brimley Johnson, 1903), p.42.

26 Walpole, *Recollections*, p.24.

27 Sir N.W. Wraxall, *Historical Memoirs of His Own Time*, vol. 2 (new edn, London: Richard Bentley, 1836), p.229.

28 *The Life of the Right Honorable Charles James Fox, Late Principal Secretary of State for Foreign Affairs…* (London: Albion Press, 1807), p.18.

29 A.M.W. Stirling, *Annals of a Yorkshire House from the Papers of a Macaroni and His Kindred*, 2 vols (London: John Lane, 1911), vol. 1, p.323.

30 Report on 'His Majesty's Birthday', *Bon Ton* (June 1791), pp.141–2.

31 John Heneage Jesse, *George Selwyn and His Contemporaries; with Memoirs and Notes* (London: Richard Bentley, 1843), vol. 2, p.113.

32 Edward Maeder, 'Made in England? An 18th-century Trade Embargo of Foreign Embroidery Raises Interesting Questions about the Meaning of "Foreign"', *Rotunda: The Magazine of the Royal Ontario Museum*, vol. 30, no. 3 (Spring 1998), pp.34–40. On the smuggling of silks, see Natalie Rothstein, 'Nine English Silks', *Bulletin of the Needle and Bobbin Club*, vol. 48, nos 1–2 (1964), p.21; William Farrell, 'Smuggling Silks into Eighteenth-century Britain: Geography, Perpetrators, and Consumers', *Journal of British Studies*, vol. 55, no. 2 (2016), pp.268–94.

33 Maeder, 'Made in England?', p.38.

34 Natalie Rothstein (ed.), *Barbara Johnson's Album of Fashions and Fabrics* (London: Thames and Hudson, 1987), p.30.

35 Walpole, *Recollections*, p.27.

36 The bill and suit are in the City of Birmingham Museum. See C. Willett Cunnington and Phillis Cunnington, *Handbook of English Costume in the Eighteenth Century* (Boston: Plays Inc., 1972 [1964]), p.15.

37 Susan Sloman, *Gainsborough in Bath* (New Haven and London: Paul Mellon Centre for Studies in British Art and Yale University Press, 2002), p.213.

38 Stirling, *Annals*, vol. 1, p.326.

39 Alfred Spencer (ed.), *Memoirs of William Hickey*, vol. 1, 1749–75 (London: Hurst and Blackett, 1919), p.140.

40 Ian Dunlop, *Marie Antoinette: A Portrait* (London: Phoenix, 1993), p.75.

41 Walpole, *Recollections*, p.7.

42 Lars E. Troide (ed.), *The Early Journals and Letters of Fanny Burney*, vol. 2, 1774–7 (Oxford: Clarendon, 1990).

43 Garrick to Jean-Baptiste Antoine Suard, 21 August 1770, in David M. Little, George M. Kahrl (eds) and Phoebe deK. Wilson (associate ed.), *The Letters of David Garrick*, 3 vols (Oxford: Oxford University Press, 1963), pp.708–9.

44 Mitchell, *Charles James Fox*, p.140.

45 Wraxall, *Historical Memoirs*, p.229.

46 Mitchell, *Charles James Fox*, p.140.

47 Walpole, *Recollections*, p.101; Wraxall, *Historical Memoirs*, p.229.

48 Brewer, *The Common People and Politics*, p.31.

49 Walpole, *Recollections*, pp.iv–v.

50 John Gascoigne, *Joseph Banks and the English Enlightenment: Useful Knowledge and Polite Culture* (Cambridge: Cambridge University Press, 1994), p.61.

51 Julien Domercq, 'Collecting the Pacific', *Apollo* (July–August 2015), p.60.

52 J.A. Home (ed.), *The Letters and Journals of Lady Mary Coke* (Bath: Kingsmead Reprints, 1970), vol. 4, p.435.

53 Gascoigne, *Joseph Banks*, p.62.

54 Aileen Ribeiro, 'Portraying the Fashion, Romancing the Past: Dress and the Cosways', in Stephen Lloyd (ed.), *Richard and Maria Cosway: Regency Artists of Taste and Fashion* (exh. cat., Scottish National Portrait Gallery, Edinburgh, 1995), pp.101–5.

55 Rica Jones and Martin Postle, 'Gainsborough in His Painting Room', in Michael Rosenthal and Martin Myrone (eds), *Gainsborough* (exh. cat., Tate Britain, London, 2002), p.36.

56 Graham Reynolds, *English Portrait Miniatures* (Cambridge: Cambridge University Press, 1988), p.126.

57 I thank Professor Richard Read for his useful comments here.

58 FGS 713.

59 I thank Professor Read again at this point.

60 Eirwen E.C. Nicolson, 'English Political Prints and Pictorial

Argument *c.*1640–*c.*1832: A Study in Historiography and Methodology', PhD thesis (University of Edinburgh, 1994).

61 The matter of coloured prints is complicated, as washes might be added later. However, prints were also often coloured at the time of their sale. The colourists of the first French fashion periodicals were sometimes named and promoted as a selling point.

62 Diana Donald, *Followers of Fashion: Graphic Satires from the Georgian Period* (exh. cat., Hayward Gallery, London, 2002), p.10.

63 *The Macaroni Jester, and Pantheon of Wit; containing All that has lately transpired in the Regions of Politeness, Whim, and Novelty; Including A singular Variety of Jests, Witticisms, Bon-Mots, Conundrums, Toasts, Acrosticks, &c. – with Epigrams and Epitaphs, of the laughable Kind, and Strokes of Humour hitherto unequalled; which have never appeared in a Book of the Kind* (London: J. Cooke et al., n.d. [1773]), p.85.

64 George C. Williamson, *Richard Cosway R.A.* (London: George Bell & Sons, 1905), pp.101–2.

65 Fredk [*sic*] B. Daniell, *A catalogue raisonné of the Engraved Works of Richard Cosway, RA, with a memoir of Cosway by Sir Philip Currie* (London: Frederick B. Daniell, 1890), p.x.

66 Henry Angelo, in Lloyd (ed.), *Richard and Maria Cosway*, p.31.

67 Gerald Howson, *The Macaroni Parson: The Life of the Unfortunate Doctor Dodd* (London: Hutchinson, 1973), pp.60–65.

68 Money, 'The Masonic Moment', pp.359, 381.

69 George Winchester Stone Jr and George M. Kahrl, *David Garrick: A Critical Biography* (Carbondale and Edwardsville: Southern Illinois University Press, 1979), p.456.

70 Ibid., pp.456–7.

71 Ibid., p.366.

72 Alan Kendall, *David Garrick: A Biography* (London: Harrap, 1985), p.100.

73 On furnishings, see Christopher Gilbert, *The Life and Work of Thomas Chippendale* (New York: Tabard Press, 1978), p.48.

74 Gretchen Gerzina, *Black England: Life before Emancipation* (London: John Murray, 1995), p.55.

75 Sukhdev Sandhu, 'Ignatius Sancho: An African Man of Letters', in Reyahn King, Sukhdev Sandhu, Jane Girdham and James Walvin (eds), *Ignatius Sancho: An African Man of Letters* (London: National Portrait Gallery, 1997), p.51.

76 Gerzina, *Black England*, p.56.

77 Ibid., p.47.

78 James Walvin, 'Ignatius Sancho: The Man and His Times', in King et al. (eds), *Ignatius Sancho*, p.97.

79 FGS 500. Stephens notes that American black men were associated with tight-fitting striped dress at this time.

80 Caryl Phillips, Foreword, in King et al. (eds), *Ignatius Sancho*, p.13.

81 Michael Rosenthal and Martin Myrone, 'Thomas Gainsborough: Art, Society, Sociability', in Rosenthal and Myrone (eds), *Gainsborough*, p.25.

Chapter 4

1 John Heneage Jesse, *George Selwyn and His Contemporaries; with Memoirs and Notes* (London: Richard Bentley, 1843), vol. 2, p.112. Selwyn was a contemporary and friend of Horace Walpole.

2 'There is no country in the universe where fashion reigns with such

authority as in France.' François-Charles Gaudet, *Bibliotheque des Petits-Maitres, ou Mémoires pour servir à l'histoire du bon ton & de l'extrêmement bonne compagnie* (Paris: Palais-Royal, Chez la petite Lolo, Marchande de Galanteries, à la Frivolité, 1762), p.28.

3 Christopher J. Berry, *The Idea of Luxury: A Conceptual and Historical Investigation* (Cambridge: Cambridge University Press, 1994); Maxine Berg, *Luxury and Pleasure in Eighteenth-century Britain* (Oxford: Oxford University Press, 2007).

4 On Italian eighteenth-century waistcoats, see Grazietta Butazzi, *Una Raccolta di sottovesti settecentesche ricamate al Castello Sforzesco* (Milan: Comune di Milano, 1976). On French waistcoats, see Pierre Arizzoli-Clémentel, *Gilets brodés: Modèles du XVIIIe* (Lyons: Musée des Tissus, 1993); Richard Davin, Introduction, in *18th-century Waistcoats* (exh. cat., Rougemont House, Museum of Costume and Lace, Exeter, 28 March–21 May 1988).

5 Victoria de Grazia, 'Introduction', in Victoria de Grazia and Ellen Furlough (eds), *The Sex of Things: Gender and Consumption in Historical Perspective* (Berkeley and London: University of California Press, 1996), pp.2, 4.

6 Jane Bridgeman, '"Condecenti et netti...": Beauty, Dress and Gender in Italian Renaissance Art', in F. Ames Lewis and M. Rogers, *Concepts of Beauty in Renaissance Art* (Aldershot: Ashgate, 1998), pp.44–6.

7 Ibid., p.46.

8 *The Spectator* (May 1711).

9 Carolyn Sargentson, *Merchants and Luxury Markets: The Marchands Merciers of Eighteenth-century Paris* (London: V&A, 1996), pp.113–15.

10 Linda Colley, *Britons: Forging the Nation 1707–1837* (London: Vintage, 1996 [1992]), Chapter 1.

11 John Andrews, *An Account of the Character and Manners of the French ...* (London: E. and C. Dilly, J. Robson, J. Walter, 1770), vol. 1, pp.68, 139. See also Aileen Ribeiro, 'Fashion in the Eighteenth Century: Some Anglo-French Comparisons', *Textile History*, vol. 22, no. 2 (Autumn 1991), pp.329–45.

12 Tobias Smollett, *Travels through France and Italy*, ed. Frank Felsenstein (Oxford: Oxford University Press, 1979 [1766]), vol. 1, p.102.

13 Philip Thicknesse, *Observations on the Customs and Manners of the French Nation ...* (London: Robert Davis, G. Kearsley, N. Young, 1766), p.25.

14 Smollett, *Travels*, vol. 1, p.97.

15 Walter Stanhope to Mrs S., Paris, 17 June 1769, cited in A.M.W. Stirling, *Annals of a Yorkshire House from the Papers of a Macaroni and His Kindred* (London: John Lane, 1911), vol. 1, p.237.

16 Smollett, *Travels*, vol. 1, p.98.

17 Dominic Janes, 'Gender and Sexuality', in Peter McNeil (ed.), *A Cultural History of Dress and Fashion in the Age of Enlightenment* (London and New York: Bloomsbury, 2017), pp.105–22.

18 *Oxford Dictionary of National Biography* (Oxford: Oxford University Press, 2004); online edn, January 2008 <http://www.oxforddnb.com/view/article/25655 [Accessed 10 October 2017].

19 Smollett, *Travels*, vol. 1, p.13.

20 The reference to 'French knavery' is in the title of Chapter 12 of *The Gentleman's Guide, in His Tour through France ...* (Bristol: S. Farley, n.d. [1766]).

21 Kimberly Chrisman-Campbell, '"He is not dressed without a muff"': Muffs, Masculinity, and *la mode* in English Satire', in Elizabeth C. Mansfield and Kelly Malone (eds), *Seeing Satire in the Eighteenth Century*, vol. 2 (Oxford: Voltaire Foundation, 2013), pp.131–44.

22 Kimberly Chrisman, '*L'émigration à la mode*: Clothing Worn and Produced by the French Émigré Community in England from the Revolution to the Restoration', MA dissertation (Courtauld Institute of Art, History of Dress, 1997), p.6.

23 Lena Rangström (ed.), *Lions of Fashion: Male Fashions of the 16th, 17th, 18th Centuries (Modelejon Manligt Mode: 1500-tal, 1600-tal, 1700-tal)* (Stockholm: Livrustkammaren Atlantis, 2002), p.319.

24 Robert Halsband, *Lord Hervey: Eighteenth-century Courtier* (Oxford: Clarendon Press, 1973), p.79.

25 *The Gentleman's Guide*, p.12.

26 Ibid., p.109.

27 Samuel Foote, *A Trip to Calais: A Comedy in Three Acts* (London: T. Sherlock, 1778), pp.21–2.

28 G.F.R. Molé, *Histoire des Modes Françaises, ou Révolutions du costume en France, depuis l'établissement de la Monarchie jusqu'à nos jours, contenant tout ce qui concerne la tête des Français, avec des recherches sur l'usage des Chevelures artificielles chez les Anciens* (Amsterdam and Paris: Costard, 1773), p.127.

29 Smollett, *Travels*, vol. 1, p.105.

30 See 'Maniere de ce faire coeffer à l'Angloise', in J. Grand-Carteret, *Les Mœurs et la caricature en France* (Paris: Librairie Illustrée, 1888), p.33.

31 Smollett, *Travels*, vol. 1, p.120.

32 David Garrioch, *The Making of Revolutionary Paris* (Berkeley: University of California Press, 2002), p.89.

33 Kimberly Chrisman-Campbell, *Fashion Victims: Dress at the Court of Louis XVI and Marie-Antoinette* (New Haven and London: Yale University Press, 2015), p.103.

34 Aileen Ribeiro, *The Art of Dress: Fashion in England and France 1750–1820* (New Haven and London: Yale University Press, 1995).

35 James Thompson, 'Jean-Baptiste Greuze', *Metropolitan Museum of Art Bulletin*, vol. 47, no. 3 (Winter 1989–90), p.27.

36 Daniel Roche, *The Culture of Clothing: Dress and Fashion in the 'Ancien Régime'*, trans. Jean Birrell (Cambridge: Cambridge University Press, 1994 [1989]), p.279.

37 Andrews, *An Account of the Character and Manners*, vol. 1, p.64.

38 Ibid., pp.65–6.

39 Ibid., p.68.

40 Ibid., p.75.

41 Ibid., vol. 2, p.287.

42 Guy Chaussinand-Nogaret, *The French Nobility in the Eighteenth Century: From Feudalism to Enlightenment*, trans. William Doyle (Cambridge: Cambridge University Press, 1985), p.58.

43 Halsband, *Lord Hervey*, p.25; George Winchester Stone Jr and George M. Kahrl, *David Garrick: A Critical Biography* (Carbondale and Edwardsville: Southern Illinois University Press, 1979), p.296.

44 Halsband, *Lord Hervey*, p.25.

45 John Carr, *The Stranger in France, or, a tour from Devonshire to Paris, illustrated by engravings in aqua tinta of sketches taken on the spot* (London: J. Johnson, 1803), p.234.

46 *Letters on the French Nation: by a Sicilian Gentleman, residing at Paris, to his friend in his own Country. Containing an useful and impartial Critique on that City, and the French Nation, translated from the original* (London: T. Lownds, 1749), pp.25–6.

47 Thicknesse, *Observations on the Customs and Manners*, p.25.

48 Carr, *The Stranger in France*, p.241.

49 Smollett, *Travels*, vol. 1, p.120.

50 *The French dancing-master and the English soldier: or, the difference betwixt fidling and fighting, displayed in a dialogue betwixt an Englishman and a Frenchman* (London: n.p. [1666]).

51 *The Baboon A-la-Mode: A Satyr against the French, by a Gentleman* (London: S. Malthus, 1704 [inscribed Jan. 1705 in a contemporary hand]), pp.4, 22.

52 Kristina Straub, *Sexual Suspects: Eighteenth-century Players and Sexual Ideology* (Princeton: Princeton University Press, 1992), pp.62–3.

53 M.L. Kekewich (ed.), *Princes and Peoples: France and the British Isles, 1620–1714* (Manchester and New York: Manchester University Press, 1994), p.158.

54 Cited in Sargentson, *Merchants and Luxury Markets*, p.114.

55 G.J. Barker-Benfield, *The Culture of Sensibility: Sex and Society in Eighteenth-century Britain* (Chicago and London: University of Chicago Press, 1992).

56 LWL card cat.

57 Stone and Kahrl, *David Garrick*, p.140.

58 David Garrick, *The Plays of David Garrick: Edited with an Introduction by Gerald M. Berkowitz* (New York and London: Garland, 1981), vol. 1, pp.16–17.

59 Anon., *The Devil upon Crutches in England, or Night Scenes in London: A Satirical Work by a Gentleman of Oxford* (London: Philip Hodges, 1755), p.4.

60 Anon., *Fashion: or, a Trip to a Foreign C--t. A Poem* (London: R. Baldwin, 1777), pp.4–14.

61 Baldassare Castiglione, *Etiquette for Renaissance Gentlemen*, trans. George Bull (abridged edn, London: Penguin, 1995 [1967]), p.10.

62 [William Darrell], *A Gentleman Instructed in the Conduct of a Virtuous and Happy Life. Written for the Instruction of a Young Nobleman* (London: E. Evets, 1704), pp.39–40.

63 Ibid., p.40.

64 Lars E. Troide (ed.), *The Early Journals and Letters of Fanny Burney*, vol. 2, 1774–7 (Oxford: Clarendon Press, 1990), p.33.

65 Fanny Burney, Letter, 1 December 1774, ibid., p.63.

66 Michèle Cohen, *Fashioning Masculinity: National Identity and Language in the Eighteenth Century* (London and New York: Routledge, 1996), p.49.

67 [Darrell], *A Gentleman Instructed*, p.45.

68 Anon., *The Gentleman's Library, Containing rules for conduct in all parts of life, written by a Gentleman* (London: W. Mears and J. Browne, 1715), pp.52–3, 59.

69 Anon., *The Man of Manners: or, Plebeian Polished . . .* (London: printed for J. Roberts, n.d.), p.12.

70 Letter, 23 March 1775, in Susan M. Radcliffe (ed.), *Sir Joshua's Nephew: Being Letters Written, 1769–1778, by a Young Man to His Sisters* (London: John Murray, 1930), p.96.

71 John Sekora, *Luxury: The Concept in Western Thought, Eden to Smollett* (Baltimore and London: Johns Hopkins University Press, 1977); Berry, *The Idea of Luxury*; Sargentson, *Merchants and Luxury Markets*; Berg, *Luxury and Pleasure*.

72 Anon., *Modern Refinement, a Satire. By the author of the Register of Folly, or, Characters and Incidents at Bath and the Hotwells; with a Trip to Bristol Vauxhall, now first added to the third edition of that poem* (Bath: S. Hazard, 1777), pp.18–19.

73 Andrews, *An Account of the Character and Manners*, pp.82–4.

74 John Andrews, *Remarks on the French and English Ladies, in a Series of Letters; Interspersed with various anecdotes, and additional matter, arising from the subject* (London: T. Longman and G. Robinson, 1783), p.345.

75 Stella Tillyard, *Aristocrats: Caroline, Emily, Louisa, and Sarah Lennox 1740–1832* (New York: Farrar, Straus and Giroux, 1994), p.205.

76 Cohen, *Fashioning Masculinity*, p.83.

77 Ralph Schomberg, *Fashion. A Poem. Addressed to the Ladies of Great-Britain. In two books. Book First* (2nd edn, London: J. Williams, 1778), p.3.

78 R. Dodsley, *Fashion: an Epistolary Satire to a Friend* (London: T. Cooper, 1742), p.6.

79 Barker-Benfield, *The Culture of Sensibility*, p.174.

80 Ibid., p.113.

81 *Tatler*, c.1710, cited in Colin McDowell, *The Literary Companion to Fashion* (London: Sinclair-Stevenson, 1995), p.23.

Chapter 5

1 [Philautus], *The Pretty Gentleman; or, Softness of Manners Vindicated From the false Ridicule exhibited under the Character of William Fribble, Esq.* (London: 1747; ed. Edmund Goldsmid, Bibliotheca Curiosa reprint, Edinburgh, 1885), p.30.

2 *London Chronicle* (9–12 April 1757), i.348. B.

3 Henri Misson, *M. Misson's Memoirs and observations in his travels over England. With some account of Scotland and Ireland. Dispos'd in alphabetical Order. Written originally in French and translated by Mr Ozell* (London: D. Browne, 1719).

4 For an overview of this historiographical debate, see Vincent Quinn and Mary Peace, 'Luxurious Sexualities', *Textual Practice*, vol. 11, no. 3 (1997), pp.405–16. See also Julie Peakman (ed.), *A Cultural History of Sexuality in the Enlightenment* (Oxford and New York: Berg, 2011).

5 Patrick Higgins (ed.), *A Queer Reader* (London: Fourth Estate, 1993), p.93.

6 Robert Halsband, *Lord Hervey: Eighteenth-century Courtier* (Oxford: Clarendon Press, 1973), p.176.

7 Cited in C. Willett Cunnington and Phillis Cunnington, *Handbook of English Costume in the Eighteenth Century* (Boston: Plays Inc., 1972 [1964]), p.15.

8 Matthew McCormack, *Embodying the Militia in Georgian England* (Oxford: Oxford University Press, 2015), p.61.

9 Lars E. Troide (ed.), *The Early Journals and Letters of Fanny Burney*, vol. 2, 1774–7 (Oxford: Clarendon Press, 1990), p.32.

10 *The Macaroni Jester, and Pantheon of Wit; containing All that has lately transpired in the Regions of Politeness, Whim, and Novelty; Including A singular Variety of Jests, Witticisms, Bon-Mots, Conundrums, Toasts, Acrosticks, &c. – with Epigrams and Epitaphs, of the laughable Kind, and Strokes of Humour hitherto unequalled; which have never appeared in a Book of the Kind* (London: J. Cooke et al., n.d. [c.1773]), p.50.

11 Ellen G. D'Oench, *'Copper into Gold': Prints by John Raphael Smith 1751–1812* (New Haven and London: Yale University Press, 1999), pp.66–8.

12 On the masquerade, see Warwick Wroth and Arthur Edgar Wroth, *The London Pleasure Gardens of the Eighteenth Century* (Hamden, CT: Archon Books, 1979 [1896]); Aileen Ribeiro, *The Dress Worn at Masquerades in England, 1730 to 1790, and Its Relation to Fancy Dress in Portraiture* (New York: Garland, 1984); Terry Castle, *The Female Thermometer: Eighteenth-century Culture and the Invention of the Uncanny* (New York and Oxford: Oxford University Press, 1995).

13 'Maquerades [*sic*]', in 'The Characters of the Public Amusements of London, concluded', *London Amusements*, vol. 27, no. 2050 (22–24 August 1770), in *The New London Spy, London Spy of 24 Hours Ramble illustrated with Curious Prints and Portraits* (London, 1760), extra-illustrated copy, 21, LWL Quarto 724/77/N.

14 Terry Castle, *Masquerade and Civilization: The Carnivalesque in Eighteenth-century English Culture and Fiction* (Stanford: Stanford University Press, 1986), p.7.

15 Amanda Vickery, 'Venice-on-Thames', *London Review of Books*, vol. 35, no. 3 (7 February 2013), pp.31–2.

16 DG, pp.73–4.

17 Henry Angelo, 'Reminiscences', cited in Norah Waugh, *The Cut of Men's Clothes, 1600–1900* (London: Faber, 1964), p.105.

18 Michel Pastoureau, *L'Étoffe du diable: Une histoire des rayures et des tissus rayés* (Paris: Éditions du Seuil, 1991).

19 'A Mask' [nom de plume], *Town and Country Magazine*, vol. 4 (May 1772), p.237.

20 Madeleine Kahn, *Narrative Transvestism: Rhetoric and Gender in the Eighteenth-century English Novel* (Ithaca, NY, and London: Cornell University Press, 1991), p.37.

21 FGS, p.714.

22 John Summerson, *Georgian London* (3rd edn, London: Barrie and Jenkins, 1978 [1945]), p.152.

23 Wayne Dynes, *Homolexis: A Historical and Cultural Lexicon of Homosexuality*, Gai Saber Monograph no. 4 (New York: Gay Academic Union, 1985), pp.28–9.

24 FGS, p.761.

25 *Short Remarks upon the Original and Pernicious Consequences of Masquerades* (1721), cited in Castle, *Masquerade and Civilization*, p.46.

26 Wayne Koestenbaum, *The Queen's Throat: Opera, Homosexuality and the Mystery of Desire* (New York: Vintage, 1994 [1993]).

27 [Philautus], *The Pretty Gentleman*, pp.15–17.

28 Cited in Aileen Ribeiro, *Dress in Eighteenth-century Europe, 1715–1789* (London: B.T. Batsford, 1984), p.142.

29 David Adshead, 'Clandon Inventory', no. 17 (typescript), courtesy of the National Trust, Clandon Park.

30 I viewed this painting in c.2003. It is listed but not illustrated in the National Trust handbook *Clandon Park, Surrey* (London: National Trust Enterprises, 2002), p.16. I was kindly sent the notes on this painting written by Alastair Laing, the National Trust's picture adviser, by the Clandon House staff. On the work, see Karen Stanworth, 'Picturing a Personal History: The Case of Edward Onslow', *Art History*, vol. 16, no. 3 (September 1993), pp.408–23. Recently some reservations have been newly expressed

by the family regarding whether the attribution is correct. In May 2013 Alison Harpur, Assistant Curator of Pictures and Sculptures, National Trust, wrote to me: 'As far as we are aware, the identification of the sitter in the dark blue jacket at the left of the portrait remains that of Edward Onslow, younger brother of the 2nd Earl, although it is recorded as tentative.' The candour of the Trust, considered by some a conservative body, in labelling this painting in such a frank manner, is to be commended.

31 James Peller Malcolm, *Anecdotes of the manners and customs of London, during the eighteenth century . . .*, 2 vols (London: Longman, Hurst, Rees and Orme, 1808–11).

32 Ibid., p.176.

33 Fanny Burney, *Evelina, or A Young Lady's Entrance into the World*, Letter X (London: 1964), p.24, cited in Valerie Steele, 'A Queer History of Fashion: From the Closet to the Catwalk', in Valerie Steele (ed.), *A Queer History of Fashion: From the Closet to the Catwalk* (New Haven and London: Yale University Press, 2013), p.9.

34 *Bon Ton* (March 1794), p.36.

35 Randolph Trumbach, 'Modern Sodomy: The Origins of Homosexuality, 1700–1800', in Matt Cook (ed.), with H.G. Cocks, Robert Mills and Randolph Trumbach, *A Gay History of Britain: Love and Sex between Men since the Middle Ages* (Oxford and Westport, CT: Greenwood World Publishing, 2007), p.89.

36 FGS, p.742.

37 Ibid., p.770.

38 Ibid., pp.cviii–cix.

39 Timothy Mowl, *Horace Walpole: The Great Outsider* (London: John Murray, 1996), pp.12, 204.

40 Laetitia Hawkins's description, cited in ibid., p.52.

41 The habit for certain Grand Tourists to be painted by Thomas Patch in Florence is not incidental here. The art historian F.J.B. Watson later made notes by hand from primary sources on the matter in the extra-illustrated copy of his 1939 article on the artist. F.J.B. Watson, 'Thomas Patch (1725–1782): Notes on his Life, together with a catalogue of his known works', special printing as published in *Walpole Society*, vol. 27 (1939–40), pp.15–50. LWL Quarto 75.P27.S940 Extra Ill.

42 FGS, pp.783–4.

43 *Macaroni, Scavoir Vivre, and Theatrical Magazine* (March 1774), p.241.

44 *Universal Magazine of Knowledge and Pleasure*, vols 50–51 (1772), pp.173–4.

45 Iona Opie and Moira Tatem, *A Dictionary of Superstitions* (Oxford: Oxford University Press, 1989), p.135.

46 *Town and Country Magazine*, vol. 4 (May 1772), p.243.

47 *Macaroni Jester*, pp.7–8.

48 *Bon Ton* (December 1791), pp.371–2.

49 Tobias Smollett, *The Adventures of Roderick Random*, ed. Paul-Gabriel Boucé (Oxford: Oxford University Press, 1979), pp.194–5.

50 Ibid., p.196.

51 Ibid., p.459.

52 *Walker's Hibernian Magazine* (1771), p.459.

53 Vincent Carretta, *George III and the Satirists from Hogarth to Byron* (Athens and London: University of Georgia Press, 1990), opp. p.150.

54 *Macaroni Jester*, p.79.

55 Terry Eagleton, 'Grub Street Snob. Review of *Fanny Hill in Bombay: The Making and Unmaking of John Cleland* by Hal Gladfelder', *London Review of Books*, vol. 34, no. 17 (13 September 2012), p.27.

56 Rictor Norton, 'The Macaroni Club: Homosexual Scandals in 1772', *Homosexuality in Eighteenth-century England: A Sourcebook* (19 December 2004, updated 11 June 2005) <http://rictornorton.co.uk/eighteen/macaroni.htm> [Accessed 27 September 2015].

57 DG 4915.

58 'This Animal tho Not so well known as many Among the polite Circle Nevertheless can claim as Much folly to his Share as those of higher Rank, but so peculiar to himself, that it can cause Emulation in none, but such as Jack Catch [Ketch] and the Devil hath reservd for their Own private purposes Sing / I wonder we ant better company upon Tyburn tree.' DG 148.

59 J.R. Wood, 'Jack Ketch in John Dryden's "A Discourse Concerning Satire"', *The Explicator*, vol. 71, no. 1 (2013), p.64.

60 Ibid., p.63.

61 DG 140.

62 *Macaroni, Scavoir Vivre, and Theatrical Magazine* (March 1774), p.241.

63 Edward Carpenter, *The Intermediate Sex* (1908), cited in D.A. Miller, 'Cage aux folles: Sensation and Gender in Wilkie Collins's *The Woman in White*', in Catherine Gallagher and Thomas Laqueur (eds), *The Making of the Modern Body: Sexuality and Society in the Nineteenth Century* (Berkeley and London: University of California Press, 1987), pp.134–5.

64 See Halsband, *Lord Hervey*, p.176.

65 I am grateful to an anonymous reader here.

66 Watson, 'Thomas Patch (1725–1782)', pp.15–50, pencil note opposite p.34. LWL Quarto 75.P27.S940 Extra Ill.

67 Gillian Russell, *Women, Sociability and Theatre in Georgian London* (Cambridge: Cambridge University Press, 2007), p.61.

68 Anon., *The Vauxhall Affray; or, The Macaronies Defeated: Being a compilation of all the Letters, Squibs, &c. on both Sides of that Dispute* (2nd edn, London: J. Williams, 1773).

69 Miles Ogborn, 'Locating the Macaroni: Luxury, Sexuality and Vision in Vauxhall Gardens', *Textual Practice*, vol. 11, no. 3 (1997), p.455.

70 Ibid., p.456.

71 *Vauxhall Affray*, pp.58–9.

72 'St James' Evening', in *Vauxhall Affray*, p.100.

73 Wroth and Wroth, *London Pleasure Gardens*, p.307.

74 See the broadsheet *This is not the Thing, or Molly Exalted* (1762), which includes a print of a pilloried molly before he was killed by the crowd, in Richard Davenport-Hines, *Sex, Death and Punishment: Attitudes to Sex and Sexuality in Britain since the Renaissance* (London: Collins, 1990), p.99. A satirical French text noted that the whores of Paris were trying to have sodomites outlawed and forced to wear hats surmounted by a sign resembling a penis. Anon., *Les Petits Bougres au Manège, ou Réponse de M. xxx. Grand Maître des Enculeurs, et de ses adhérents, défendeurs, à la requête des fouteuses, des macquerelles et des branleuses, demanderesses* (Enculons and Paris: Pierre Pousse-Fort, n.d. [1793]), p.26.

75 *Universal Magazine* (May 1772), p.269.

76 3 January 1751. Philip Dormer Stanhope Chesterfield (4th Earl),

Letters of Lord Chesterfield to His Son and Others (London, Toronto and New York: J.M. Dent, 1929), p.190.

77 Kostenbaum, *The Queen's Throat*, p.85.

78 Billie Bullivant to Cecil Beaton, 17 November 1922, cited in Hugo Vickers, *Cecil Beaton: The Authorized Biography* (London: Weidenfeld and Nicolson, 1985), p.33.

79 Moe Meyer, 'Introduction: Reclaiming the Discourse of Camp', in Moe Meyer (ed.), *The Politics and Poetics of Camp* (London and New York: Routledge, 1994), p.4.

80 Nancy Armstrong, *Desire and Domestic Fiction: A Political History of the Novel* (New York: Oxford University Press, 1989).

81 Dominic Janes, *Oscar Wilde Prefigured: Queer Fashioning and British Caricature, 1750–1900* (Chicago: University of Chicago Press, 2016).

82 Dynes, *Homolexis*, p.14.

83 Ibid.

Chapter 6

1 [Robert Hitchcock], *The Macaroni, a comedy as it is performed at the Theatre-Royal in York* (York: A. Ward, 1773), 'Prologue'. The play was reprinted in London in 1773 and in Dublin in 1774.

2 Shearer West, *The Image of the Actor: Verbal and Visual Representation in the Age of Garrick and Kemble* (New York: St Martin's Press, 1991), p.5.

3 Claire Tomalin, *Mrs Jordan's Profession: The Story of a Great Actress and a Future King* (London: Viking, 1994), p.14. Stella Tillyard, *Aristocrats: Caroline, Emily, Louisa, and Sarah Lennox 1740–1832* (New York: Farrar, Straus and Giroux, 1994), p.164.

4 Marc Baer, *Theatre and Disorder in Late Georgian London* (Oxford: Clarendon Press, 1992), p.106.

5 Ann Bermingham, 'Introduction' to Ann Bermingham and John Brewer (eds), *The Consumption of Culture 1600–1800: Image, Object, Text* (London and New York: Routledge, 1995), p.10.

6 H. James Jensen, *Signs and Meanings in Eighteenth-century Art: Epistemology, Rhetoric, Painting, Poesy, Music, Dramatic Performance, and G.F. Handel* (Oxford: Peter Lang, 1997), p.1.

7 Anon., *A Dictionary of Love, with Notes. Wherein is the Description of a Perfect Beauty; the Picture of a Fop or Macaroni; and a key to all the arch-phrases and difficult terms used in that universal language* (London: J. Bew et al., 1777), n.p., listed under 'Fop'.

8 Stephen Orgel, *Impersonations: The Performance of Gender in Shakespeare's England* (Cambridge: Cambridge University Press, 1996), p.61.

9 The engraving was taken from Zoffany's portrait of Garrick in the role. Alan Kendall, *David Garrick: A Biography* (London: Harrap, 1985), p.18.

10 Heather McPherson, 'Painting, Politics and the Stage in the Age of Caricature', in Robyn Asleson (ed.), *Notorious Muse: The Actress in British Art and Culture 1776–1812* (New Haven and London: Yale University Press, 2003), p.173.

11 Daniel O'Quinn, *Staging Governance: Theatrical Imperialism in London, 1770–1800* (Baltimore: Johns Hopkins University Press, 2005), p.6.

12 *She Stoops to Conquer; or The Mistakes of a Night* (1773), in Oliver Goldsmith, *'The Good Natur'd Man' and 'She Stoops to Conquer'* (Boston and London: D.C. Heath and Co., 1903), p.223.

13 Goldsmith, *'The Good Natur'd Man'*, pp.271–2.

14 David Garrick, *Plays by David Garrick and George Colman the Elder*, ed. E.R. Wood (Cambridge: Cambridge University Press, 1982), p.16.

15 Ibid., p.114.

16 Leigh Woods, *Garrick Claims the Stage: Acting as Social Emblem in Eighteenth-century England* (Westport, CT, and London: Greenwood Press, 1984), pp.113–14. Such scenes of the morals of the town infecting the mores of the countryside also provided the opening scene and premise of Goldsmith's *She Stoops to Conquer*.

17 Brian E. Maidment, *Reading Popular Prints, 1790–1870* (Manchester and New York: Manchester University Press, 1996), pp.98–9.

18 Jensen, *Signs and Meanings in Eighteenth-century Art*, p.2.

19 Hannah Greig, *The Beau Monde: Fashionable Society in Georgian London* (Oxford: Oxford University Press, 2013), p.118.

20 West, *Image of the Actor*, p.17.

21 'E.F.', 'Mr Garrick's Conduct as a Manager ...' (1747), cited in George Winchester Stone Jr and George M. Kahrl, *David Garrick: A Critical Biography* (Carbondale and Edwardsville: Southern Illinois University Press, 1979), p.133.

22 West, *The Image of the Actor*, pp.130–31.

23 Woods, *Garrick Claims the Stage*, p.74.

24 Ibid., pp.112, 116.

25 Stone and Kahrl, *David Garrick*, Appendix B, performances 1741–6: 59 performances.

26 Ibid., p.209.

27 Ibid., pp.209–10.

28 *Miss in Her Teens*, in David Garrick, *The Plays of David Garrick*, ed. Gerald M. Berkowitz (New York and London: Garland, 1981), vol. 1, pp.20–21.

29 Ibid., p.21.

30 Ibid.

31 Ibid., p.23.

32 Stone and Kahrl, *David Garrick*, p.210.

33 Baer, *Theatre and Disorder*, pp.57–8.

34 Stone and Kahrl, *David Garrick*, p.139.

35 David Thomas (ed.), *Theatre in Europe, a Documentary History: Restoration and Georgian England, 1660–1788* (Cambridge: Cambridge University Press, 1989), p.408.

36 Garrick, *Plays of David Garrick*, vol. 2, 'Prologue'.

37 29 January 1747, cited in J.D. Hainsworth, 'David Garrick and Thomas Fitzpatrick', *Notes and Queries*, vol. 19, no. 6 (June 1972), pp.227–8.

38 8 September 1786, in Sophie Von La Roche, *Sophie in London, 1786: Being the Diary of Sophie V. La Roche*, trans. Clare Williams (London: Jonathan Cape, 1933 [1786]), p.122.

39 Stone and Kahrl, *David Garrick*, p.216.

40 Garrick, *Plays of David Garrick*, vol. 1, p.17.

41 Act 1, scene 1, in Garrick, *Plays by David Garrick and George Colman*, p.197.

42 Ibid., p.198.

43 Ibid., p.199.

44 Dated *c*.1775, cited in Thomas, *Theatre in Europe*, p.381.

45 Stone and Kahrl, *David Garrick*, p.497. This was his fourth most-performed role, with 105 such performances.

46 Unattributed cutting, dated in pencil 7 February 1776, BL 1825–40, cited in Thomas, *Theatre in Europe*, p.382.

47 A good example of this may be seen in the engravings by John Raphael Smith. In his mezzotint *Mademoiselle Clermont* (1777), the composition and hairstyle are directly copied from a French fashion periodical.

48 Cited in Christopher Anstey, *An Election Ball*, Introduction and notes by Gavin Turner (Bristol: Broadcast Books, 1997 [1776]), p.112.

49 Horace Walpole to Sir William Hamilton, letter from Arlington St, 10 February 1776, LWL 7914414 Mss Group 1, File 3. This letter is a new acquisition that is not in the published correspondence.

50 *Literary Gazette and Journal of Belles Lettres*, vol. 8 (July 1826), p.429, cited in Mary Webster, *Johann Zoffany, RA, 1733–1810* (New Haven and London: Yale University Press, 2011), p.2.

51 Matthew Craske, *Art in Europe 1700–1830* (Oxford: Oxford University Press, 1997), pp.148–9.

52 Stone and Kahrl, *David Garrick*, p.457.

53 Ibid., pp.456–7.

54 David M. Little, George M. Kahrl (eds) and Phoebe deK. Wilson (associate ed.), *The Letters of David Garrick* (Oxford: Oxford University Press, 1963), vol. 2, pp.828–9.

55 John O'Keeffe, *Recollections of His Life* (London: Colburn, 1826), vol. 1, pp.153–5, cited in Thomas, *Theatre in Europe*, p.408.

56 7 September 1786. Von La Roche, *Sophie in London*, p.95.

57 [Philautus], *The Pretty Gentleman; or, Softness of Manners Vindicated From the false Ridicule exhibited under the Character of William Fribble, Esq.* (London: 1747; ed. Edmund Goldsmid, Bibliotheca Curiosa reprint, Edinburgh: privately printed, 1885), Foreword.

58 Ibid., p.10.

59 Ibid., p.9.

60 Ibid., p.13. A toy-shop is a luxury purveyor.

61 Ibid., p.14.

62 Ibid., p.26.

63 Ibid., p.31.

64 Arthur Murphy, *Life of David Garrick* (London: 1801), vol. 1, p.118, cited in Hainsworth, 'David Garrick and Thomas Fitzpatrick', p.228.

65 Garrick, *Plays of David Garrick*, vol. 1, p.17.

66 Thady Fitzpatrick was an Irish stage-manager imagined as 'fribble' or 'trifler' within the verse-satire by Charles Churchill, *The Rosciad* (1761). His non-English and Celtic background was connected with a non-metropolitan and 'tribal' persona, displaying ambiguous male and female characteristics in a monstrous combination. See Declan William Kavanagh, '"Of Neuter Gender, tho' of Irish growth": Charles Churchill's Fribble', *Irish University Review*, vol. 43, no. 1 (2013), pp.119–30.

67 Stone and Kahrl, *David Garrick*, p.149.

68 Ibid., p.150.

69 Hainsworth, 'David Garrick and Thomas Fitzpatrick', p.228.

70 Thomas Davies, *Memoirs of the Life of David Garrick* (1808), vol. 2, p.20, cited in FGS, p.40.

71 David Garrick, *The Fribbleriad* (London: J. Coote, 1761), p.8.

72 FGS, p.viii.

73 Garrick, *The Fribbleriad*, pp.2–5.

74 Ibid., p.12.

75 FGS, p.40.

76 *Fizgig's Triumph. A New Song to the Tune of Stand around my brave Boys*, written by Murdoch O Blaney, printed by Tristram Shandy, Fleet St, 1763. LWL 763/o/5P. PM IV.13.53.

77 Lothar Altmann, *The Bustelli Statuettes in Nymphenburg Porcelain* (Munich: Staatliche Porzellan-Manufaktur Berlin, 1999).

78 James Peller Malcolm, *Anecdotes of the manners and customs of London, during the eighteenth century*, 2 vols (London: Longman, Hurst, Rees and Orme, 1808–11), pp.136–7. Meissen invented new forms of 'cabinet pieces' designed for contemplation in a private room in an apartment from the 1760s, and at German 'tavern parties' some aristocrats dressed in plebeian dress that resembled the porcelain figures adorning their tables. See Ulrich Pietsch and Claudia Banz (eds), *Triumph of the Blue Swords: Meissen Porcelain for Aristocracy and Bourgeoisie, 1710–1815* (Dresden: Staatliche Kunstsammlungen, 2010), pp.64–9.

79 FGS, p.41.

80 Kendall, *David Garrick*, p.89.

81 [Hitchcock], *The Macaroni*, p.1.

82 Ibid., p.6.

83 Ibid., p.3.

84 'When Popish Jemmy rul's this Land / He rul's it like a King', from *Charnwood Opera* (c.1753), cited in E.P. Thompson, *Customs in Common* (London: Penguin, 1993 [1991]), p.105.

85 [Hitchcock], *The Macaroni*, p.70.

86 Ibid.

87 Ibid., pp.78–9.

88 'The search after happiness'; newspaper item pasted on the back of the pamphlet 'epilogue', 1773. LWL. 'Theatre of Georges', p.20, 1773, no. 5.

89 John Brewer, *The Common People and Politics, 1750–1790s* (Cambridge: Chadwyck-Healey, 1986), p.23.

90 Anon., *A Lecture on Heads, by the Celebrated George Stevens; which has been exhibited upwards of three hundred successive nights to crowded audiences, and met with the most universal applause* (London: J. Pridden, n.d. [c.1765]), p.2.

91 *Couffures nouvelles* (May 1726), illustrated in 'Exposition sur la Gravure de Mode, Bibliothèque Nationale, Galerie Mansart, avril 1961', BN Est. Ad 392, unpag. Women are surrounded by busts with wigs. One has hair hanging down in two pigtails with ribbons, very much like the macaroni pigtail.

92 From Murphy's farce *The Upholsterer or What News?* (1757), in which tradesmen discuss politics, one of them being 'Quidnunc', an upholsterer.

93 Stone and Kahrl, *David Garrick*, p.456.

94 It has been argued that Salvador Dalí's sculpture *Buste de femme rétrospectif* (1933), for example, is a sculpture with 'qualified reference to eighteenth century ideals of feminine beauty'. Johanna Malt, *Obscure Objects of Desire: Surrealism, Fetishism, and Politics* (Oxford: Oxford University Press, 2004), p.114.

95 *Lecture on Heads*, heads nos 38–9.

96 Ibid., p.4.

97 Kristina Straub, *Sexual Suspects: Eighteenth-century Players and Sexual Ideology* (Princeton: Princeton University Press, 1992), p.16.

98 *Lecture on Heads*, p.4.

99 Edward Beetham, *Moral Lectures on Heads* (Newcastle upon Tyne: T. Robson, 1780), pp.29–31.

100 Samuel Foote, *The Nabob. A Comedy in Three Acts: As It is Performed at the Theatre-Royal in the Haymarket* (London: T. Sherlock, 1778), pp.31–2.

101 Aileen Ribeiro, *Dress in Eighteenth-century Europe, 1715–1789* (London: B.T. Batsford, 1984), p.142.

102 C. Willett Cunnington and Phillis Cunnington, *Handbook of English Costume in the Eighteenth Century* (Boston: Plays Inc., 1972 [1964]), p.23.

103 O'Quinn, *Staging Governance*, p.1.

104 Baer, *Theatre and Disorder*, p.11.

105 Thompson, *Customs in Common*, pp.45–6.

106 Ibid., p.72.

107 Ibid., pp.45–6.

108 Thompson put forward these ideas in a series of journal articles in the 1970s. See Baer, *Theatre and Disorder*, p.9.

109 Anon., *The Polite Academy, or School of Behaviour for Young Gentlemen and Ladies* ... (3rd edn, London: R. Baldwin and B. Collins, 1765), p.A2.

110 Richard Sennett, *Flesh and Stone: The Body and the City in Western Civilization* (London: Faber and Faber, 1994), p.100.

Chapter 7

1 'Fashion Victims' was the title of my PhD thesis submitted in 1999 (University of Sydney), which began my macaroni journey, and I had very much hoped to use it for the title of this work. The title has subsequently been well and imaginatively used by Alison Matthews-David and Kimberly Chrisman-Campbell for monographs published in 2015.

2 Walter Vaughan, *An Essay Philosophical and Medical Concerning Modern Clothing* (London: Robinsons, 1792).

3 FGS, p.xliv.

4 Marilyn Butler, 'Antiquarianism (Popular)', in Iain McCalman (ed.), *An Oxford Companion to the Romantic Age: British Culture, 1776–1832* (Oxford: Oxford University Press, 2001), p.330.

5 John Caspar Lavater, *Essays on Physiognomy, designed to promote the knowledge and the love of mankind*, trans. Henry Hunter (London: John Murray, 1789), vol. 2, part 1, p.35.

6 Ibid., vol. 1, part 1, p.82.

7 Ibid., vol. 3, part 1, p.213.

8 Ibid., vol. 3, part 1, opp. p.225.

9 Ibid., vol. 3, part 1, p.225.

10 Ibid., vol. 1, p.156.

11 Henry Siddons, *Practical Illustrations of Rhetorical Gesture and Action, Adapted to the English Drama. From a work on the same subject by M. Engel, Member of the Royal Academy of Berlin, embellished with numerous engravings, expressive of the various passions, and representing the modern costume of the London Theatres* (London: Richard Phillips, 1807), p.27.

12 Ibid., p.95.

13 *Political Review* (November 1809), cited in Marc Baer, *Theatre and Disorder in Late Georgian London* (Oxford: Clarendon Press, 1992), p.204.

14 Hazlitt, 'On Actors and Acting', *Examiner* (January 1817), cited in ibid., pp.195–6.

15 'His Majesty's Birthday', *Bon Ton* (June 1794), p.154.

16 Aileen Ribeiro, 'The Macaronis', *History Today*, vol. 28, no. 7 (July 1978), p.468.

17 Jane Austen, *Persuasion*, ed. D.W. Harding (Harmondsworth: Penguin, 1986 [1818]), p.36.

18 Charles Dickens, *The Pickwick Papers (The Posthumous Papers of the Pickwick Club)*, ed. Robert L. Patten (London: Penguin, 1986 [1836–7]), pp.584–5.

19 A.M.W. Stirling, *Annals of a Yorkshire House from the Papers of a Macaroni and His Kindred* (London: John Lane, 1911), vol. 1, p.322.

20 Beatrice Grimshaw, 'Victorian Family Robinson: A Story of Love and Adventure', *Australian Women's Weekly* (13 April 1935), p.5.

21 '*Blood and Gold* by Van Harrison', *Australian Women's Weekly* (5 March 1938), p.24. Galloping Larry, a highwayman in this story, says, 'So why shouldn't I kill 'im, eh? Wi' two thousand I could go anywhere – far enough from the Lunnon catchpolls – be safe for life – live like a Macaroni –'.

22 Advertisement/trade-card, Yarra Library, Melbourne. Courtesy of Virginia Wright.

23 Equestrian references related to foppery include a racehorse named Fribble in the 1760s and the Newmarket Macaroni Stakes for 'old and aged horses', including Bubble and Squeak in the late 1780s–90s. For Fribble, see Rictor Norton (ed.), 'The Fribbleriad, 1761', in *Homosexuality in Eighteenth-century England: A Sourcebook* (18 March 2003, updated 3 January 2006) <http://rictornorton. co.uk/eighteen/fribbler.htm> [Accessed 17 July 2017]. For the Stakes, see 'Sporting Intelligence', *World*, no. 1043 (7 May 1790), unpag.

Selected Bibliography

Abbreviations used in the notes, bibliography and captions

BL   British Library, London

BM   British Museum, London

BN   Bibliothèque Nationale de France, Paris

DG   M. Dorothy George, *Catalogue of poiPolitical and Personal Satires Preserved in the Department of Prints and Drawings in the British Museum*, vol. 5, 1771–83 (London: Trustees of the British Museum, 1935)

Est.   Estampes

exh. cat.   exhibition catalogue

FGS   Frederic George Stephens and Edward Hawkins, *Catalogue of Prints and Drawings in the British Museum. Division I. Political and Personal Satires*, vol. 4, 1761–*c*.1770 (London: Trustees of the British Museum, 1883). Stephens began cataloguing the collection in the 1860s, building on the earlier work of Hawkins. (DG and FGS are used at times in my text to refer to caricature prints held by the British Museum, rather than the more common abbreviation 'BM', because at times I distinguish between the entries written by the different cataloguers of the collection. All the prints are assigned a number by these authors.)

LWL   Lewis Walpole Library, Yale University

M.   Monsieur, abbreviated as such in some eighteenth-century texts

n.d.   no date

n.p.   no place; no publisher

pub.   published

ROM   Royal Ontario Museum, Toronto

unpag.   unpaginated

V&A   Victoria and Albert Museum, London

[]   indicates the opinions of cataloguers or extraneous material

The location of certain rare pamphlets and prints is indicated.

I Manuscript Sources

Miscellaneous prints and pamphlets relating to eighteenth-century fashion, including 'Suite consacrée aux élégantes et petits maîtres' [1778], BN Est. Oa 20 mat. (1–2)

[Banks, Sophia S.], 'A catalogue of books, etc. in the main house at 32 Soho Square, prepared by Sarah Banks', n.d., BL 460 d.13

Banks Collections [S.S.], 'Political and Miscellaneous Broadsides: Topography', 9 vols, BL LR 301 h 3–11

'Costumes d'Angleterre' (recueil) [scrapbook], BN Est. Ob. 101. pet. in-f

'IIe Suite d'Habillemens à la mode en 1779', BN Est. Oa 82. pet-fol

Diary and accounts of a minor aristocrat, resident near Chateaurenard and Barbanten, just south of Avignon, 1753–78 (Private collection, south of France)

'Etchings by Henry William Bunbury, Esq. and After His Designs: Horace Walpole's scrapbook collection of 280 etchings, prints and drawings in the Lewis Walpole Library', 2 vols, fol. 49/3563./v.1.2, at p.2, prepared by Walpole *c*.1776–82, LWL 765 0 85dr

'Exposition sur la Gravure de Mode, Bibliothèque Nationale, Galerie Mansart, avril 1961' [folio of photographs of the exhibition], BN Est. Ad 392

'Grande-Bretagne. Costumes & Mœurs, I. Hommes' (folio) [scrapbook], BN Est. Ob. 100

'Grande-Bretagne. Mœurs & Costumes, II. Femmes' (folio) [scrapbook], BN Est. Ob 100a

'Grande-Bretagne. Costumes & Mœurs. Mœurs. XVIe–1839', BN Est. Ob. 100e f

'Ier Cahier de la Collection d'Habillements Modernes et Galants, avec les habillements des Princes et Seigneurs', BN Est. Oa 83. pet.-fol.

Watson, F.J.B., 'Thomas Patch (1725–1782): Notes on his Life, together with a catalogue of his known works', special printing as published in *Walpole Society*, vol. 27 (1939–40), LWL Quarto 75.P27.S940 Extra Ill. [box containing miscellaneous papers on Patch, including a private extra-illustrated copy gifted by Watson to W.S. Lewis, with numerous annotations and cuttings]

–– 'Thomas Patch: Some New Light on his Work', *Apollo* (May 1967); n.p., expressly reprinted for W.S. Lewis, Farmington, CT, heavily corrected by Lewis with extensive annotations. LWL Quarto 75.P27.S940 Extra Ill

Theses

Chrisman, Kimberly, '*L'émigration à la mode*: Clothing Worn and Produced by the French Émigré Community in England from the Revolution to the Restoration' (MA, Courtauld Institute of Art, History of Dress, 1997)

Greig, Hannah, 'The Beau Monde and Fashionable Life in Eighteenth-century London, *c*.1688–1800' (Diss., Royal Holloway, University of London, 2003)

Nicolson, Eirwen E.C., 'English Political Prints and Pictorial Argument *c*.1640–*c*.1832: A Study in Historiography and Methodology' (PhD, University of Edinburgh, 1994)

II Primary Sources

Abdeker: or, the Art of Preserving Beauty, translated from an Arabic manuscript (London: A. Millar, 1754)

The Baboon A-la-Mode: A Satyr against the French, by a Gentleman (London: S. Malthus, 1704 [inscribed Jan. 1705 in a contemporary hand])

The Bottle and Friends Garland, containing Four Excellent New Songs . . . V. The Macaroni (n.p.: n.d. [*c*.1765])

The Devil upon Crutches in England, or Night Scenes in London: A Satirical Work by a Gentleman of Oxford (London: Philip Hodges, 1755)

A Dictionary of Love, with Notes. Wherein is the Description of a Perfect Beauty; the Picture of a Fop or Macaroni; and a key to all the arch-phrases and difficult terms used in that universal language (London: J. Bew et al., 1777), BL 8415 aa 53

The English Lady's Complete Catechism setting forth the pride and vanity of the English Quality, in relieving Foreigners before their own Country-Folks (n.p., n.d. [*c*.1790])

Fashion: or, a Trip to a Foreign C--t. A Poem (London: R. Baldwin, 1777)

The French dancing-master and the English soldier: or, the difference betwixt fidling and fighting, displayed in a dialogue betwixt an Englishman and a Frenchman (London: n.p., 1666 [single sheet])

The Gentleman's Companion, and Tradesman's Delight . . . (London: J. Stone, 1735)

The Gentleman's Guide, in His Tour through France. Wrote by an Officer in the Royal-Navy, who lately travelled on a principle, which he most sincerely recommends to his Countrymen, viz. Not to spend more money in the Country of our natural enemy, than is requisite to support with decency the character of an Englishman (Bristol: S. Farley, n.d. [1766])

The Gentleman's Library, Containing rules for conduct in all parts of life, written by a Gentleman (London: W. Mears and J. Browne, 1715)

The Gentleman's Library: Containing rules for conduct in all parts of life, written by a Gentleman (5th edn, London: D. Browne, G. Keith, J. Richardson and B. Law and Co., 1760)

A Lecture on Heads, by the Celebrated George Stevens; which has been exhibited upwards of three hundred successive nights to crowded audiences, and met with the most universal applause (London: J. Pridden, n.d. [c.1765])

Letters on the French Nation: by a Sicilian Gentleman, residing at Paris, to his friend in his own Country. Containing an useful and impartial Critique on that City, and the French Nation, translated from the original (London: T. Lownds, 1749)

The Life of the Right Honorable Charles James Fox, Late Principal Secretary of State for Foreign Affairs . . . (London: Albion Press, 1807)

The Macaroni Jester, and Pantheon of Wit; containing All that has lately transpired in the Regions of Politeness, Whim, and Novelty; Including A singular Variety of Jests, Witticisms, Bon-Mots, Conundrums, Toasts, Acrosticks, &c. – with Epigrams and Epitaphs, of the laughable Kind, and Strokes of Humour hitherto unequalled; which have never appeared in a Book of the Kind (London: J. Cooke et al., n.d. [c.1773])

The Man of Manners: or, Plebeian Polished . . . (London: printed for J. Roberts, n.d.)

The Merry Andrew; or, Macaroni Jester. A Choice Collection of Funny Jokes, Merry Stories, Droll Adventures, Frolicksome Tales, Witty Quibbles, Youthful Pranks . . . (London: n.p., 1786)

Modern Refinement, a Satire. By the author of the Register of Folly, or, Characters and Incidents at Bath and the Hotwells; with a Trip to Bristol Vauxhall, now first added to the third edition of that poem (Bath: S. Hazard, 1777)

'The Natural History of a Macaroni', *Walker's Hibernian Magazine* (July 1771), pp.458–9

Les Petits Bougres au Manège, ou Réponse de M. xxx. Grand Maître des Enculeurs, et de ses adhérents, défendeurs, à la requête des fouteuses, des macquerelles et des branleuses, demanderesses (Enculons and Paris: Pierre Pousse-Fort, an II [1793]), BN Enfer 746

The Polite Academy, or School of Behaviour for Young Gentlemen and Ladies . . . (3rd edn, London: R. Baldwin and B. Collins, 1765)

Remarks on the French and English Ladies, in a Series of Letters; Interspersed with various anecdotes, and additional matter, arising from the subject (London: T. Longman and G. Robinson, 1783)

Select Trials for Murders, Robberies, Rapes, Sodomy, Coining, Frauds and other offences. At the Sessions House in the Old-Bailey. To which are added Genuine Accounts of the Lives . . . of the most eminent Convicts, 4 vols (2nd edn, London: n.p., 1742), vols 2–3

Tableau Général du Goût, des Modes et Costumes de Paris, par une société d'artistes et de gens de lettres (Paris: 'chez Gide, Librairie', 1797–9)

The Vauxhall Affray; or, The Macaronies Defeated: Being a compilation of all the Letters, Squibs, &c. on both Sides of that Dispute (2nd edn, London: J. Williams, 1773)

Andrews, John, *An Account of the Character and Manners of the French; with occasional Observations on the English, in two volumes* (London: E. and C. Dilly, J. Robson, J. Walter, 1770)

– – *Remarks on the French and English Ladies, in a Series of Letters; Interspersed with various anecdotes, and additional matter, arising from the subject* (London: T. Longman and G. Robinson, 1783)

Anstey, Christopher, *The New Bath Guide: or, Memoirs of the B--R--D Family. In a Series of Poetical Epistles* (7th edn, London: J. Dodsley, 1770)

– – *Liberality; or, The Decayed Macaroni. A Sentimental Piece* (London: Dodsley, Robson, Cadell and Dilly, n.d. [c.1788])

– – *The New Bath Guide*, Introduction and notes by Gavin Turner (Bristol: Broadcast Books, 1994 [1766])

– – *An Election Ball*, Introduction and notes by Gavin Turner (Bristol: Broadcast Books, 1997 [1776])

Austen, Jane, *Persuasion*, ed. D.W. Harding (Harmondsworth: Penguin, 1986 [1818])

Beetham, Edward, *Moral Lectures on Heads* (Newcastle upon Tyne: T. Robson, 1780)

Boswell, James, *Boswell's London Journal 1762–1763*, ed. Frederick A. Pottle (Melbourne, London and Toronto: William Heinemann, 1950)

Burney, Frances, *Cecilia, or Memoirs of an Heiress*, Introduction by Judy Simons (London: Virago, 1986 [1st edn 5 vols, 1782])

[Caraccioli, Louis-Antoine de], *Dictionnaire Critique, Pittoresque et Sentencieux, propre à faire connoître les usages du siècle, ainsi que ses bisarreries*, 3 vols (Lyons: Benoît Duplain, 1768)

– – *La Critique des dames et des Messieurs à leur toilette* [pamphlet, inscribed '1770'], BN Z 3230 no. 23/2

Carr, John, *The Stranger in France, or, a tour from Devonshire to Paris, illustrated by engravings in aqua tinta of sketches taken on the spot* (London: J. Johnson, 1803)

Castiglione, Baldassare, *Etiquette for Renaissance Gentlemen*, trans. George Bull (abridged edn, London: Penguin, 1995 [1967])

Chambers, R. (ed.), *The Book of Days: A Miscellany of Popular Antiquities in connection with the Calendar, including anecdote, biography, and history, curiosities of literature and oddities of human life and character*, vol. 2 (7 July 1864)

Chesterfield, Philip Dormer Stanhope, Earl of, *Letters of Lord Chesterfield to His Son and Others* (London, Toronto and New York: J.M. Dent, 1929)

Cleland, John, *Fanny Hill, or Memoirs of a Woman of Pleasure*, ed. Peter Wagner (Harmondsworth: Penguin, 1985 [1748–9])

[Darrell, William], *A Gentleman Instructed in the Conduct of a Virtuous and Happy Life. Written for the Instruction of a Young Nobleman* (London: E. Evets, 1704)

Dickens, Charles, *The Pickwick Papers (The Posthumous Papers of the Pickwick Club)*, ed. Robert L. Patten (London: Penguin, 1986 [1836–7])

Dodsley, R., *Fashion: an Epistolary Satire to a Friend* (London: T. Cooper, 1742)

Edwards, Hugh, *Macaroni* (London: Geoffrey Bles, 1938)

Egan, Pierce, *Grose's Classical Dictionary of the Vulgar Tongue, revised and corrected, with the addition of numerous slang phrases, collected from tried authorities* (London: for the Editor, 1823 [1785, revised edn])

Foote, Samuel, *The Nabob; A Comedy in Three Acts. As It is Performed at the Theatre-Royal in the Haymarket* (London: T. Sherlock, 1778)

– – *A Trip to Calais: A Comedy in Three Acts* (London: T. Sherlock, 1778)

Garrick, David, *The Fribbleriad* (London: J. Coote, 1761)

–– *The Plays of David Garrick. Edited with an Introduction by Gerald M. Berkowitz*, 4 vols (New York and London: Garland, 1981)

–– *Plays by David Garrick and George Colman the Elder. Edited with an Introduction and Notes by E.R. Wood* (Cambridge: Cambridge University Press, 1982)

Gaudet, François-Charles, *Bibliotheque des Petits-Maitres, ou Mémoires pour servir à l'histoire du bon ton & de l'extrêmement bonne compagnie* (Paris: Palais-Royal, Chez la petite Lolo, Marchande de Galanteries, à la Frivolité, 1762)

Goldsmith, Oliver, '*The Good Natur'd Man' and 'She Stoops to Conquer'* (Boston and London: D.C. Heath and Co., 1903)

[Hitchcock, Robert], *The Macaroni, a comedy as it is performed at the Theatre-Royal in York* (York: A. Ward, 1773; 2nd edn, London: W. Nicoll and J. Bell, 1773; Dublin: G. Allen, 1774)

Home, J.A. (ed.), *The Letters and Journals of Lady Mary Coke*, 4 vols (Bath: Kingsmead Reprints, 1970)

[Jacquin, Abbé Armand-Pierre], *De la Santé, ouvrage utile à tout le monde . . .* (Paris: Durand, 1762)

Jesse, John Heneage, *George Selwyn and His Contemporaries; with Memoirs and Notes*, 2 vols (London: Richard Bentley, 1843)

Latham, Robert Gordon, *A Dictionary of the English Language . . .*, 2 vols (London: n.p., 1870)

Lavater, John Caspar, *Essays on Physiognomy, designed to promote the knowledge and the love of mankind*, 5 vols, trans. Henry Hunter, from the French (London: John Murray, 1789)

Le Chevalier de la Bxxx, M., *Les Confessions d'un Fat* (n.p., 1749 [in 2 parts]; [1741])

Lewis, Wilmarth S. (ed.), *The Yale Edition of Horace Walpole's Correspondence*, 48 vols (New Haven and London: Yale University Press, 1937–83)

Little, David M., George M. Kahrl (eds) and Phoebe deK. Wilson (associate ed.), *The Letters of David Garrick*, 3 vols (Oxford: Oxford University Press, 1963)

Malcolm, James Peller, *Anecdotes of the manners and customs of London, during the eighteenth century: including the charities, depravities, dresses and amusements of the citizens of London, during that period: with a review of the state of society in 1807: to which is added, a sketch of the domestic architecture, and of the various improvements in the metropolis: illustrated by forty-five engravings*, 2 vols (London: Longman, Hurst, Rees and Orme, 1808–11)

Misson, Henri, *M. Misson's Memoirs and observations in his travels over England. With some account of Scotland and Ireland. Dispos'd in alphabetical Order. Written originally in French and translated by Mr Orzell* (London: D. Browne, 1719); LWL holds Horace Walpole's own copy with annotations

Molé, G.F.R., *Histoire des Modes Françaises, ou Révolutions du costume en France, depuis l'établissement de la Monarchie jusqu'à nos jours, contenant tout ce qui concerne la tête des Français, avec des recherches sur l'usage des Chevelures artificielles chez les Anciens* (Amsterdam and Paris: Costard, 1773)

[Philautus], *The Pretty Gentleman; or, Softness of Manners Vindicated From the false Ridicule exhibited under the Character of William Fribble, Esq.* (London: 1747; ed. Edmund Goldsmid, Bibliotheca Curiosa reprint, Edinburgh: privately printed, 1885)

Powell, G.H., *Reminiscences and Table-talk of Samuel Rogers. Banker, Poet and Patron of the Arts 1763–1855. Collected from the Original Memoirs of Dyce and Sharpe, with Introduction and Index* (London: R. Brimley Johnson, 1903)

Radcliffe, Susan M. (ed.), *Sir Joshua's Nephew: Being Letters Written, 1769–1778, by a Young Man to His Sisters* (London: John Murray, 1930)

Roche, Sophie Von La, *Sophie in London, 1786: Being the Diary of Sophie V. La Roche*, trans. Clare Williams (London: Jonathan Cape, 1933 [1786])

Rousseau, Jean-Jacques, *Emile*, trans. Barbara Foxley (London: J.M. Dent, 1993 [1762])

[Sandys, W. (ed.)], *Specimens of Macaronic Poetry* (London: Richard Beckley, 1831)

Schomberg, Ralph, *Fashion. A Poem. Addressed to the Ladies of Great-Britain. In two books. Book First* (2nd edn, London: J. Williams, 1778)

Siddons, Henry, *Practical Illustrations of Rhetorical Gesture and Action, Adapted to the English Drama. From a work on the same subject by M. Engel, Member of the Royal Academy of Berlin, embellished with numerous engravings, expressive of the various passions, and representing the modern costume of the London Theatres* (London: Richard Phillips, 1807)

Smollett, Tobias, *Travels through France and Italy. Containing Observations on Character, Customs, Religion, Government, Police, Commerce, Arts, and Antiquities, with a particular description of the Town, Territory, and Climate of Nice: to which is added, a Register of the Weather, kept during a residence of Eighteen Months in that City*, 2 vols (London: R. Baldwin, 1766)

–– *The Adventures of Roderick Random*, ed. Paul-Gabriel Boucé (Oxford: Oxford University Press, 1979)

–– *Travels through France and Italy*, ed. Frank Felsenstein (Oxford: Oxford University Press, 1979 [1766])

Stirling, A.M.W., *Annals of a Yorkshire House from the Papers of a Macaroni and His Kindred*, 2 vols (London: John Lane, 1911)

Thicknesse, Philip, *Observations on the Customs and Manners of the French Nation, in a series of letters, in which that nation is vindicated from the misrepresentations of some late writers* (London: Robert Davis, G. Kearsley, N. Young, 1766)

–– *Useful Hints to those who make the tour of France, in a series of letters written from that Kingdom* (London: R. Davis, G. Kearsley, H. Parker, 1768)

Tissot, M., MD, *The Lady's Physician. A Practical Treatise on the various disorders incident to the fair sex. With proper directions for the cure thereof . . . translated . . .* (London: J. Pridden, 1766)

Tissot, Mr [Samuel A.], *Avis au Peuple sur sa Santé*, 2 vols (3rd edn, Paris: P. Franç. Didot le jeune, 1767)

Toynbee, Paget (ed.), *Satirical Poems Published Anonymously by William Mason with Notes by Horace Walpole, Now First Printed from His Manuscript* (Oxford: Clarendon Press, 1926)

Troide, Lars E. (ed.), *The Early Journals and Letters of Fanny Burney*, vol. 2 (1774–7) (Oxford: Clarendon, 1990)

Vandermonde, M. [Charles-Augustin], *Essai sur la manière de perfectionner l'espèce humaine*, 2 vols (Paris: Vincent, 1756)

Vaughan, Walter, *An Essay Philosophical and Medical Concerning Modern Clothing* (London: Robinsons, 1792)

Vigée-Lebrun, Elisabeth, *The Memoirs of Elisabeth Vigée-Lebrun*, trans. Sian Evans (London: Camden Press, 1989 [1st pub. Paris, 3 vols, 1835–7])

Walpole, B.C., *Recollections of the Life of the Late Right Honorable Charles*

James Fox; exhibiting a faithful account of the most remarkable events of his political career, and a delineation of his character as a statesman, senator, and man of fashion . . . (London: James Cundee, 1806)

Ward, Edward, *The History of the London Clubs, or, the Citizens Pastime, particularly, The Lying Club, the Yorkshire Club . . . with a sermon preach'd to a gang of high-way-men, part I, by the author of the London Spy* (London: J. Dutten, 1709)

–– *The History of the London Clubs . . . The Second Part of the London Clubs: Containing. The No Nose Club, The Beaus Club, The Mollies Club, The Quacks Club* (London, 1709; facsimile reprint by F[red] M[archmont], n.d.)

Wraxall, Sir N.W., *Historical Memoirs of His Own Time*, vol. 2 (new edn, London: Richard Bentley, 1836)

III Secondary Sources

Indispensables accessoires XVIe–XXe siècle (exh. cat., Musée de la Mode et du Costume, Paris, 1983), p.117

Allemagne, Henry René d', *Les Accessoires du costume et du mobilier, depuis le treizième jusqu'au milieu du dixneuvième siècle*, vols 1–3 (Paris: Schemit, 1928)

Allen, Robert J., *The Clubs of Augustan London* (Hamden, CT: Archon Books, 1967)

Altmann, Lothar, *The Bustelli Statuettes in Nymphenburg Porcelain* (Munich: Staatliche Porzellan-Manufaktur Berlin, 1999)

Arizzoli-Clémentel, Pierre, *Gilets brodés: Modèles du XVIIIe* (Lyons: Musée des Tissus, 1993)

Armstrong, Nancy, *Desire and Domestic Fiction: A Political History of the Novel* (New York: Oxford University Press, 1989)

Atherton, Herbert M., *Political Prints in the Age of Hogarth: A Study of the Ideographic Representation of Politics* (Oxford: Clarendon Press, 1974)

Ayling, Stanley, *Fox: The Life of Charles James Fox* (London: John Murray, 1991)

Baer, Marc, *Theatre and Disorder in Late Georgian London* (Oxford: Clarendon Press, 1992)

Barker-Benfield, G.J., *The Culture of Sensibility: Sex and Society in Eighteenth-century Britain* (Chicago and London: University of Chicago Press, 1992)

Beckett, J.V., *The Aristocracy in England, 1660–1914* (Oxford and New York: Basil Blackwell, 1986)

Bell, Quentin, *On Human Finery* (2nd edn, London: Hogarth Press, 1976 [1st edn 1947])

Bentman, Raymond, 'Horace Walpole's Forbidden Passion', in Martin Duberman (ed.), *Queer Representations: Reading Lives, Reading Cultures* (New York and London: New York University Press, 1997), pp.276–89

Berg, Maxine, *Luxury and Pleasure in Eighteenth-century Britain* (Oxford: Oxford University Press, 2007)

Bermingham, Ann, and John Brewer (eds), *The Consumption of Culture 1600–1800: Image, Object, Text* (London and New York: Routledge, 1995)

Berry, Christopher J., *The Idea of Luxury: A Conceptual and Historical Investigation* (Cambridge: Cambridge University Press, 1994)

Betsky, Aaron, *Queer Space: Architecture and Same-sex Desire* (New York: William Morrow and Co., 1997)

Boucher, François, *A History of Costume in the West*, trans. John Ross (new edn, London: Thames and Hudson, 1987 [1966])

Breward, Christopher, *The Culture of Fashion: A New History of Fashionable Dress* (Manchester and New York: Manchester University Press, 1995)

–– *The Hidden Consumers: Masculinities, Fashion and City Life, 1860–1914* (Manchester and New York: Manchester University Press, 1999)

Brewer, John, *The Common People and Politics, 1750–1790s* (*The English Satirical Print 1600–1832*) (Cambridge: Chadwyck-Healey, 1986)

–– and Roy Porter (eds), *Consumption and the World of Goods* (London: Routledge, 1993)

Browning, J.D. (ed.), *Satire in the 18th Century* (New York and London: Garland, 1983)

Buck, Anne, *Dress in Eighteenth-century England* (New York: Holmes & Meier, 1979)

Burke, Peter, *Popular Culture in Early Modern Europe* (London: Temple Smith, 1978)

–– *The Fortunes of the Courtier: The European Reception of Castiglione's Cortegiano* (University Park, PA: Penn State University Press, 1996)

Butazzi, Grazietta, *Una Raccolta di sottovesti settecentesche ricamate al Castello Sforzesco* (Milan: Comune di Milano, 1976)

Butler, Judith, *Gender Trouble: Feminism and the Subversion of Identity* (New York: Routledge, 1990)

Butler, Marilyn, 'Antiquarianism (Popular)', in Iain McCalman (ed.), *An Oxford Companion to the Romantic Age: British Culture, 1776–1832* (Oxford: Oxford University Press, 2001)

Calthrop, Dion Clayton, *English Costume Painted and Described* (London: Adam & Charles Black, 1907)

Campbell, Timothy, *Historical Style: Fashion and the New Mode of History, 1740–1830* (Philadelphia: University of Pennsylvania Press, 2016)

Carretta, Vincent, *George III and the Satirists from Hogarth to Byron* (Athens and London: University of Georgia Press, 1990)

Carter, Harold B., *Sir Joseph Banks (1743–1820): A Guide to Biographical and Bibliographical Sources* (Winchester and London: St Paul's Bibliographies and British Museum, 1987)

Carter, Philip, 'Men about Town: Representations of Foppery and Masculinity in Early Eighteenth-century Urban Society', in Hannah Barker and Elaine Chalus (eds), *Gender in Eighteenth-century England: Roles, Representations, and Responsibilities* (New York: Longman, 1997), pp.31–57

Castle, Terry, *Masquerade and Civilization: The Carnivalesque in Eighteenth-century English Culture and Fiction* (Stanford: Stanford University Press, 1986)

–– *The Female Thermometer: Eighteenth-century Culture and the Invention of the Uncanny* (New York and Oxford: Oxford University Press, 1995)

Chancellor, E. Beresford, *The XVIIIth Century in London: An Account of Its Social Life and Arts* (London: B.T. Batsford, n.d. [1920])

Chaussinand-Nogaret, Guy, *The French Nobility in the Eighteenth Century: From Feudalism to Enlightenment*, trans. William Doyle (Cambridge: Cambridge University Press, 1985 [Hachette, 1976])

Cheeser, Lucy, 'Cross Dressing, Sexual (Mis)Representation and Homosexual Desire, 1863–1893', in David L. Phillips and Graham Willett (eds), *Australia's Homosexual Histories: Gay and Lesbian Perspectives 5* (Sydney and Melbourne: Australian Centre for Lesbian and Gay Research and the Australian Lesbian and Gay Archives, 2000)

Chenoune, Farid, *A History of Men's Fashion* (Paris: Flammarion, 1993)

Chrisman-Campbell, Kimberly, '"He is not dressed without a muff": Muffs, Masculinity, and *la mode* in English Satire', in Elizabeth C.

Mansfield and Kelly Malone (eds), *Seeing Satire in the Eighteenth Century*, vol. 2 (Oxford: Voltaire Foundation, 2013), pp.131–44

–– *Fashion Victims: Dress at the Court of Louis XVI and Marie-Antoinette* (New Haven and London: Yale University Press, 2015)

Christie, Ian R., *Stress and Stability in Late Eighteenth-century Britain: Reflections on the British Avoidance of Revolution. The Ford Lectures Delivered in the University of Oxford, 1983–1984* (Oxford: Clarendon Press, 1984)

Cohen, Michèle, *Fashioning Masculinity: National Identity and Language in the Eighteenth Century* (London and New York: Routledge, 1996)

Colley, Linda, *Britons: Forging the Nation 1707–1837* (London: Vintage, 1996 [1992])

Craske, Matthew, *Art in Europe 1700–1830* (Oxford: Oxford University Press, 1997)

Cuisenier, Jean (ed.), *Costume, coutume* (exh. cat., Grand Palais, Paris, 1987)

Cunnington, C. Willett, and Phillis Cunnington, *Handbook of English Costume in the Eighteenth Century* (Boston: Plays Inc., 1972 [1964])

Daniell, Fredk [*sic*] B., *A catalogue Raisonné of the engraved Works of Richard Cosway, RA, with a memoir of Cosway by Sir Philip Currie* (London: Frederick B. Daniell, 1890)

Davenport-Hines, Richard, *Sex, Death and Punishment: Attitudes to Sex and Sexuality in Britain since the Renaissance* (London: Collins, 1990)

Davin, Richard, 'Introduction', in *18th-century Waistcoats* (exh. cat., Rougemont House, Museum of Costume and Lace, Exeter, 28 March–21 May 1988)

D'Oench, Ellen G., *'Copper into Gold': Prints by John Raphael Smith 1751–1812* (New Haven and London: Yale University Press, 1999)

Donald, Diana, *The Age of Caricature: Satirical Prints in the Reign of George III* (New Haven and London: Yale University Press, 1996)

–– *Followers of Fashion: Graphic Satires from the Georgian Period* (exh. cat., London: Hayward Gallery, 2002)

Duberman, Martin Bauml, Martha Vicinus and George Chauncey Jr (eds), *Hidden from History: Reclaiming the Gay and Lesbian Past* (London: Penguin, 1991 [New American Library, 1989])

Duffy, Michael, *The Englishman and the Foreigner* (The English Satirical Print 1600–1832) (Cambridge: Chadwyck-Healey, 1986)

Dunlop, Ian, *Marie Antoinette: A Portrait* (London: Phoenix, 1993)

Dyce, Alexander, *Reminiscences and Table-talk of Samuel Rogers* (London: R. Brimley Johnson, 1903)

Dynes, Wayne, *Homolexis: A Historical and Cultural Lexicon of Homosexuality*, Gai Saber Monograph no. 4 (New York: Gay Academic Union, 1985)

Ellis, Havelock, *Studies in the Psychology of Sex*, vol. 1, part 4 (New York: 1901)

Fleming, Juliet, *Graffiti and the Writing Arts of Early Modern England* (London: Reaktion Books, 2001)

Flügel, J.C., *The Psychology of Clothes* (London: Hogarth Press, 1930)

Gallagher, Catherine, and Thomas Laqueur (eds), *The Making of the Modern Body: Sexuality and Society in the Nineteenth Century* (Berkeley and London: University of California Press, 1987)

Garrioch, David, *The Making of Revolutionary Paris* (Berkeley: University of California Press, 2002)

Gascoigne, John, *Joseph Banks and the English Enlightenment: Useful Knowledge and Polite Culture* (Cambridge: Cambridge University Press, 1994)

George, M. Dorothy, *England in Johnson's Day* (London: Methuen, 1928)

–– *Catalogue of Political and Personal Satires Preserved in the Department of Prints and Drawings in the British Museum*, vol. 5, 1771–83 (London: Trustees of the British Museum, 1935) [DG]

–– *London Life in the Eighteenth Century* (Harmondsworth: Penguin, 1966 [1925])

–– *Hogarth to Cruikshank: Social Change in Graphic Satire* (London: Allen Lane/Penguin, 1967)

Gerard, Kent, and Gert Hekma (eds), *The Pursuit of Sodomy: Male Homosexuality in Renaissance and Enlightenment Europe* (New York and London: Haworth Press, 1989) [also pub. as *Journal of Homosexuality*, vol. 16, nos 1–2, 1988]

Gerzina, Gretchen, *Black England: Life before Emancipation* (London: John Murray, 1995)

Gilbert, Christopher, *The Life and Work of Thomas Chippendale* (New York: Tabard Press, 1978)

Gombrich, E.H., *Meditations on a Hobby Horse and Other Essays on the Theory of Art* (4th edn, London: Phaidon, 1985)

Grand-Carteret, J., *Les Mœurs et la caricature en France* (Paris: Librairie Illustrée, 1888)

Grazia, Victoria de, and Ellen Furlough (eds), *The Sex of Things: Gender and Consumption in Historical Perspective* (Berkeley and London: University of California Press, 1996)

Greig, Hannah, *The Beau Monde: Fashionable Society in Georgian London* (Oxford: Oxford University Press, 2013)

Grunenberg, Christoph, and Max Hollein (eds), *Shopping: A Century of Art and Consumer Culture* (Ostfildern-Ruit: Hatje Cantz, 2002)

Halsband, Robert, *Lord Hervey: Eighteenth-century Courtier* (Oxford: Clarendon Press, 1973)

Harvey, John, *Men in Black* (London: Reaktion Books, 1995)

Herdt, Gilbert (ed.), *Third Sex, Third Gender: Beyond Sexual Dimorphism in Culture and History* (New York: Zone Books, 1994)

Higgins, Patrick (ed.), *A Queer Reader* (London: Fourth Estate, 1993)

Hollander, Anne, *Sex and Suits: The Evolution of Modern Dress* (New York: Kodansha, 1995 [1994])

Howson, Gerald, *The Macaroni Parson: The Life of the Unfortunate Doctor Dodd* (London: Hutchinson, 1973)

Hunt, Lynn, *Politics, Culture, and Class in the French Revolution* (Berkeley and London: University of California Press, 1984)

–– (ed.), *Eroticism and the Body Politic* (Baltimore and London: Johns Hopkins University Press, 1991)

–– 'Freedom of Dress in Revolutionary France', in Sara E. Melzer and Kathryn Norberg (eds), *From the Royal to the Republican Body: Incorporating the Political in Seventeenth- and Eighteenth-century France* (Berkeley: University of Calfornia Press, 1998)

Janes, Dominic, *Oscar Wilde Prefigured: Queer Fashioning and British Caricature, 1750–1900* (Chicago: University of Chicago Press, 2016)

–– 'Gender and Sexuality', in Peter McNeil (ed.), *A Cultural History of Dress and Fashion in the Age of Enlightenment* (London and New York: Bloomsbury, 2017), pp.105–22

Jensen, H. James, *Signs and Meanings in Eighteenth-century Art: Epistemology, Rhetoric, Painting, Poesy, Music, Dramatic Performance, and G.F. Handel* (Oxford: Peter Lang, 1997)

Jones, Eric, 'The Fashion Manipulators: Consumer Tastes and British Industries, 1660–1800', in Louis P. Cain and Paul J. Uselding (eds), *Business Enterprise and Economic Change: Essays in Honour of Harold F. Williamson* (Kent, OH: Kent State University Press, 1973), pp.198–226

Jones, Jennifer, 'Coquettes and Grisettes: Women Buying and Selling in Ancien Régime Paris', in Victoria de Grazia and Ellen Furlough (eds), *The Sex of Things: Gender and Consumption in Historical Perspective* (Berkeley and London: University of California Press, 1996), pp.25–53

Jones, Rica, and Martin Postle, 'Gainsborough in His Painting Room', in Michael Rosenthal and Martin Myrone (eds), *Gainsborough* (exh. cat., Tate Britain, London, 2002), pp.26–39

Kekewich, Margaret Lucille (ed.), *Princes and Peoples: France and the British Isles, 1620–1714. An Anthology of Primary Sources* (Manchester and New York: Manchester University Press, 1994)

Kendall, Alan, *David Garrick: A Biography* (London: Harrap, 1985)

King, Reyahn, Sukhdev Sandhu, Jane Girdham and James Walvin (eds), *Ignatius Sancho: An African Man of Letters* (London: National Portrait Gallery, 1997)

King, Thomas A., *The Gendering of Men, 1600–1750*, vol. 1: *The English Phallus* (Madison: University of Wisconsin Press, 2004)

Koestenbaum, Wayne, *The Queen's Throat: Opera, Homosexuality and the Mystery of Desire* (New York: Vintage, 1994 [1993])

Kuchta, David, *The Three-piece Suit and Modern Masculinity: England, 1550–1850* (Berkeley and London: University of California Press, 2002)

Langford, Paul, *A Polite and Commercial People: England 1727–1783* (Oxford: Oxford University Press, 1989)

Lesley, Everett P., Jr, and William Osmun, *Conspicuous Waist: Waistcoats and Waistcoat Designs 1700–1952* (exh. cat., Cooper Union Museum for the Arts of Decoration, New York, 1952)

Lloyd, Stephen (ed.), *Richard and Maria Cosway: Regency Artists of Taste and Fashion* (exh. cat., Scottish National Portrait Gallery, Edinburgh, 1995)

McCormack, Matthew, *Embodying the Militia in Georgian England* (Oxford: Oxford University Press, 2015)

McDowell, Colin, *The Literary Companion to Fashion* (London: Sinclair-Stevenson, 1995)

McKendrick, Neil, John Brewer and J.H. Plumb, *The Birth of a Consumer Society: The Commercialization of Eighteenth-century England* (Bloomington: Indiana University Press, 1982)

McKenna, Neil, *Fanny and Stella: The Young Men Who Shocked Victorian England* (London: Faber and Faber, 2013)

McNeil, Peter (ed.), *A Cultural History of Dress and Fashion in the Age of Enlightenment* (London and New York: Bloomsbury, 2017)

McPherson, Heather, 'Painting, Politics and the Stage in the Age of Caricature', in Robyn Asleson (ed.), *Notorious Muse: The Actress in British Art and Culture 1776–1812* (New Haven and London: Yale University Press, 2003), pp.171–93

Maidment, Brian E., *Reading Popular Prints, 1790–1870* (Manchester and New York: Manchester University Press, 1996)

Malt, Johanna, *Obscure Objects of Desire: Surrealism, Fetishism, and Politics* (Oxford: Oxford University Press, 2004)

Maza, Sarah, *Private Lives and Public Affairs: The Causes Célèbres of Prerevolutionary France* (Berkeley and London: University of California Press, 1993)

Melot, Michel, 'Caricature and the Revolution: The Situation in France in 1789', in Lynne Hockman (ed.), *French Caricature and the French Revolution 1789–1799* (exh. cat., Grunwald Center for the Graphic Arts, Wight Art Gallery, Los Angeles, 1988), pp.25–32

Melzer, Sara E., and Kathryn Norberg (eds), *From the Royal to the Republican Body: Incorporating the Political in Seventeenth- and Eighteenth-century France* (Berkeley: University of Calfornia Press, 1998)

Meyer, Moe (ed.), *The Politics and Poetics of Camp* (London and New York: Routledge, 1994)

Mitchell, Leslie George, *Charles James Fox* (Oxford: Oxford University Press, 1992)

Monteyne, Joseph, *From Still Life to the Screen: Print Culture, Display, and the Materiality of the Image in Eighteenth-century London* (New Haven and London: Yale University Press, 2013)

Montgomery-Massingberd, Hugh, and Christopher Simon Sykes, *Great Houses of England and Wales* (London: Laurence King, 1994)

Moores, John Richard, *Representations of France in English Satirical Prints, 1740–1832* (Basingstoke: Palgrave Macmillan, 2015)

Motley, Mark, *Becoming a French Aristocrat: The Education of the Court Nobility, 1580–1715* (Princeton: Princeton University Press, 1990)

Mowl, Timothy, *Horace Walpole: The Great Outsider* (London: John Murray, 1996)

Norton, Rictor (ed.), 'The Fribbleriad, 1761', in *Homosexuality in Eighteenth-century England: A Sourcebook* (18 March 2003, updated 3 January 2006) <http://rictornorton.co.uk/eighteen/fribbler.htm> [Accessed 17 July 2017]

––'The Macaroni Club: Homosexual Scandals in 1772', in *Homosexuality in Eighteenth-century England: A Sourcebook* (19 December 2004, updated 11 June 2005) <http://rictornorton.co.uk/eighteen/macaroni.htm> [Accessed 27 September 2015]

O'Connell, Sheila, *The Popular Print in England 1550–1850* (exh. cat., British Museum, London, 1999)

Ogborn, Miles, 'Geographia's Pen: Writing, Geography and the Arts of Commerce, 1660–1760', *Journal of Historical Geography*, vol. 30, no. 2 (2004), pp.294–315

Opie, Iona, and Moira Tatem, *A Dictionary of Superstitions* (Oxford: Oxford University Press, 1989)

O'Quinn, Daniel, *Staging Governance: Theatrical Imperialism in London, 1770–1800* (Baltimore: Johns Hopkins University Press, 2005)

Orgel, Stephen, *Impersonations: The Performance of Gender in Shakespeare's England* (Cambridge: Cambridge University Press, 1996)

Paston, George [pseudonym of Miss E.M. Symonds], *Social Caricature in the Eighteenth Century* (London: Methuen, 1905)

Pastoureau, Michel, *L'Étoffe du diable: Une histoire des rayures et des tissus rayés* (Paris: Éditions du Seuil, 1991)

Paulson, Ronald, *Hogarth: His Life, Art, and Times*, 2 vols (New Haven and London: Yale University Press, 1971)

––'Gillray: The Ambivalence of the Political Cartoonist', in J.D. Browning (ed.), *Satire in the 18th Century* (New York: Garland, 1983), pp.147–83

Peakman, Julie (ed.), *A Cultural History of Sexuality in the Enlightenment* (Oxford and New York: Berg, 2011)

Pedersen, Mikkel, 'Status', in Peter McNeil (ed.), *A Cultural History of Dress and Fashion in the Age of the Enlightenment* (London and New York: Bloomsbury, 2017), pp. 123–38

Perry, Gill, and Michael Rossington (eds), *Femininity and Masculinity in Eighteenth-century Art and Culture* (Manchester and New York: Manchester University Press, 1994)

Pietsch, Ulrich, and Claudia Banz (eds), *Triumph of the Blue Swords: Meissen Porcelain for Aristocracy and Bourgeoisie, 1710–1815* (Dresden: Staatliche Kunstsammlungen, 2010)

Piper, David, *The English Face* (2nd edn, London: National Portrait Gallery, 1978 [1957, Thames and Hudson])

[Plunkett, C.], Lord Dunsany, *If I Were Dictator: The Pronouncements of the Grand Macaroni* (London: Methuen, 1934)

Pointon, Marcia, *Hanging the Head: Portraiture and Social Formation in Eighteenth-century England* (New Haven and London: Yale University Press, 1993)

–– *Brilliant Effects: A Cultural History of Gem Stones and Jewellery* (London and New Haven: Yale University Press, 2010)

Quicherat, J., *Histoire du costume en France depuis les temps les plus reculés jusqu'à la fin du XVIIIe siècle* (Paris: Hachette, 1875)

Rangström, Lena (ed.), *Lions of Fashion: Male Fashions of the 16th, 17th, 18th Centuries (Modelejon Manligt Mode: 1500-tal, 1600-tal, 1700-tal)* (Stockholm: Livrustkammaren Atlantis, 2002)

Rauser, Amelia, *Caricature Unmasked: Irony, Authenticity, and Individualism in Eighteenth-century English Prints* (Newark: University of Delaware Press, 2008)

Reynolds, Graham, *English Portrait Miniatures* (revised edn, Cambridge: Cambridge University Press, 1988)

Ribeiro, Aileen, *Dress in Eighteenth-century Europe, 1715–1789* (London: B.T. Batsford, 1984)

–– *The Dress Worn at Masquerades in England, 1730 to 1790, and Its Relation to Fancy Dress in Portraiture* (New York: Garland, 1984)

–– *The Art of Dress: Fashion in England and France 1750–1820* (New Haven and London: Yale University Press, 1995)

Roche, Daniel, *The Culture of Clothing: Dress and Fashion in the 'Ancien Régime'*, trans. Jean Birrell (Cambridge: Cambridge University Press, 1994) [1st pub. as *La Culture des apparences*, Librairie Arthème Fayard, 1989]

Rosenthal, Michael, and Martin Myrone (eds), *Gainsborough* (exh. cat., Tate Britain, London, 2002)

Rothstein, Natalie (ed.), *Four Hundred Years of Fashion* (London: V&A, 1984)

–– (ed.), *Barbara Johnson's Album of Fashions and Fabrics* (London: Thames and Hudson, 1987)

–– 'The Excellence of English Brocades', in Regula Schorta and Natalie Rothstein (eds), *Seidengewebe des 18. Jahrhunderts: Die Industrien in England und in Nordeuropa* (Riggisberg: Abegg-Stiftung, 2000)

Russell, Gillian, *Women, Sociability and Theatre in Georgian London* (Cambridge: Cambridge University Press, 2007)

Sargentson, Carolyn, *Merchants and Luxury Markets: The Marchands Merciers of Eighteenth-century Paris* (London: V&A, 1996)

Sekora, John, *Luxury: The Concept in Western Thought, Eden to Smollett* (Baltimore and London: Johns Hopkins University Press, 1977)

Sennett, Richard, *Flesh and Stone: The Body and the City in Western Civilization* (London: Faber and Faber, 1994)

Silverman, Kaja, 'Fragments of a Fashionable Discourse', in Tania Modleski (ed.), *Studies in Entertainment: Critical Approaches to Mass Culture* (Bloomington: Indiana University Press, 1986), pp.139–52

–– *Male Subjectivity at the Margins* (New York and London: Routledge, 1992)

Sinfield, Alan, *The Wilde Century: Effeminacy, Oscar Wilde and the Queer Moment* (London and New York: Cassell, 1994)

Sloman, Susan, *Gainsborough in Bath* (New Haven and London: Paul Mellon Centre for Studies in British Art and Yale University Press, 2002)

Smith, Charles Saumarez, *Eighteenth-century Decoration: Design and the Domestic Interior in England* (London: Weidenfeld and Nicolson, 1993)

Société de l'Histoire du Costume, *Exposition de costumes anciens* (exh. cat., Paris: Musée des Arts Décoratifs, 6 May–10 October 1909)

Spencer, Alfred (ed.), *Memoirs of William Hickey*, vol. 1, 1749–75 (London: Hurst and Blackett, 1919)

Steele, Valerie, 'A Queer History of Fashion: From the Closet to the Catwalk', in Valerie Steele (ed.), *A Queer History of Fashion: From the Closet to the Catwalk* (New Haven and London: Yale University Press, 2013), pp.7–75

Steorn, Patrik, 'Object in Focus', *Fashioning the Early Modern Website* <http://www.fashioningtheearlymodern.ac.uk/object-in-focus/swedish-faience-tray/> [Accessed 5 September 2015]

Stephens, Frederic George, and Edward Hawkins, *Catalogue of Prints and Drawings in the British Museum. Division I. Political and Personal Satires*, vol. 4, 1761–c.1770 (London: Trustees of the British Museum, 1883) [FGS]

Stone, George Winchester, Jr, and George M. Kahrl, *David Garrick: A Critical Biography* (Carbondale and Edwardsville: Southern Illinois University Press, 1979)

Straub, Kristina, *Sexual Suspects: Eighteenth-century Players and Sexual Ideology* (Princeton: Princeton University Press, 1992)

Styles, John, *The Dress of the People: Everyday Fashion in Eighteenth-century England* (New Haven and London: Yale University Press, 2007)

Summerson, John, *Georgian London* (3rd edn, London: Barrie and Jenkins, 1978 [1945])

Tetteris, Karin, 'Pocket Watch with Châteleine', in Lena Rangström (ed.), *Lions of Fashion: Male Fashion of the 16th, 17th, 18th Centuries (Modelejon Manligt Mode: 1500-tal, 1600-tal, 1700-tal)* (Stockholm: Livrustkammaren Atlantis, 2002), p.389

Thoen, Irma, *Strategic Affection? Gift Exchange in Seventeenth-century Holland* (Amsterdam: Amsterdam University Press, 2007)

Thomas, David (ed.), *Theatre in Europe, a Documentary History: Restoration and Georgian England, 1660–1788* (Cambridge: Cambridge University Press, 1989)

Thomas, Keith, 'Introduction', in Jan Bremmer and Herman Roodenburg (eds), *A Cultural History of Gesture* (Ithaca, NY: Cornell University Press, 1991)

Thompson, E.P., *Customs in Common* (London: Penguin, 1993 [1991])

Tillyard, Stella, *Aristocrats: Caroline, Emily, Louisa, and Sarah Lennox 1740–1832* (New York: Farrar, Straus and Giroux, 1994)

Tomalin, Claire, *Mrs Jordan's Profession: The Story of a Great Actress and a Future King* (London: Viking, 1994)

Trevelyan, George Otto, *The Early History of Charles James Fox* (London: Longmans, Green and Co., 1880)

Trumbach, Randolph, 'Modern Sodomy: The Origins of Homosexuality, 1700–1800', in Matt Cook (ed.), with H.G. Cocks, Robert Mills and Randolph Trumbach, *A Gay History of Britain: Love and Sex between Men since the Middle Ages* (Oxford and Westport, CT: Greenwood World Publishing, 2007)

Van der Meer, Theo, 'Sodomy and the Pursuit of a Third Sex in the Early Modern Period', in Gilbert Herdt (ed.), *Third Sex, Third Gender: Beyond Sexual Dimorphism in Culture and History* (New York: Zone Books, 1994)

Vrignaud, Gilberte, *Vêture et parure en France au dix-huitième siècle* (Paris and Chennevières-sur-Marne: Éditions Messene, 1995)

Waterhouse, Ellis, *Painting in Britain 1530 to 1790* (London: Penguin, 1953)

Weatherill, Lorna, *Consumer Behaviour and Material Culture in Britain, 1660–1760* (2nd edn, London and New York: Routledge, 1996 [1988])

Webster, Mary, *Johann Zoffany, RA, 1733–1810* (New Haven and London: Yale University Press, 2011)

Weeks, Jeffrey, *Sexuality and Its Discontents: Meanings, Myths and*

Modern Sexualities (London, Melbourne and Henley: Routledge and Kegan Paul, 1985)

–– 'Inverts, Perverts, and Mary-Annes: Male Prostitution and the Regulation of Homosexuality in England in the Nineteenth and Early Twentieth Centuries', in Martin Bauml Duberman, Martha Vicinus and George Chauncey Jr (eds), *Hidden from History: Reclaiming the Gay and Lesbian Past* (New York: Penguin Putnam, 1990 [1981]), pp.195–211

Wenzel, Siegfried, *Macaronic Sermons: Bilingualism and Preaching in Late-medieval England* (Ann Arbor: University of Michigan Press, 1994)

West, Shearer, *The Image of the Actor: Verbal and Visual Representation in the Age of Garrick and Kemble* (New York: St Martin's Press, 1991)

Woods, Leigh, *Garrick Claims the Stage: Acting as Social Emblem in Eighteenth-century England* (Westport, CT, and London: Greenwood Press, 1984)

Wroth, Warwick, and Arthur Edgar Wroth, *The London Pleasure Gardens of the Eighteenth Century* (Hamden, CT: Archon Books, 1979 [facsimile of 1896 edn, London: Macmillan])

IV Journal Articles

Beckson, Karl, 'Aesthetics and Eros in Wilde' [review of Patricia Flanagan Behrendt, *Oscar Wilde: Eros and Aesthetics*], *English Literature in Translation, 1880–1920*, vol. 36, no. 2 (1993), pp.212–18

Carter, Philip, 'An "Effeminate" or "Efficient" Nation? Masculinity and Eighteenth-century Social Documentary', *Textual Practice*, vol. 11, no. 3 (1997), pp.429–43

Chilton, Meredith, 'The Spaghetti Eaters', *Metropolitan Museum Journal*, vol. 37 (2002), pp.223–9

Eagleton, Terry, 'Grub Street Snob. Review of *Fanny Hill in Bombay: The Making and Unmaking of John Cleland* by Hal Gladfelder', *London Review of Books*, vol. 34, no. 17 (13 September 2012), pp.27–8

Evans, James, '"The Dullissimo Maccaroni": Masculinities in *She Stoops to Conquer*', *Philological Quarterly*, vol. 90, no. 1 (2011), pp.45–65

Farrell, William, 'Smuggling Silks into Eighteenth-century Britain: Geography, Perpetrators, and Consumers', *Journal of British Studies*, vol. 55, no. 2 (2016), pp.268–94

Fawcett, Trevor, 'Eighteenth-century Shops and the Luxury Trade', *Bath History*, vol. 3 (1990), pp.49–75

Festa, Lynn M., 'Personal Effects: Wigs and Possessive Individualism in the Long Eighteenth Century', *Eighteenth-century Life*, vol. 29, no. 2 (2005), pp.47–90

Ford, Brinsley, 'Thomas Patch: A Newly Discovered Painting', *Apollo*, vol. 77 (March 1963), pp.172–6

Fradenburg, Louise O., and Carla Freccero (eds), 'Premodern Sexualities in Europe', special issue of *GLQ: A Journal of Lesbian and Gay Studies*, vol. 1, no. 4 (1995)

Hainsworth, J.D., 'David Garrick and Thomas Fitzpatrick', *Notes and Queries*, vol. 19, no. 6 (June 1972), pp.227–8

Hyde, Melissa, 'Confounding Conventions: Gender Ambiguity and François Boucher's Painted Pastorals', *Eighteenth-century Studies*, vol. 30, no. 1 (Fall 1996), pp.25–57

Kates, Gary, 'Fashioning Gender: Introduction', *Eighteenth-century Studies*, vol. 30, no. 1 (Fall 1996), pp.1–4

Kavanagh, Declan William, '"Of Neuter Gender, tho' of Irish growth": Charles Churchill's Fribble', *Irish University Review*, vol. 43, no. 1 (2013), pp.119–30

Kerfoot, Alicia, 'Declining Buckles and Movable Shoes in Frances Burney's *Cecilia*', *Burney Journal*, vol. 11 (2011), pp.55–79

Kwass, Michael, 'Big Hair: A Wig History of Consumption in Eighteenth-century France', *American Historical Review*, vol. 3, no. 3 (2006), pp.631–59

Lemire, Beverly, 'Developing Consumerism and the Ready-made Clothing Trade in Britain, 1750–1800', *Textile History*, vol. 15, no. 1 (Spring 1984), pp.21–44

Lochnan, Katharine A., 'Caricatures and Fashion Plates', *The Magazine Antiques*, vol. 153 (January 1998), pp.196–205

Lubbock, Jules, 'Adolf Loos and the English Dandy', *Architectural Review*, vol. 169, no. 1038 (August 1983), pp.43–9

McNeil, Peter, '"That Doubtful Gender": Macaroni Dress and Male Sexualities', *Fashion Theory: The Journal of Dress, Body and Culture*, vol. 3, no. 4 (1999), pp.411–47

–– 'Macaroni Masculinities', *Fashion Theory: The Journal of Dress, Body and Culture*, vol. 4, no. 4 (2000), pp.373–404

–– and Patrik Steorn, 'The Medium of Print and the Rise of Fashion in the West', *Konsthistorisk tidskrift/Journal of Art History*, vol. 82, no. 3 (September 2013), pp.135–56

McWilliam, Neil, '*The Age of Caricature* by Diana Donald' [review], *Art History*, vol. 20, no. 1 (March 1997), pp.178–80

Maeder, Edward, 'Made in England? An 18th-century Trade Embargo of Foreign Embroidery Raises Interesting Questions about the Meaning of "Foreign"', *Rotunda: The Magazine of the Royal Ontario Museum*, vol. 30, no. 3 (Spring 1998), pp.34–40

Meyer, Arline, 'Re-dressing Classical Statuary: The Eighteenth-century "Hand-in-waistcoat" Portrait', *Art Bulletin*, vol. 77, no. 1 (March 1995), pp.45–63

Money, John, 'The Masonic Moment: Or, Ritual, Replica, and Credit: John Wilkes, the Macaroni Parson, and the Making of the Middle-class Mind', *Journal of British Studies*, vol. 32 (1993), pp.358–93

Ogborn, Miles, 'Locating the Macaroni: Luxury, Sexuality and Vision in Vauxhall Gardens', *Textual Practice*, vol. 11, no. 3 (1997), pp.445–61

Olson, Kelly, 'Matrona and Whore: The Clothing of Women in Roman Antiquity', *Fashion Theory: The Journal of Dress, Body and Culture*, vol. 6, no. 4 (2002), pp.387–420

Quinn, Vincent, and Mary Peace, 'Luxurious Sexualities', *Textual Practice*, vol. 11, no. 3 (1997), pp.405–16

Rauser, Amelia Faye, 'Hair, Authenticity, and the Self-made Macaroni', *Eighteenth-century Studies*, vol. 38, no. 1 (2004), pp.101–17

Rempal, Lora, 'Carnal Satire and the Constitutional King: George III in James Gillray's *Monstrous Craws at a New Coalition Feast*', *Art History*, vol. 18, no. 1 (March 1995), pp.4–23

Ribeiro, Aileen, 'The Macaronis', *History Today*, vol. 28, no. 7 (July 1978), pp.463–8

–– 'Fashion in the Eighteenth Century: Some Anglo-French Comparisons', *Textile History*, vol. 22, no. 2 (Autumn 1991), pp.329–45

–– 'Re-fashioning Art: Some Visual Approaches to the Study of the History of Dress', *Fashion Theory: The Journal of Dress, Body and Culture*, vol. 2, no. 4 (December 1998), pp.315–26

Roche, Daniel, 'Equestrian Culture in France from the Sixteenth to the Nineteenth Century', *Past and Present*, no. 199 (May 2008), pp.113–45

Rothstein, Natalie, 'Nine English Silks', *Bulletin of the Needle and Bobbin Club*, vol. 48, nos 1–2 (1964), pp.5–36

Senelick, Laurence, 'Mollies or Men of Mode? Sodomy and the
  Eighteenth-century London Stage', *Journal of the History of
  Sexuality*, vol. 1, no. 1 (1990), pp.33–67

Siegfried, Susan, 'Portraits of Fantasy, Portraits of Fashion',
  Nonsite.org, no. 14 (15 December 2014) <http://nonsite.org/article
  portraits-of-fantasy-portraits-of-fashion> [Accessed 2 November
  2015]

–– 'The Visual Culture of Fashion and the Classical Ideal in Post-
  revolutionary France', *Art Bulletin*, vol. 97, no. 1 (March 2015),
  pp.77–99

Sloman, Susan Legouix, '"The immaculate Captain Wade": "Arbiter
  Elegantiae"', *Gainsborough's House Review* (1993–4), pp.46–62

Stanworth, Karen, 'Picturing a Personal History: The Case of Edward
  Onslow', *Art History*, vol. 16, no. 3 (September 1993), pp.408–23

Steele, Valerie, 'The Social and Political Significance of Macaroni
  Fashion', *Costume*, vol. 19, no. 1 (1985), pp.94–109

Steorn, Patrik, 'Migrating Motifs and Productive Instabilities: Images
  of Fashion in Eighteenth-century Swedish Print Culture',
  Konsthistorisk tidskrift / Journal of Art History, vol. 82, no. 3 (September
  2013), pp.219–34

Thompson, James, 'Jean-Baptiste Greuze', *Metropolitan Museum of
  Art Bulletin*, vol. 47, no. 3 (Winter 1989–90), pp.1–51

Vickery, Amanda, 'Venice-on-Thames', *London Review of Books*, vol. 35,
  no. 3 (7 February 2013), pp.31–2

West, Shearer, 'The Darly Macaroni Prints and the Politics of Private
  Man', *Eighteenth-century Life*, vol. 25, no. 2 (2001), pp.170–82

Wilton-Ely, John, '"Gingerbread and sippets of embroidery": Horace
  Walpole and Robert Adam', *Eighteenth-century Life*, vol. 25, no. 2
  (Spring 2001), pp.147–69

Wood, J.R., 'Jack Ketch in John Dryden's "A Discourse Concerning
  Satire"', *The Explicator*, vol. 71, no. 1 (2013), pp.60–64

V Periodicals (see also Primary Sources)

Bon Ton (June 1791 – June 1794)

The Lady's Magazine: or, the Universal Entertainer, vol. 1, no. 1 (18 November
  1749), to vol. 3, no. 28 (9–23 December 1752) (Oxford, Jasper
  Goodwill)

*The Lady's Magazine; or Entertaining Companion for the Fair Sex,
  appropriated solely to their use and amusement*, vol. 7 (London,
  G. Robinson, 1776)

The London Magazine, vol. 97, no. 41 (April 1772)

Macaroni, Scavoir Vivre, and Theatrical Magazine (October 1773 –
  October 1774) (London, John Williams)

New Monthly Magazine and Literary Journal, vol. 10 (1824)

The Spectator (May 1711)

*Town and Country Magazine, or Universal Repository of Knowledge,
  Instruction, and Entertainment*, vol. 4 (London, 1772)

Universal Magazine of Knowledge and Pleasure, vols 50–51 (London, 1772)

Walker's Hibernian Magazine (1771)

Photographic Acknowledgements

Bath, © Victoria Art Gallery, Bath and North East Somerset Council /
Bridgeman Art Library: fig. 2.12

© Christie's Images / Bridgeman Art Library: fig. 3.20

Geneva, Collection Musée Ariana, Ville de Genève / Nicolas Lieber:
fig. 7.2

Geneva, © Musée d'Art et d'Histoire, Ville de Geneve 1913-0068: fig. 7.1

Helsinki, Finnish National Museum / Janne Mäkinen: fig. 2.23

Holkham Hall, Norfolk, © Collection of the Earl of Leicester /
Bridgeman Art Library: fig. 2.16

London, © The Trustees of the British Museum: figs 1.9, 1.10, 1.15, 1.21,
2.24, 3.22, 4.2, 5.3–5.5, 5.10, 5.13, 6.7, 6.10, 6.15

© Look and Learn / Peter Jackson Collection / Bridgeman Art Library:
fig. 5.1

Peter McNeil, 2014: p.11

Melbourne, Johnston Trust / Mark Chew: fig. 4.18

National Trust Photographic Library / Prudence Cuming: fig. 2.17;
/ John Hammond: fig. 5.7; / Angelo Hornak / Bridgeman Art Library:
fig. 3.4; / Neville Taylor: fig. 5.8

New York, © The Metropolitan Museum of Art. Image source:
Art Resource, NY: figs 1.14, 3.19

Oxford, © Ashmolean Museum, University of Oxford, WA1845.61: fig. 6.3

© 2018 Her Majesty Queen Elizabeth II / Bridgeman Art Library:
figs 2.22, 3.21

Stockholm, © Nationalmuseum / Greta Lindström: fig. 1.11

Toronto, © 2017 Bata Shoe Museum. Photo: Shannon Linde and
Hayley Mills: fig. 3.6

Index

First published by Yale University Press 2018

302 Temple Street, P.O. Box 209040, New Haven, CT 06520-9040

47 Bedford Square, London WC1B 3DP

yalebooks.com / yalebooks.co.uk

ISBN 978-0-300-21746-9 HB

Library of Congress Control Number: 2017954568

10 9 8 7 6 5 4 3 2 1

2022 2021 2020 2019 2018

Designer: Myfanwy Vernon-Hunt, This-Side.co.uk

Printed in China

Illustrations

Front cover, left: M. Darly, *Buckles and Buttons. I Am the Thing. Dem-me*, 7 February 1777 (page 91; detail); right: Henry William Bunbury, *Monr. le Frizuer*, 12 May 1771 (page 138; detail, reversed)

Page 2: Richard Cosway, *Self-portrait*, *c*.1770–75 (page 106)

Page 4: William Humphrey (printmaker), *Steel Buttons I,* 29 April 1777 (page 91)

Page 7: Thomas Gainsborough, *Richard Paul Jodrell*, *c*.1774 (page 59)

Page 12: *A French Macarony Eating of Macaroons*, 22 July 1772 (page 35; detail)

Page 36: 'Brandoin pinxt.', James Caldwell (printmaker), *Now Sr, You'r a compleat Macaroni*, 6 May 1772 (page 47; detail)

Page 82: M. Darly, *Buckles and Buttons. I Am the Thing. Dem-me*, 7 February 1777 (page 91; detail)

Page 122: Henry William Bunbury, *Monr. le Frizuer*, 12 May 1771 (page 138; detail, reversed)

Page 150: *The Macaroni Jester, and Pantheon of Wit* (1773). Frontispiece (page 168; detail)

Page 184: 'Fizgig', in David Garrick, *The Fribbleriad* (1761). Frontispiece (page 206; detail)

Page 218: Christopher Anstey, *Liberality; or, The Decayed Macaroni. A Sentimental Piece* (*c*.1788). Frontispiece (page 228; detail)

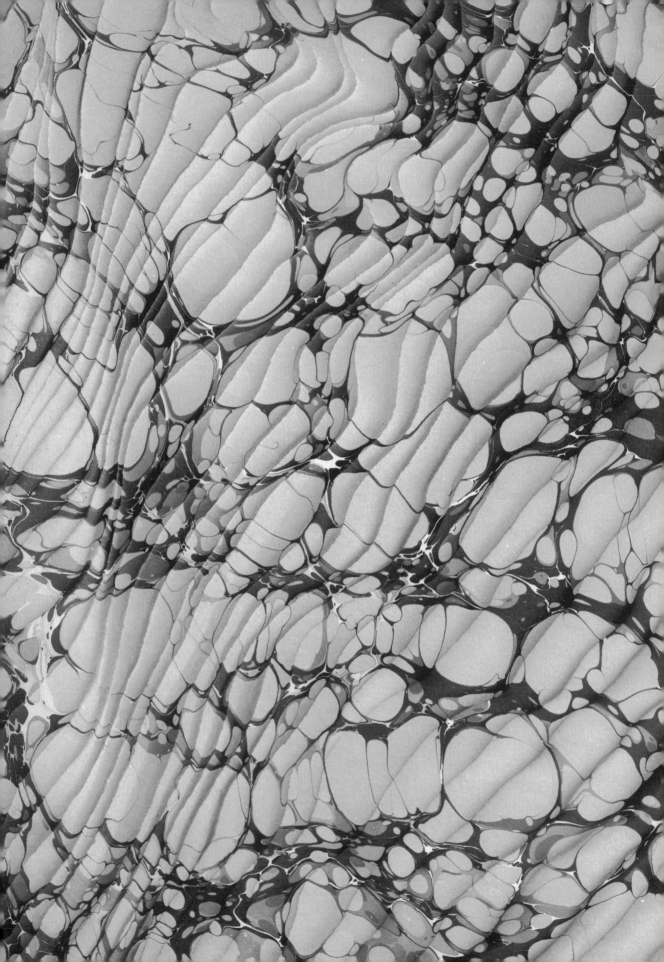

NO STEP SITTING ONLY

DANGER

FREE KUWAIT

RESCUE

820

DESERT FIST

ALLIED AIRPOWER FOR DESERT STORM
A PILOT'S VIEW

IAN BLACK

Airlife
England

ACKNOWLEDGEMENTS

The Author would like to thank the following: Canon Cameras (UK), Nikon Cameras (UK), all the aircrew who helped in capturing the air-air photographs, the kindness of the photographers/journalists of the *Daily Mail*, *Today*, *Daily Mirror* and *Times Newspapers*. I owe you!

Photograph Page 1: On recovery. DJ (Delta Juliet) recovers to the Saudi air base of Dhahran at medium altitude. The fully armed aircraft is carrying two 2500-litre underwing tanks normally carried for combat air control.

Photograph Previous Page: Equipped with a 9G capable centreline fuel tank, an F15 C fighter taxis along a sand and rubble bordered runway at the start of its two-hour training mission.

Copyright © Ian Black, 1991

First published in the UK in 1991
by Airlife Publishing Ltd.

British Library Cataloguing in Publication Data available.

   ISBN 1 85310 295 4 (Hardback)
   ISBN 1 85310 289 X (Paperback)

Printed and bound in Singapore by Kyodo Printing Co (S'pore) Pte Ltd.

Airlife Publishing Ltd.

101 Longden Road, Shrewsbury SY3 9EB, England.

INTRODUCTION

On 2 August 1990 Iraqi forces invaded Kuwait taking possession of the country in a matter of days. The events which followed are now history but involved the largest formation of land, sea and air forces since World War II.

Within days Allied fighters, bombers and helicopters were dispatched from their bases in the United States, the United Kingdom and Europe to the Gulf region. Men and machines were deployed on a scale not seen in recent times. F15s flew nonstop 12-hour sorties from the United States, RAF Tornados flew in from Germany, C141 Starfighters, C130 Hercules and C5 Galaxy transport aircraft flew sorties round the clock delivering vital equipment to the region.

Whilst the waiting game started Allied forces continued to mount training sorties as well as continuous Combat Air Patrol (CAP) missions along the Saudi-Iraqi border. Every day was spent honing the edge, preparing for war. Early familiarization flights in theatre proved invaluable to Allied aircrew normally used to flying over the varied terrain of North America and Europe. Low flying across miles of featureless, barren desert required the use of quickly acquired new skills.

The United Nations set a deadline of 15 January 1991 for Iraqi forces to leave Kuwait. By 16 January 1991 Allied forces were faced with no alternative but to use force in a battle that was over by 26 February 1991. More so than in any other conflict, air power was the key to success in 'Operation Desert Storm'. The photographs in this book were taken by the author, a serving RAF Tornado pilot, during the build up to war.

Overleaf: Framed against a dramatic cumulonimbus backdrop three Jaguar GR1A strike aircraft return to their Muharraq air base in Bahrain following a successful low level training sortie. All three aircraft carry the overwing Sidewinder rails previously only fitted to the Jaguar International.

Below: Mounted under the fuselage of this Tornado GR1 a CPU-123B Paveway laser-guided weapon, with suitably inscribed messages from the aircraft's ground crew.
(Photo: Ian McDonald-Webb)

Opposite: A Tornado GR1 in desert camouflage shows the obvious signs of many missions over occupied territory. Small black palm trees indicate the number of missions flown over enemy territory whilst the black bombs beneath indicate the bombs dropped. Aircraft carried five 1000lb bombs on each sortie. Enthusiastic ground crew have nicknamed this aircraft *Miss Behavin.* (Photo: Ian McDonald-Webb)

Below: Against the setting sun a Royal Air Force Tornado F3 air defence fighter taxis back to its dispersal at the Royal Saudi Air Force base of Dhahran. The aircraft carries a full war load of four x Sky flash radar guided missiles, four underwing Sidewinder infra-red missiles, 23mm Mauser gun and 2 x 1500-litre underwing fuel tanks.

RESCUE

miss. Behavin'

Opposite: A Tornado F3 from the RAF Leeming detachment at Dhahran breaks away from the camera ship displaying its underwing and under fuselage air-to-air missiles.

Below: Breaking out of close formation a Tornado GR1 from the RAF detachment at Bahrain peels away from the Sidewinder equipped Tornado F3. Showing signs of obvious hard use the sand pink camouflage of this Tornado blends in well with the scorching desert below.

Overleaf: Looking more like Dumbo the elephant than an operational Royal Air Force TriStar tanker, this large wide-bodied tanker-transport had been hastily repainted in desert camouflage when hostilities broke out on 16 January 1991.
(Photo: M. Heaton)

Opposite: Buccaneer bombers were used to enhance the precision bombing capability of the Royal Air Force's Tornado force. Equipped with an AN-AVQ23E pave spike laser designator on the port inner pylon, the Buccaneers were assigned to marking aircraft shelters and bridges for Tornados armed with laser-guided bombs to destroy. Buccaneers deployed to the Gulf were hastily repainted in desert pink.

Below: CF — A Tornado GR1 of the Royal Air Force detachment in Dhahran in Saudi Arabia shows obvious signs of makeshift battle damage repair on the forward portion of the aircraft's fin.
(Photo: Ian McDonald-Webb)

Overleaf: A small pale blue and pink roundel on the aircraft's port wing are the only clues to the national identity of this Tornado GR1. The aircraft flying in its normal training fit carries two 1500-litre external fuel tanks, a bolt-on refuelling probe at the forward right of the cockpit and underwing ECM and Chaff dispensers.

Opposite: Wings swept back to 67° and flight refuelling probe in the extended position, a Tornado F3 taxis out from its temporary sun shelter at Dhahran in Saudi Arabia prior to an air combat training mission. The aircraft devoid of underwing fuel tanks carries a Phimat Chaff dispensing pod on the starboard wing pylon. Behind, the aircraft's playmate taxis out.

Below: Pink Puma. A Royal Air Force Puma, rotors running, awaits take-off clearance from the tarmac to recover to its desert airstrip in the north of Saudi Arabia.

Overleaf: A pair of Tornado fighters plug into a Royal Air Force VC10 tanker over the Arabian Gulf. Tanker crews, often the unsung heroes of any conflict, contributed greatly to the success of both air and ground attack missions.

Opposite: Plan view of the Royal Air Force Tornado F3 low over the Saudi desert. Once airborne the aircraft's modern air conditioning equipment allowed the crews some relief from the baking Saudi heat.

Below: Looking after Allied assets, a guard of the Bahraini defence force patrols the line of Tornado GR1 strike attack bombers. Temporarily based at Muharraq in Bahrain.

Opposite: Wings swept back for high speed flight, this Tornado
F3 skims across the Saudi sand dunes whilst on low level combat
air patrol.

Below: Awaiting its crew prior to another night mission, two
Tornado GR1s of the Royal Air Force sit side by side on the
Bahrain apron. The furthest tail fin, coded ER (Echo Romeo) has
had the patriotic addition of a small II between the E and the R.
Unlike the fighter variant the Tornado GR1 has a refuelling probe
bolted to the forward starboard side of the aircraft.

Opposite: Sharing the row of sun shelters with a Royal Saudi Air Force F15 C Eagle, this Tornado F3 sits fully armed awaiting its crew prior to a night combat air patrol.

Below: Mission complete. A Tornado F3 and two Tornado GR1s break out of formation to return to their respective home bases.

Overleaf: A quartet of Jaguar GR1 strike aircraft fly in arrow
formation whilst returning to their home base of Muharraq.
Devoid of unit markings, the aircraft carry a small black letter for
identification on the tail fin.

Opposite: RAF Tornado GR1s bore the brunt of the early low
level night attacks on Iraqi airfields using a variety of weapons
including the Hunting JP233 airfield denial weapon.

Below: *Luscious Lizzie* indicating 38 missions flown and 50,000lbs
of bombs dropped. The aircraft sits in its Dhahran sun shelter
ready for further missions. *(Photo: Ian McDonald-Webb)*

Opposite: A Tornado F3 crosses the desert towards the Bahraini coastline, the aircraft carries two 1500-litre drop tanks mounted under each wing painted in a hastily applied desert camouflage.

Below: A Royal Air Force Tornado pilot runs quickly through his pre-flight checks prior to the start of a four to five-hour combat air patrol mission. During this time perhaps one or two visits to the airborne tanker force will be necessary to sustain the aircraft on CAP (Combat Air Patrol).

Overleaf: A pair of Jaguar fighters peel away from the camera ship. The aircraft are equipped in their training fit of centreline fuel tank, Phimat Chaff pod, ECM pod and overwing mounted Sidewinder missiles.

Opposite: A Jaguar GR1A of the Royal Air Force which was used during Operation Desert Storm on battlefield support duties including raids on Republican Guard bases on the Iraqi-Kuwaiti border.

Below: Against a setting sun and dramatic backdrop, a Tornado F3 fighter peels away from the author displaying its awesome weapon load. Flying over the Saudi desert provided new challenges for Allied air crew with flat barren landscape for miles upon miles, a judgement of height whilst flying at low level was particularly difficult.

Opposite: A close view of *ZE961* whilst on combat air patrol close to the Iraqi-Kuwaiti border. The crews wear white painted helmets to avoid heat stress caused by the strong midday sun.

Below: Taxiing back into an Arabian sunset the four semi-recessed Sky Flash missiles show prominently in this view of a Tornado F3 of the Royal Air Force detachment at Dhahran.

Opposite: Hiding against a desert backdrop, this near planform shot of a Tornado GR1 shows how easy it is to hide over the desert when using the correct paint scheme.

Below: Sitting in front of a VC10 tanker, this Tornado GR1 is serviced by its hardworking ground crew. The outboard ECM pods are covered to avoid heat damage by the sun.

Opposite: Tornado GR1 (GE) *ZE396* carries the under fuselage Hunting JP233 airfield denial weapon used successfully during the opening stages of Desert Storm.

Below: Aptly named *Dhahran Annie*, this Tornado GR1 carries two under fuselage laser-guided 1000 pound bombs.

Overleaf: This ancient Dakota sat in the corner of this Saudi airfield, obviously not having moved for several years. How the aircraft came to be in this location was unclear.

Opposite: During the workup phase to deploy to the Gulf the Royal Air Force used Phantoms of 56 and 74 Squadron to simulate Iraqi Flogger aircraft. Seen at the end of a day's flying are a line-up of both 56 and 74 Squadron Phantom aircraft.

Below: This Jaguar GR1A carries the under fuselage recce pod normally associated with aircraft of 41 (F) Fighter Squadron based at Coltishall in Norfolk.

Opposite: Training continued during Operation Desert Storm
with this Royal Saudi Air Force Jet Stream aircraft operated by a
crew from British Aerospace at Warton. The aircraft are used to
train navigators for the Saudi Air Force Tornado IDS and
Tornado ADV aircraft.

Below: Saudi Air Force. One corner of this Saudi airfield was
littered with aircraft from the 1950s including F86 Sabre jets, T33
Shooting Stars and other military hardware.

CUT HERE IN EMERGENCY

ROYAL SAUDI AIR FORCE   القوات الجوية الملكية السعودية

Opposite: Two 13 Squadron RSAF F15 fighters, both in full
re-heat roll down the Dhahran runway. In the background the
Patriot air-to-air missile system which proved itself so effective
against the Iraqi Scud missiles. The lead aircraft is a single F15 C
fighter, whilst the two seat is an F15 B trainer.

Below: A Royal Saudi Air Force McDonnell Douglas F15 C
fighter of 13 Squadron Dhahran. The Saudi Air Force took
delivery from the United States Air Force of additional F15
fighters from both Germany and Holland during Desert Storm to
supplement their existing stocks. Obvious from this view is the
excellent all round visibility of the F15 cockpit.

Opposite: A Royal Saudi F15 fighter in full re-heat launches from
its Saudi base on to a combat air patrol along the Iraqi border. It
carries a full warload of four underwing Sidewinder missiles and
four Sparrow fuselage mounted radar-guided missiles. Combat
air patrols during the conflict were flown 24 hours a day by air
forces of the United Kingdom, Saudi Arabia and the United States
of America.

Below: A Tornado IDS of 7 Squadron Dhahran taxis prior to a
training sortie loaded with live 1000lb conventional bombs. The
aircraft are housed in concrete revetments which allow both
access from the front and the rear.

Overleaf: A Royal Saudi Air Force Tornado F3 and McDonnell
Douglas F15 C fighter sit inside the huge McDonnell Douglas
hangar at Dhahran, northeast Saudi Arabia. Together these two
aircraft form the backbone of the Royal Saudi Air Force Air
Defence network.

Opposite: The crew of this Tornado IDS of the Royal Saudi Air
Force run through their lengthy pre-flight checks prior to their
mission. The refuelling probe is extended indicating that the
aircraft may be involved in an air-to-air refuelling either from
Hercules or KC135 tanker aircraft.

Below: A British Aerospace Hawk T1 combat trainer taxis back,
canopy open after the completion of an air-to-air combat training
mission.

Opposite: A well worn McDonnell Douglas Saudi F15 C fighter sits in its unhardened sun shelter on the eastern base of Dhahran.

Below: Looking somewhat out of place in its desert camouflage a Lightning F (Mark 52) of the Royal Saudi Air Force stands on its concrete plinth outside the headquarters of a large air base. The aircraft had previously been in service with the Royal Air Force.

Opposite: President of the United States, George Bush, visited Dhahran in November 1990. One of the many aircraft present was the specially painted Black Hawk helicopter.

Below: Amongst the many civil and military transport aircraft that visited Dhahran during the period of August to December 1990 was this unmarked Boeing 707 operated by the United States. The aircraft is unusual in having two Pitot probes mounted on the top surfaces of each wing.

Overleaf: Several squadrons of McDonnell Douglas F15 C Eagle fighters were located at bases in the northern half of Saudi Arabia, with almost 100 aircraft available drawn from the 1st, 33rd and 36th Tactical Fighter Wings based at Langley, Virginia. Here one of four F15 C fighters runs through his pre-flight checks prior to a combat training mission.

Opposite: Guarding valuable military aircraft became an increasing but necessary task during the Gulf conflict.

Below: A UH-60A Black Hawk of the US Army.

Opposite: A Fairchild A10 Thunderbolt aircraft passes over a
stray camel train in northern Saudi Arabia. The A10 armed with
deadly GAU-8-A cannon was used to successfully knock out
enemy tanks.

Below: Two F15 fighters await their pilots on the Dhahran ramp.
These American air superiority fighters retained their air
superiority grey camouflage whilst over the desert landscape.

Opposite: Framed by the silver tail of a C-141 Starlifter, a green and grey European style camouflage Starlifter starts its engines on the Dhahran ramp prior to another airlift sortie.

Below: Work-horse of the US military airlift command, a Lockheed C130 transport aircraft decorated with colourful caricature and named *Sand Shark*, returns to Europe to collect more military supplies for the massive supply operation of Desert Shield.

Opposite: Evening and night time provided the few opportunities to service and maintain the front line aircraft of the Allied air forces. Here a US Air Force F15 fighter undergoes routine maintenance.

Below: The Bell UH1H Iroquois helicopters were used extensively during the Vietnam war. Here a medi-vac equipped Iroquois taxis out past a line of Saudi UH1 and US Army Black Hawk helicopters on the massive helicopter ramp at Dhahran. In the background are Kuwaiti Air Force A4 Sky Hawk bombers.

Opposite: A dual controlled McDonnell Douglas F15 D fighter trainer awaits take off clearance at the last chance check-point at an airfield in northern Saudi Arabia.

Below: Pilot and ground crew discuss the Hell Fire missile fitted to this Cobra helicopter prior to a live training sortie. The helicopter is a US Marine Corps AH1W Supercobra which carries a crew of two and up to eight Hell Fire missiles. During the conflict Cobra gun ships together with Air Force A10 Warthog aircraft conducted close air support missions against Iraqi armour and infantry.

Opposite: On the morning of 24 February 1991, the largest helicopter assault in history was launched deep into Iraq to set up Cobra, a forward operations base for attack helicopters. Used in the assault were US Army McDonnell Douglas AH64 Apache helicopters similar to this.

Below: The massive C5 Galaxy transport aircraft causes a visible heat haze whilst taxiing in to deliver more munitions and stores to the US Air Force.

Opposite: Throughout the war small transport aircraft provided vital communications between forward operating bases and the headquarters in Riyadh.

Below: This Black Hawk helicopter of the US Army is obviously equipped for long range missions judging by the massive external fuel tank mounted on the left outer pylon. Also visible on the top of the fuselage is the infra-red decoy device and also on the left fuselage the infra-red flare decoy box.

Opposite: A pair of VMFA 333 F18A Hornet fighter bombers cross the Arabian coastline near their home base. The aircraft from Beaufort, eastern United States, were among the first fighters to deploy to the Gulf.

Below: An F15 Eagle pilot runs through the aircraft maintenance schedule with the ground technician. The aircraft from the 71st Tactical Fighter Wing at Langley was among the first F15 fighters to arrive in Saudi Arabia during early August 1990. Most F15's flew the sortie from the United States to Saudi Arabia nonstop, requiring several air-to-air refuellings.

Opposite: A C141 Starlifter begins its pre-flight checks before recovering to Ramstein in Germany to collect more stores and equipment.

Below: United States Marine and Navy C130 tanker aircraft were used extensively during the conflict to top up F18, F14 and A6 carrier borne aircraft operating in the Gulf.

Opposite: Two C5 Galaxy aircraft of the United States Military Airlift Command unload a vast quantity of weapons and munitions. Whilst the aircraft are unloading, refuelling bowsers refuel the aircraft to allow them to be airborne again in the shortest possible time. Most US transports routed through Frankfurt in Germany collecting tanks, trucks and also disassembled helicopters.

Below: Amongst the many military aircraft that were used to airlift supplies and weapons to the Gulf, many civil companies were used to transport troops and personnel into theatre.

Opposite: An OV10 Bronco forward air control aircraft of the United States Marine Corps taxis to the holding point. The dangerous mission of these aircraft was highlighted during the early phases of the war with the loss of two aircraft engaged in forward air control sorties inside Kuwait.

Below: An Apache anti-tank helicopter, rotors running awaits take-off clearance from the Dhahran helicopter ramp. Behind the helicopter two Kuwaiti Air Force Sky Hawk fighter bombers undergo maintenance in the open fronted hangar.

Opposite: RAF Tornado F3 crews flew against US Marine Corps F18 fighter bombers who proved to be an excellent adversary not dissimilar to the Iraqi MiG 29 Fulcrum fighter. Most affiliation training was against aircraft from VMFA 450, 451, and here the VMFA 333.

Below: Owned by Kalita Airlines, an ageing DC8 airliner awaits its turn to be unloaded on the Dhahran flight line.

Opposite: Mirage 2000 Interceptor aircraft taxi out from Hofuf in
south eastern Saudi Arabia. The aircraft come from Orange Air
Force Base in southern France. Like most air defence aircraft
which took part in the Gulf operations they retain their air
superiority colour scheme.

Below: To keep the cockpits as cool as possible silver foil is
wrapped across the inside of the canopy to reflect as much heat
as possible. The French Air Force detachment included twelve
Jaguar bombers, some of which were already in the region
operating from Chad.

Opposite: Surrounded by support equipment this French Jaguar aircraft has its engines run after some post-flight rectification.

Below: Mission complete. French ground crew remove the gun camera film from this Mirage F1 CR fighter recce aircraft.

Opposite: An Orange-based 5e Escadre de Chasse Mirage 2000 armed with Magic air-to-air missiles and centreline fuel tank.

Below: French ground technicians finish refuelling this Mirage fighter ready for the next mission.

Opposite: Several French Jaguar aircraft which took part in battlefield interdiction missions into Kuwait during the early parts of the Gulf War were hit by small arms ground fire including one pilot who was slightly injured when a bullet penetrated his cockpit.

Below: Despite having flown a two hour reconnaissance mission on the Iraqi border, this French Air Force fighter pilot still manages to look debonair, wearing a desert lightweight flying suit and life vest complete with underarm personal weapon, seen walking back to his operations building to debrief his mission.

Opposite: In its desert camouflage this Mirage F1 CR fighter recce aircraft was used extensively prior to the start of hostilities in Operation Desert Storm. The Iraqi Air Force operated numerous variants of this aircraft both in the air superiority and ground attack roles.

Below: Desert camouflage French Air Force Jaguar bomber.

Opposite: In addition to the French Army operating Puma helicopters, Pumas were also used by the British Royal Air Force, Kuwaiti Air Force and Saudi Air Force.

Below: A Mirage 2000 pilot runs through his pre-flight checks on the Hofuf flight line.

Opposite: Jaguar tails. Displaying a variety of camouflage this
line up of Jaguar strike aircraft shows the markings of the various
units involved in the Allied Gulf air campaign.

Below: A Mirage F1 CR normally based at Strasbourg, northern
France.

Opposite: Servicing of the Kuwaiti Air Force Sky Hawks was undertaken by US civilians. Here a contract ground crew gives the pilot the relevant flap and hand signals during the pre-flight checks of this small but versatile fighter bomber.

Below: A British Aerospace Hawk trainer of the Kuwaiti Air Force sits with its canopy covered awaiting repair. The aircraft was flown by its Kuwaiti pilot during the early days of the war when Iraq occupied Kuwait. Unsure of future developments, the aircraft canopy was destroyed to prevent unauthorised flight of the aircraft.

Overleaf: A line of three Kuwaiti Air Force Sky Hawk bombers wait whilst two A10 Warthog anti-tank aircraft of the US Air Force land at Dhahran.

Opposite: Having completed a (DACT) Dissimilar Air Combat Training Sortie, this Kuwaiti Air Force A4 Sky Hawk closes into formation for the recovery to base.

Below: The Commanding Officer of No.9 Squadron Free Kuwait Air Force, sits in the cockpit of his A4 Sky Hawk prior to simulated range sortie in December 1990. The wing mounted gun has obviously been used recently judging by the amount of carbon deposits along the side of the fuselage.

Opposite: Taxiing out from a busy flight line, a Free Kuwait Air Force A4 Sky Hawk prior to a low level strike training mission. At least eighteen (the majority) of the Kuwaiti Air Force's Sky Hawk force managed to flee Kuwait during the early part of the invasion of Kuwait. Many Kuwaiti Air Force pilots told brave stories of flying from unprepared airfields and at night against Iraqi armoured divisions during the first two days of the war. During the Gulf conflict Kuwaiti pilots returned to their home base to bomb Iraqi positions which had occupied their airfield.

Below: Free Kuwait Air Force A4 Sky Hawks at the start of the day's flying. At the time of the Iraq-Kuwait conflict the Kuwaiti Air Force were due to replace the Sky Hawk with F18 fighter bombers.

Overleaf: The author, Ian Black, on patrol high over the Saudi desert.

Final page: Low over the Saudi desert. Sky Hawk number *819* joins into close formation for the recovery to Dhahran. Although on the nose of the aircraft a refuelling probe is visible, the Kuwaiti Air Force does not have air-to-air refuelling tankers, nor does it practice air-to-air refuelling. The A4 Sky Hawk is similar in size and appearance to the British Hawk, but has twice the thrust and a similar turning performance.